7-7-06

Weight Matters
for Young People

A complete guide to weight, eating and fitness

Rachel Pryke

General Practitioner
Member, Worcestershire Obesity Reduction and Prevention Strategy Group

Foreword by

Ann McPherson

General Practitioner
Chair of the Adolescent Task Force, RCGP

Radcliffe Publishing
Oxford • Seattle

Radcliffe Publishing Ltd
18 Marcham Road
Abingdon
Oxon OX14 1AA
United Kingdom

www.radcliffe-oxford.com
Electronic catalogue and worldwide online ordering facility.

British Library Cataloguing in Publication Data

A catalogue record for this book is available from the British Library.

ISBN-10 1 85775 772 6
ISBN-13 978 1 85775 772 9

Typeset by Anne Joshua & Associates, Oxford
Printed and bound by TJ International Ltd, Padstow, Cornwall

Contents

Foreword

This book is very timely as 'obesity' is now seen as the new plague. Dieting is the new cure all, with tomes high on the best seller lists, promising instant and totally unproven success: teenage magazines focus on slim models, encouraging eating disorders and obsession about unfulfilled weight reduction.

It is therefore refreshing to read a book that not only deals with diet, healthy eating, exercise and weight – but actually sees these from a young person's perspective. It does not preach; it does not victim blame; it does not claim to have all the answers.

Instead it looks objectively at the different cogs that make up the fat of the subject – including the food industry, the way that we eat, the way we buy our food, the way that food is advertised, and the different social and financial pressures on young people and their parents.

It puts weight in perspective in terms of 'real life' and takes the broader view. It deals with the myths and even if it doesn't have all the answers, it is an excellent basis for asking the questions.

I learnt a great deal reading it, and this book will certainly help me when answering the many difficult questions on 'diet and weight' that I am emailed on www.teenagehealthfreak.org, as well as giving food for thought when I am consulting with young people in the surgery.

Ann McPherson CBE, MBBS, FRCGP, FRCP
General Practitioner
Chair of the Adolescent Task Force, Royal College of General Practitioners
January 2006

Preface

Many people, from parents, health workers to young people themselves, care about the health and lifestyle of today's youngsters. *Weight Matters for Young People* applies to all, because whilst teenagers are in the process of becoming independent and making up their own minds, their family will still have some influence over lifestyle issues. This practical book contains safe, evidence-based nutritional information plus the answers to common weight-related queries and plenty of further resources.

It is not simply obesity that is on everyone's mind – more families fear eating disorders than the misery of being overweight, not to mention anxieties over additives, confusion over hard-sell advertising and bewilderment at the national obsession with dieting. This book looks at the full spectrum and, above all, tackles the common underlying thread – *self-esteem* – because if this is missing, any nutritional advice will seem useless and unworkable. People look after the things they value, so the best start is to value oneself.

It begins with all the things that influence how young people make choices, and includes tips on wising up to the persuasive tactics used by the food industry. It then looks at practical nutrition: the Food Frequency Framework solves family meal dilemmas, whilst the Safe Dieting Assessment Guide looks at all the common dieting regimes to see which are safe or worthwhile. There is a chapter on eating disorders as well as an A to Z of common weight-related conditions. Finally, the Top Teen Health Plan shows young people how to assess the strengths and weaknesses of their current lifestyle, with practical advice on adopting change.

All the nutritional information is consistent with highly respected sources, including the British Heart Foundation, the Food Standards Agency, the Food Commission and the World Health Organization. Additionally, this book contains the essential psychology that lies behind putting this advice successfully into practice.

Weight Matters for Young People is a complete reference book that can put young people confidently in charge of their own health.

Rachel Pryke
January 2006

About the author

Rachel Pryke MBBS, MRCGP trained at King's College Hospital, London. She is now a GP in Worcestershire with particular interests in family medicine, women's health and weight management. She is a regular contributor to medical magazines and writes on a wide variety of topics.

In *Weight Matters for Young People* she has combined the most up-to-date evidence and advice on adolescent nutrition and psychology with the practical knowledge that comes from being both a practising doctor and a parent.

Rachel comes from a medical and musical family and is married to a GP. They have three boys plus a naughty shoe-stealing dog called Tiffin.

Acknowledgements

My sincere thanks go to my family and many friends who have tolerated my one-track conversation and interest in recent months. In particular, my parents, husband and children have been unwavering in their support.

Thank you to Jane Deville-Almond for her infectious enthusiasm, to Helen Mercer for her trusted nutritional advice and to Sally and Lyndon Simkin for allowing me to mix business with pleasure. Their help has again been crucial.

The input from all the young people who helped with assessing the food diary was most appreciated and I would like to thank, in particular, Charlotte Cameron and Phoebe and Jacob Hugh for their ideas and help with the front cover. Deb Hugh played a crucial role in developing the Top Teen Health Plan, thank you.

I am most grateful to John Short and to Tam Fry of the Child Growth Foundation for their help with providing growth charts and I felt honoured that Ann McPherson agreed to write the foreword, thank you.

Radcliffe Publishing have given me tremendous help, in particular Susan Rabson for her regular tutorials on the publishing world and Jamie Etherington for editing my writing.

My love goes to my brothers Nick and Tim for their friendship and, above all, their inspiration. What luck to come from such a family.

In honour and in loving memory of my lovely brother, Steve Hugh.

Section 1

Looking at things from a young person's viewpoint

The first section takes a look at issues from a young person's viewpoint to see what factors influence their choices, interests and emotions, because these all contribute to whether young people choose a healthy lifestyle or not. Exploring risk taking is a normal part of growing up and this will often have a big effect on lifestyle. Parents gradually lose some of their influence whilst young people look to other role models and sources of information to guide their views.

Chapter 1

Does weight really matter to young people?

This chapter looks at barriers that prevent young people from eating healthily and making good lifestyle choices. It outlines the basic concept of a healthy diet that is suitable for young people, using *The Balance of Good Health* eating plan (*see* p. 5), and explains the decision-making process, particularly in relation to food and exercise, so that young people can take charge over creating a healthy lifestyle.

Does weight really matter?

It should and it does. Most young people are highly sensitive to body image, self-esteem and fitting in, which means trying to keep weight in line with other young people in order not to stand out from the crowd. But far from being merely a cosmetic detail, lifestyle trends that are established during the teenage years are very likely to set the scene for adult life too. Fitness and weight have a huge effect on health throughout life, affecting the types of illness people are prone to and their sense of self-esteem and body satisfaction. This in turn affects how people feel on a daily basis, colouring the choices they make and the reactions they get from other people. In short, a healthy weight is one of life's fundamentals – get it right and it can be put on the back burner. Get it wrong and the repercussions run and run.

Healthy habits that begin in adolescence are likely to persist into later years, but unhealthy trends are also likely to persist. Hence finding ways to help young people put health higher up their own priority list is a great investment for their short- and long-term futures.

This book shows how to put weight into perspective with lifestyle overall, so that a person's weight is not the focus of life but becomes a simple indicator of how a person values him or herself. By getting this perspective right – which means valuing all aspects of ourselves so that we feel able to make good choices whatever the issue – young people can look at lifestyle improvements without the need for short-term diets or forays into risk-taking behaviour.

Achieving this involves making sense of practical nutrition and improving ordinary meals, but also understanding about eating tendencies and how people make food choices, because these are affected by so many different things. Whilst young people need to learn to make their own choices – and mistakes – parents can still help to improve their lifestyles, without argument and conflict.

Why do young people need a different approach from both children and adults?

Adolescence is a time when emotions take on huge importance and colour everything, in particular the decision-making process. Young people have specific needs in terms of their diet because they are still growing, and in terms of lifestyle because this is a time when most young people experiment to some degree with taking risks. The specific nutritional needs of young people are discussed in Chapter 5.

Young people are no longer children who can be simply told what to do, but neither do they have the experience and maturity that are acquired during adulthood. In order to engage young people in thinking about their health it is important to provide information that feels both relevant and achievable, otherwise many will continue to give their health no thought at all.

Depending on age, young people may find themselves unable to make choices either at home or in a legal sense, despite feeling quite sure of their own opinions. Equally, some young people find themselves dealing with situations that even grown adults may struggle with, but with no adult experience to fall back on for guidance. They may be hindered from taking advice because of:

- a lack of information as to why the advice is relevant to them
- a desire to find out things for themselves
- a need to make choices that reflect who they are, which sometimes leads young people to rebel
- practical barriers that prevent young people from carrying out intentions. For example, despite a desire to eat healthily, a young person may not be in charge of shopping and cooking at home and so have difficulty in changing eating habits
- poor communication. If communication is strained and awkward between young people and adults then opportunities to discuss problems are limited.

It is normal for young people to pass through difficult times when mistakes are made. The approaches in this book aim to help young people move on into adulthood, taking with them positive messages about healthy eating and exercise and valuing themselves, so that even if success is limited initially, they will have a clear idea about the basics of a healthy lifestyle ready for when they want to make it a priority.

With so much information available, how do young people know which advice to follow?

Information overload can be almost as problematic as no information at all. As far as health is concerned information is everywhere, from advertising and aggressive marketing, health campaigns, rumours, myths and government edicts. It is enough to make some people switch off altogether, meaning that health is ignored, whilst others fall for bizarre lifestyles and fad diets because of clever marketing, misleading claims or conflicting views about whether they are worth trying.

In essence, a healthy diet is very simple – plenty of fresh, simple ingredients and not too much of all those tempting, rich, sugary and fatty foods. However, many people find that achieving a healthy diet on a regular basis can take initial effort and understanding, because hectic lives in combination with a powerful food industry make convenience foods highly attractive. By gradually changing the approach to meals and eating habits, using the varied approaches outlined in this book, a healthy diet can become the most enjoyable way to eat, and once people learn to enjoy healthy food then that is what they will continue to choose.

This book uses the United Kingdom (UK) national food guide, a system called *The Balance of Good Health*, to explain how to get the basics of the diet right so that occasional rich treats will not be a problem. *The Balance of Good Health* is easy to follow and uses a great deal of common sense too. The system is suitable for all people from the age of five upwards because it contains plenty of the essential building blocks that everyone needs, particularly when actively growing (although the under-fives may benefit from making the diet a little more energy-dense).

Two other eating plans are outlined later in the book: the Food Frequency Framework shows how to adjust family meals to fit with *The Balance of Good Health* (*see* Chapter 7) and the Top Teen Health Plan, towards the end of the book (*see* p. 173), explores ways for young people to tweak an existing diet of junk and convenience meals so that nutrition is improved. A family guide to help young people adopt this plan is outlined in Chapter 6.

Introducing *The Balance of Good Health*: the perfect diet for young people

The Balance of Good Health shows the proportions of each of the five different food groups that a healthy diet should contain. Obviously there is no single meal plan that would suit everyone, but certain principles apply:

- the diet should be well balanced, and that means varied
- individual preferences should be taken into account
- the diet should be practical, bearing in mind lifestyle and the rest of the family.

What is meant by a 'well-balanced' diet? Too much of some things are just as bad as not enough of others. Without having to read labels or calculate recommended daily allowances (RDAs), it is possible to eat a well-balanced diet by choosing as wide a variety of foods as possible. This will give a hotchpotch of all the necessary ingredients whilst avoiding dietary deficiencies that a more restrictive diet may lead to.

The Balance of Good Health is extremely flexible and so can easily take individual preferences into account, such as vegetarian or halal eating. The Food Frequency Framework and the Top Teen Health Plan both demonstrate ways of making a healthy diet as practical as possible.

Figure 1.1 UK national food guide: *The Balance of Good Health*. Reproduced by kind permission of the Foods Standard Agency.

How to use the guide

The plate in Figure 1.1 shows what proportions of the five different food groups should appear in the diet over an average day. Roughly a third of mouthfuls (not calories) should come from fruit and vegetables; another third should come from bread, potatoes and cereals, especially wholegrain. The remaining third of the diet should be made up of protein-containing foods, such as meat and fish, dairy products and milk, plus a small amount of fatty and sugary foods.

- This balance does not need to be achieved at each meal, but should guide eating throughout the day. So, for example, breakfast consisting of cereals and milk is fine if fruit and vegetables feature in meals and snacks later in the day.
- The guide does not require any calorie counting, but guides what proportions should appear on the plate.
- Portion sizes for a particular person tend to be fairly constant – a person who usually has two potatoes is unlikely to suddenly choose five, and so it doesn't matter that the guide does not specify exactly what a portion size is. Details of suitable fruit and vegetable portion sizes for young people are described in Chapter 5.
- By getting these proportions roughly right throughout each day, there is no need to worry about individual foods because the overall balance will be good. Eating fatty and sugary foods too frequently will upset the balance, and may mean that healthier parts of the diet are 'pushed off the plate'.
- For foods made up of several ingredients, such as pies, looking at the main listed ingredient will indicate which group it fits best. This will be the first item listed in the ingredients on the packaging. Some foods will fit into two food groups, such as cheesy potato bake. The Food Frequency Framework looks into this in more depth.
- No foods are banned in the guide; if the existing diet contains too much fatty or sugary food, then it can be improved by making those portion sizes smaller or less frequent whilst increasing the number of portions of healthier items.
- The diet will be healthier if there is variety within each food group. For example, eating five portions of carrots each day might provide plenty of vitamin A, but will not supply the full variety of vitamins that a mixture of fruit and vegetables will.
- Although cooking methods are not specified in the guide, it is recommended to use low-fat methods such as grilling rather than frying, and to choose lower-fat meat and dairy products on the whole.
- Fruit and vegetables can be fresh, frozen, chilled, canned, dried or served as juice – all will provide an array of vitamins, minerals and fibre.
- Where possible, choosing wholegrain cereals and breads will maximise the amount of micronutrients and fibre in the diet.
- For celebrations, put *The Balance of Good Health* to one side and enjoy whatever is on offer!

By aiming to eat healthily at least some of the time and by generating interest and enthusiasm for a good lifestyle, young people will find that they feel happy to miss out some of the junk food and explore how to make their diet work for rather than against them.

What influences the way that young people like to eat?

Despite having an idea about which foods are healthy and which are not, young people don't always use this knowledge. What governs the choices they make?

This question has many answers, which can be divided into three themes:

1 a young person's upbringing
2 the lure of different foods
3 physical factors such as fullness, hunger and energy requirements.

The next section of this chapter looks at each theme to build up an understanding of why young people eat the way they do and thus find avenues for change.

A young person's upbringing

By the time a person reaches the teenage years they have usually settled into an eating routine with a clear knowledge of what they do and don't like. In general, they have already learned to make choices as a result of the following factors:

- copying parents and other role models
- the choice worked last time, i.e. they are choosing something familiar
- the choice might annoy parents, and that can be highly satisfying
- the choice is relevant to them, i.e. they sense it's good for them
- they couldn't think of a good alternative, i.e. that's how the family does things
- the choice was easy rather than an effort
- they had some control over the choice, even if that meant getting it wrong, i.e. it *was* a choice!

Familiarity is a vital part of a food's popularity

Despite a baby's tendency to spit out new foods, if the same thing keeps reappearing it becomes familiar so that eventually the baby will accept it. This works more easily if it is cooked or served in a variety of ways, especially in combination with other more familiar ingredients. It usually takes anything from five to ten exposures for a new food to become familiar and this principle continues to apply as children grow older. Even adults can teach themselves to develop a liking for a new food that initially seemed unpleasant by repeatedly trying it, particularly if they see other people enjoying it. Thus many adults have successfully swapped from butter to low-fat spreads, from full-fat to semi-skimmed milk or from sweetened fizzy drinks to sugar-free versions. The crucial factor to remember is that those people who eat healthy foods enjoy healthy foods. Making healthy foods familiar by serving them regularly is a great way to make them popular.

Expectation is the key to making ordinary food enjoyable

If a person expects frequent rich treats, then there will be disappointment when they are missing, but if they are not expected, then they will not be missed.

Expectation colours our acceptance of what is served. Imagine the disappointment of turning up to a banquet at the Ritz hotel and being served tinned spaghetti on toast, or looking forward to egg and chips in a greasy Joe's café and finding the menu only offers a seafood salad or roasted aubergine with quails' eggs! If the venues were swapped round, however, no one would be disappointed because expectations would have been met.

Parents have a big influence on the type, quantity and frequency of family foods, and can improve acceptance of a healthy diet by working on the family's expectations.

A person who has been brought up to eat a healthy diet with only occasional treat items will think that that diet is normal – not great, not bad, just normal. The bonus is that treats will seem far more special than they would to someone who has treats at every meal and in between.

Food does not need to be the centre of life. Despite the attractions of exotic designer menus and the constant supply of tempting new foods, there are plenty of inedible amusements that can fill the 'entertainment gap'. Of course, rich foods are there to be enjoyed from time to time, but it is important to get the balance right. The Top Teen Health Plan family guide looks at ways of reducing the impact of comfort eating in more detail (*see* p. 83).

Household routines can both help and hinder

Families often slip into habits without much thought. Popping out on two consecutive Fridays for fish and chips may suddenly mean a household tradition has started – popular, easy and perhaps a bit of fun, particularly as it fits with the old adage 'Fish on Fridays'. Depending on the diet throughout the rest of the week, eating this high-calorie and high-fat meal regularly may turn an otherwise okay diet into a cause of weight gain. Rich treats that appear too frequently are a common cause of trouble, particularly as families will learn to see them as 'normal' if they appear each week and therefore feel a sense of loss if they then disappear during health drives.

Snacks or meals in front of the television form another household routine that can upset an otherwise healthy lifestyle. Television is a big distraction, which means that people who snack whilst watching are more likely to eat to excess and are more likely to eat food that is advertised – which usually means high-fat or sugar foods.

Healthy household routines include eating meals as a family whilst sitting at the table. This gives the family the opportunity to be a team, to share jokes, to check out the gossip and to pick up on problems. When mealtimes form the opportunity to talk then there is less pressure on the food itself to be the main attraction and so ordinary foods are more successful. There are plenty of ways to make meals special or interesting without resorting to rich foods (*see* 'Variety night ideas', p. 105 or 'Ideas for making ordinary meals special', p. 104).

The type of meal is another routine that needs reviewing from time to time. As young people grow and become more independent it may no longer be suitable for the main meal of the day to be in the evening. If a large canteen lunch is served then a light evening snack may be more suitable. Or if there is no time to eat much at lunchtime then grabbing snack foods may have become a convenient but unhealthy option. An alternative would be to have a larger breakfast so that a quick snack for lunch is adequate without resorting to too much junk food. Whatever the day's agenda, young people will benefit from forward planning and being organised. Even if this approach seems unpopular at the time, as young people get a bit older and feel their health is becoming more important they will have these good ideas to fall back on.

Do pushy parents end up with compliant youngsters?

Yes and no. There is a fine balance between setting a good example to encourage the good things and putting people off. When it comes to choice, people resent being forced regardless of how reasonable the option. If young people are backed into corners then it is usually a recipe for war as to who will back down first and risk losing face.

Parents may find it hard to back away when young people seem intent on making the wrong decision, but simply insisting is not usually the best approach. Depending on the nature of the youngster, a parent who puts their foot down will find their child reacts either with defiance and aggression or with timid and insecure compliance. Taking this a stage further, if a parent goes so far as to ban something then rather than producing respectful obedience, young people usually feel the need to explore further and try it anyway just to see for themselves what all the fuss is about. Chapter 3 takes a look at how parents can let young people get on with their own decision-making processes whilst retaining some influence and control.

Faddy eating tendencies in adults will rub off on the rest of the family

In the same way that young people use family role models to guide their routines and views, they will also pick up abnormal habits too. The commonest example is learning dieting behaviour and to feel guilty about eating.

When adults 'go on a diet' they tend to eat differently from the rest of the household and make numerous remarks such as 'I'm not allowed that' or 'I shouldn't'. This dietary restraint is actually associated with greater feelings of hunger and a strong sense of denial. Dieting is often associated with feeling moody and is definitely linked to guilt when forbidden foods are eaten. Girls in particular are sensitive to copying dieting behaviour that they see around them and even if they don't apply much restraint, they may still develop a sense of guilt about eating enjoyable food.

If a parent is trying to diet then the rest of the family will benefit from hearing positive comments about the healthy things that the diet recommends, rather than sensing how much the parent misses what seem to be the good things in life. If fruit and vegetables form a significant part of the diet, then make sure they are served to the whole household. Healthy eating is not only for people who want to lose weight. Chapter 9 takes a detailed look at dieting.

The lure of different foods

Why are some foods tastier than others? Why do some foods create that feel-good factor whereas others bring up horrid memories? Are some foods actually addictive? This section looks at flavour and the desire to eat.

Why are some foods tastier than others?

The popularity of a food depends only partly on its flavour. Texture, freshness, moisture, fat and sugar content all count towards a food's overall appeal. In addition, food eaten at a time of illness or emotional upset may forever be linked with that memory, colouring its appeal, whereas food linked with excitement and celebration tends to remain prized.

Flavour sometimes tells people quickly about its richness: a high fat content gives what is described as 'a creamy mouth-feel', which many people find pleasing but others may use as a warning to steer clear of fatty foods. Flavour also usefully shows if food is going off.

Even so, there must be other factors in operation or coffee cake would be just as popular as chocolate cake. Looking back to early childhood can reveal some of the mechanisms for how preference for flavours develops: food is rarely used solely for nutrition. If nutrition was the only concern then everyone would stick to the same basic food every day without another thought. Instead, food is used to keep young children quiet, for rewards, to cheer people up and as a cure for boredom. Many parents spend significant effort in trying to please their children at mealtimes because it is rewarding to see young children eat well but worrying when they won't eat.

The more particular foods, such as chocolate or crisps, are used to distract and entertain young children then the more prized and popular they become, whereas if a whole variety of different foods are used, such as chopped carrots or cucumber, nuts, breadsticks, a packet of raisins, or occasionally chocolate or crisps, then the link with wanting certain foods when bored or for comfort will not be so strong.

In short, from a very early age most children have been conditioned to like rich and highly flavoured snacks because they are regularly and successfully used to make life better. However, the battle is not lost, and older people can find ways to broaden the things they like and to 'grow out' of childhood favourites.

The 'feel-good' factor is most strongly linked to a food's image, not its flavour

Somehow, even ordinary and unappetising food can gain an image of wholesome goodness, warmth or irresistible allure if it is given the marketing once-over. The food industry uses a whole variety of techniques to make food appetising or to link it with a glamorous aspect of life so that some of that appeal rubs off on the food. Celebrity endorsements (such as using sports stars to promote fizzy drinks or crisps), product placement (for example, burger chain sponsorship of events so that the logo appears on every surface to boost its familiarity and induce brand loyalty) and endless 'special offers' (to make a food appear good value) are a few tricks of the marketing trade.

Before a new product is launched, the age group of the target market is decided upon and then an advertising campaign is developed to firmly establish the product within that age group's consciousness. For products aimed at young people, the manufacturers usually try to get celebrity endorsements from pop stars, comedians or sports stars and try to make the product appear cool, sexy or in some way controversial to boost both its appeal and the amount of media interest it receives.

Young people could be forgiven for finding traditional plain old favourites a trifle dull when they are constantly bombarded with images of foods claiming to enrich life.

Chapter 4 looks at marketing and advertising tactics so that young people can wise up to the hard sell.

Do chocoholics really exist?

There are a number of people who believe they are addicted to a food, which is most commonly chocolate. A variety of studies have looked at whether chocolate really is addictive but have found little compelling evidence that it is. Whilst eating chocolate may give a lift to boredom or feeling glum, this is probably related to earlier childhood conditioning, as explained above, where chocolate snacks provided a reliable way to feel better. When life is tough or when families have tended towards emotional eating, it could appear as if chocolate were pretty much the only thing that could lift mood or give a true feeling of satisfaction, so giving the impression that chocolate is essential and that the person must therefore be addicted.

Oddly, in studies, few people claiming a chocolate addiction were found to eat much more than a moderate amount of chocolate and most preferred milk chocolate rather than plain. Seeing as milk chocolate contains a lower amount of cocoa solids (which would provide the addictive element) but a higher amount of sugar and fat, it is more likely that chocoholics have simply become accustomed to feeling better after a tasty and sugary chocolate 'fix' rather than there being an addictive element.

Young people will eat what they can reach

Most young people lead busy and sometimes disorganised lives, where meals and snacks are fitted in as a necessity rather than a main concern. Health in general may not be high up the priority list, so that wholesome eating may seem irrelevant – convenience and flavour are all that count. Therefore, convenience foods may seem like the answer, particularly as they are widely available, cheap, tasty and filling. By the time they have suffered a few parental lectures on the virtues of veg and the power of protein, the chances are that sticking to junk food will be a good way to state their independence, plus a way of testing the boundaries of authority at home.

Most young people are likely to go through a phase of choosing junk food in preference to healthier items, but with a bit of guidance the phase can be kept short. If young people find ways to value themselves in general terms, then they will find that including the basics of a balanced diet becomes a positive choice rather than a naff alternative for nerds!

Physical factors such as fullness, hunger and energy requirements

The ability to recognise the sense of fullness and then to act on it – i.e. to stop eating – is becoming a rare talent. A whole series of factors may reduce a person's own control of portion sizes and how much is eaten, resulting in the tendency to eat too much. This, in combination with reduced activity levels, is leading to problems of overweight or even obesity. Tuning in to fullness 'cues' is an important step in eating appropriately.

How do people know when they are full?

Everyone is born with an appetite 'switch' so that during eating a sense of slight bloating or completeness gradually comes on, indicating when to stop eating. This sensation is not always the strongest feeling and it can easily be overridden by tempting food or by pressure to eat more from other people. It also takes a while to kick in, so if people eat very quickly they may eat too much before the sense of bloating hits them.

At a main meal, on average it takes around 900 calories (kcal) for an adult to feel full, although people quickly become accustomed to expecting more or less if different-sized meals are the norm.

If there is no interference, people adjust how much they eat over each 24-hour period rather than at each meal: for example, a large meal at lunchtime may be compensated for by a smaller meal in the evening, or appetite might increase if a lot of extra energy has been used up earlier in the day. The trouble is that most people find all sorts of interference in how they regulate their eating, whether it be from well-meaning relatives serving larger portions than needed or tempting snacks that seem too good to turn down or a dose of 'the blues' that requires a bit of indulgence therapy!

Studies suggest that overweight people have poorer 'fullness' cues than people of normal weight, which may partly explain why they eat more than they need. A significant reason why this tendency comes about is the amount of mealtime coaxing by a parent during earlier childhood. Rather than helping, parents who try to control what and how much their children eat end up with children who show the least ability to regulate their eating when not with their parents.

It is important to allow people to tune in to their own signals that say when to stop eating and some young people may need to relearn this skill if they were brought up with parents taking control of portion sizes and insisting on their clearing the plate. Parents cannot be sufficiently aware of either a young person's hunger or energy requirements each day. Energy requirements vary according to growth, activity levels and whether extra calories have been consumed that day in the form of drinks or snacks. A young person is in the best position to know all this and has an inbuilt mechanism to recognise it: hunger – if allowed to use it. The Top Teen Health Plan family guide looks at ways of improving a young person's awareness of both fullness and hunger.

Hunger is not always what it seems

In the same way that people may not recognise when they are full, their ability to recognise hunger may be a bit hazy too. Of course, the typical feelings of a rumbling tummy and gnawing emptiness seem obvious; and by the time that shaking sensation starts most people feel the answer is simple – food. And fast. However, hunger is more complex – why should someone who is very over-weight feel hungry at all, when they already have oodles of energy stored in their body fat? Oddly, it is often the most overweight people who feel the hungriest.

Hunger has many triggers:

- Blood sugar. If there is a rapid fall in blood sugar it triggers that empty feeling that makes many people crave something sweet. In fact, a sugary snack is an ineffective way to cure this problem because the sensation arises when blood sugar swings quickly. Simple sugar is the easiest thing for the body to handle and so a sugar dose will be swept rapidly out of the bloodstream, leaving the risk of the sensation coming back. It is far better to eat something starchy or containing protein so that blood sugar settles more slowly. Then the sensation will go away and stay away.

- Fat cells. When fat cells are called upon to release their energy, such as during dieting, they inform the body that they are getting empty by triggering hunger. Fat cells, in evolutionary terms, are a back-up system, an energy reserve for times of need. For this mechanism to be effective, they need a way of being restocked at a later date when food is available once more, and hunger is the way this is achieved. That is why it can be hard to keep weight off at the end of a diet – the empty fat cells are trying to restock in case of need again. For this reason, long-term weight loss is best achieved by gradual changes to lifestyle that include increasing exercise, so that the fat cells become gradually accustomed to containing less fat. Fat cells that have been rapidly starved shout the loudest.
- Boredom. Because food is generally a very effective way to lift boredom and to keep young children quiet, many people form a link between boredom and food. The more food was used to settle a fractious youngster, the stronger that link will have become, so that for some people any dull moments trigger a desire for food, with boredom and hunger appearing to be merged into one

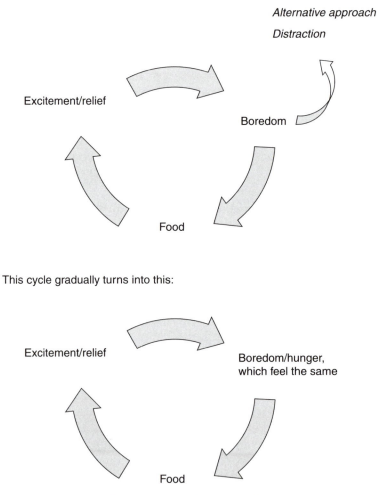

Figure 1.2 The learned cycle.

sensation (*see* Figure 1.2). People can learn to use distraction in order to quell hunger in between meals and relearn to distinguish between hunger and boredom once more.

- Expectation. Some people eat three square meals a day whereas others just eat in the evening. How hungry they all feel will depend on what they are used to and what they are expecting. Hunger is far greater when people have no idea what to expect, such as when meals and snacks vary from day to day with very little predictability. (In the same way, a journey to an unknown destination usually feels as though it has taken far longer than travelling the same distance along a familiar route.) If meals follow a regular and predictable pattern then hunger becomes far less obvious and the sense of fullness tends to become clearer too.

Family attitudes to meals may need reviewing

One long-standing issue at mealtimes is whether children are brought up to finish everything on their plate. This is commonly a learned behaviour: people tend to encourage their children to do so if that is how their own parents wanted things when they were younger.

There are many reasons for feeling that it is good parenting to encourage this (*see* Box 1.1). By looking at these reasons from the young person's viewpoint, it is possible to come to very different conclusions. The following section takes each reason in turn.

Box 1.1 Reasons why parents justify encouraging their family to eat

- It is wasteful to leave good food.
- How can we leave good food to waste when there are starving millions in Africa?
- Some people feel it is impolite to leave food uneaten.
- If a person fills up at mealtimes, there may be less chance of wanting snacks later on.
- If a person has been told to eat up during a meal, the parent may feel justified in refusing snacks later.
- If a person has to eat up everything on the plate, then perhaps healthy items will be consumed in the process, whereas if there is choice about what is eaten, won't the vegetables be left out altogether?

Is it wasteful to leave good food?

Whilst it is wasteful in one way, it must be remembered that it is the responsibility of the person preparing the meal to decide on the quantity of food provided. It is not a young person's fault if too much food is prepared, leaving some left over. Encouraging the family to finish of excess food by complaining that it will otherwise be wasted will teach them to eat in order to please the cook or because of guilt, and will encourage them to disregard their own hunger signals.

If someone has specifically requested a certain item or amount to eat then, after checking that they made a sensible request, it would be reasonable to encourage them to finish what they asked for. If a person routinely asks for more than they want, encourage them to take smaller amounts first and to request seconds if still hungry.

If the cook routinely cooks too much, find ways to either prepare less, perhaps by weighing out dry ingredients such as potatoes, pasta or rice before cooking, or by finding ideas for using up leftovers in other dishes.

Will it help starving nations if we avoid food wastage in this country?
It is sad that food availability is so uneven throughout the world, but encouraging a child in Western leafy suburbia to overeat when already full will merely increase the risk of obesity. Encouraging people to override their own 'fullness' cues will destroy the most reliable mechanism that people have for eating sensibly. Factors that encourage obesity in one country will have no benefit on food shortages elsewhere.

The most positive way to reduce food wastage is to review the amount of food prepared and served. If the family regularly leaves food untouched because they feel full, then too much food is being prepared. Preparing too little is safer than too much, as the meal can always be padded out with bread, pudding, etc. if quantities were significantly underestimated.

Leaving food might be seen as impolite
If a person has been brought up to feel that leaving food is impolite, this can be addressed by allowing people to serve themselves, but with the advice that if they have asked for or taken something then it is polite to finish it, as above. In addition, ensure that people pay attention whilst a meal is being served so they can express their views on how much they want. Make sure the family are confident about asking for small portions or saying 'no' to new things at mealtimes if they are not sure.

Untouched food could be returned to the serving dish if too much has been taken.

Explain that if a person is feeling really full, it is fine to ask politely to be excused from eating more.

Will eating well at mealtimes reduce the chance of snacking later?
If a person eats until they are full, they will be no more likely to snack later than if they had overeaten at the meal. In fact, as discussed above, if people have been taught to ignore their inner messages about being full, they will be more likely to snack following a large meal out of either boredom or habit, because the awareness of when they are full has been lost.

It is questionable whether snacking should be seen as a problem at all. Other omnivores such as monkeys tend to graze on food throughout the day, rather than sticking to set mealtimes. Rigid mealtimes are generated by society and are not a natural tendency, so perhaps it is understandable to want to eat when hungry rather than because the clock is chiming mealtime. In our society it is more convenient for families to fit in with set mealtimes because schools and workplaces follow the clock, but there are no fixed rights and wrongs about this, and it is up to individual families to decide when snacks are suitable. However, the type of snack is important – this is discussed further in Section 2 of the book.

Will insisting on a clean plate mean healthy food gets eaten?
It would be nice to think so, but as discussed earlier in this chapter, people object to things that are forced upon them. Bribing them to clear their plate by offering an unhealthy but desirable pudding will raise the pudding's profile, so increasing the chance of developing a sweet tooth, because people grow to like foods that are used as a reward. It may also encourage them to ignore when they are full. The best approach is to develop a taste for healthy foods from the start so that they are eaten out of choice and for enjoyment. Many of the approaches in this book will gradually encourage young people to achieve this.

Summary points

- Weight is important to young people, not simply due to appearances but because it influences how people feel about themselves, their fitness and their health throughout later adult life.
- Young people often go through phases of feeling that health is unimportant or temporarily irrelevant. Experimenting with taking risks may seem more alluring during the transition from childhood to adulthood.
- *The Balance of Good Health* is an ideal food guide for all young people over five. Focusing on eating plenty of healthy foods is more rewarding than worrying over whether a particular food is good or bad.
- People who choose to eat healthy foods do so because they enjoy them. Foods become more popular when they are familiar and if they form a predictable and routine part of the diet.
- Serving rich treats too frequently results in people expecting them frequently and missing them when they are absent. Learning to expect and enjoy ordinary things on ordinary days means that occasional treats will carry more impact.
- Household routines should be reviewed to see if they are causing lifestyle problems. They may be used to introduce improvements to the family's eating habits.
- Young people need space to make choices, even if it results in a few mistakes along the way. They resent being forced into a corner over an issue. Forceful parents may end up with youngsters who are defiant and uncooperative or who become timid and indecisive.
- There is more to a food's popularity than its flavour. Young people are swayed by a food's entertainment value and by marketing that makes it appear cool, sporty or good value.
- The sensation of hunger is often mixed up with that of boredom, leading to grazing in between meals.
- It is crucial to recognise the sense of fullness in order not to overeat. Encouraging people to clear their plate requires people to ignore their own fullness 'cues', so increasing the chance of weight problems.

Chapter 2

Testing times

Emotions enter into everything for teenagers, who move on from testing their parents' reactions to testing the reactions of everyone they meet by experimenting with dress, language, behaviour and sometimes eating, particularly at times of stress. Role models tend to be friends, other adults and celebrities, which can lead to experimenting with alcohol, smoking and sometimes drugs. Young people can be encouraged to broaden their view of role models and develop confidence in their own decision making.

The world looks different from a teenager's viewpoint

For most teenagers, the impact of the physical changes required to become an adult is dwarfed by the enormous emotional turmoil associated with growing up. Whilst many teenagers become temporarily obsessed with body image and appearance, this is only one symptom of normal teenage development, which also includes becoming more distant from parents, experimenting with taking risks and having fun, and finding out about who and what the teenager wants to be.

In short, emotions colour everything, so understanding teenage issues involves remembering what hard work it is wading through life whilst experiencing those daunting emotional reactions for the first time. The first crush, rejection from the opposite sex, success and failure, not looking the part, insufficient money to keep up with friends, the dumping of uncool boy- or girlfriends, teenage spots: these are just a few common dilemmas that most teenagers have to get to grips with. The scary discovery that girls – a subspecies despised by most 11-year-old boys – are now fascinating and mysterious can come as a humiliating shock.

It is easy for adults to look back at their own teenage years and wonder what all the fuss was about, whilst forgetting that teenagers are doing their best to act like adults, but without the benefit of adult experience and knowledge. It is only with practice and experience that people develop emotional confidence – teenagers start off emotionally in the dark.

However, the teenage years are a necessary evil. Just like learning a foreign language, the more you practise, the better you become. Therefore dealing with emotional relationships, fighting with parents over home boundaries and exploring how much or how little effort is needed to get by all help a teenager prepare for adulthood. Protecting children from conflict and making all their decisions for them just means that adulthood itself is postponed and may become an even scarier prospect; better to explore when parents, teachers and mentors are around to guide the process.

The teenage conspiracy theory

It is safely assumed that spotty, greasy-haired layabouts (flawlessly characterised by Harry Enfield's 'Kevin') are distasteful and loathed by all. Imagine looking in the mirror one day and realising that you have become just that! The first thing any sensible teenager will do is to check out the theory – act sweet and childlike and nothing will change, but act like a teenager and suddenly the rules will need to be written afresh. By behaving how they now feel – wanting to explore emotions, freedom and the lures of adulthood – the reactions from other adults confirm the theory that teenagers are to be despised, are different from everyone else and are thoroughly hard done by.

Even though a teenager's need for love and approval is, if anything, greater than that of a junior, outward behaviour would seem to reject and scorn it. Teenagers like to be right, and by acting aggressively and rudely they appear to prove the theory correct! The next chapter looks at how parents can help their teenagers disprove this theory, because disapproval of a young person's choices does not automatically mean that a parent is rejecting the whole person.

Common sense doesn't always apply to young people

Young people are not clones of their parents, but it can take a great deal of courage as well as a few wrong choices to find out what sort of person a teenager wants to become. Simply copying and accepting the views and values of parents is an easy option, but may not lead the teenager to where he or she wants to be. Exploring self-expression, conflict and new ideas is a normal and healthy avenue, even though it may go against the parental grain and be very hard work at the time. Despite a reactionary phase, many teenage 'handfuls' settle down to a normal life that may encompass many of the original parental values that were once scorned.

For many young people, being told what to do simply won't work. Unless they learn the hard way, they won't learn at all, which means making mistakes and then sorting the mistakes out. This doesn't mean that parental input must stop, but the decision-making process needs to evolve so that the young person, rather than the parent, is in charge of the final say. Getting things wrong doesn't have to be disastrous, particularly if there is guidance available over how to make amends and change tack.

It is worth thinking carefully about appearance and behaviour issues before taking too strong a view. Is it a situation where there is a right and wrong answer or is it just a case of different opinions, each of which may be valid depending on the point of view?

From a young person's viewpoint, it is not always the outcome that is necessarily important; the journey and experiences that arise from it may have far more impact than the outcome itself (*see* Box 2.1).

Box 2.1 Appearance gives clues to inner identity

Leanne, a quiet 15-year-old girl with mousy-brown hair, really wanted to dye her hair black, but had many arguments with her mother about it. Eventually she booked the appointment herself and used her Nan's birthday money to pay for it. She was secretly very disappointed with the outcome because she thought it made her look haggard and was suddenly struck with worry that her existing clothes wouldn't look right with black hair.

She was surprised at the repercussions her hairdo generated; she had expected her mum to be angry but hadn't thought that anyone else would pay much attention. First she heard her older brother using her example as an excuse for stretching his own boundaries when he wanted to buy an amplifier for his guitar: 'If you let Leanne stick her head in a bucket of tar, I don't see why I can't be allowed to play some decent music!'

She then noticed other people's reactions. Some of her friends were impressed with her bold and defiant move, which increased her status at school. Others laughed and called her names, but she was quite surprised that strangers related to her differently as she now looked older than her years. Initially she was very hurt by her mother's disapproval and coldness towards her, but gradually found her increased status amongst her friends made up for her mother's reaction.

Even though she had initially disliked the way she now looked, she began to experiment with dark make-up and black clothing, not because she thought she looked particularly good, but because she found the reactions that her appearance generated gave her a buzz and a clear identity that seemed more interesting than the mousy, quiet girl she had been before.

Her Nan's reaction, which Leanne had been worried about, was the most heartening: 'I don't mind how you look as long as you still visit.'

Emotions have a big impact on eating patterns

As eating is such a social, frequent activity, which generates discussion, influences how we feel and can alter our appearance, it is no wonder that the emotional turmoil of the teenage years frequently impacts on eating patterns.

From the earliest years people use food as a method of communication, and as people get older eating patterns may give information about how they feel, sometimes even more clearly than when trying to put feelings into words. The commonest example is loss of appetite when stressed or upset. Weight loss in response to a bereavement or relationship break-up is usual, although some people may find increased appetite due to comfort eating in these circumstances.

Table 2.1 contains a few examples of how emotions and eating patterns may be linked.

Table 2.1 Examples of how emotions and eating patterns may be linked

Eating pattern	Emotional issue
Dean criticises everything his mother serves, but still eats it.	Dean resents that whilst wanting to grow up and be an adult, he has no say in most household matters, and vents his frustration by being rude.
Jody has started to worry about being chubby, but still eats everything on her plate and never refuses seconds.	Jody is seeking parental approval by clearing her plate, as taught as a small child. She feels the need to comply with things her parents offer.
Rosie has taken to stealing food since her mum started a 'healthy eating' regime at home.	For Rosie, food is a comfort. Healthy eating seems like a poor excuse to leave out the good things in life – she can't see any point in joining the starvation programme that her mum seems to be promoting.
Owen has given up eating meat and become a vegetarian.	Owen has become anxious about inequalities in the world, especially since reading some Amnesty International leaflets. He feels powerless to do much, but stopping eating meat eases his conscience slightly.
Fiona has been skipping meals and then binge eating, when she will suddenly have cravings to eat anything she can get her hands on.	Fiona has been anxious about her weight and has tried to lose some by cutting out lunch. By teatime she is so hungry that her will-power gives way completely and she then overeats, after which she feels guilty.

The effect of emotions on eating patterns is not always mild or short-lived; some teenagers can become ill because their emotions are so disrupted, and the resulting eating disorders can be hard to treat. Anorexia nervosa and bulimia are examples of eating disorders and are discussed in Chapter 10, with information provided on how to obtain further help.

If there are any suspicions that a young person is developing a problem-eating pattern, seek further advice as quickly as possible, because the sooner help is available, the greater the chance of recovery. Some problems will naturally sort themselves out, but others can turn into a vicious cycle that becomes harder to break the longer it continues.

Emotions can affect many other things besides eating patterns

Even though this is a book about weight and eating problems, the following section examines other typical teenage concerns because factors that influence eating patterns may also explain why teenagers experiment with smoking, alcohol and drugs and start to engage in (sometimes risky) sexual experiences. Emotional issues underlie all these behaviours and understanding them will give a better idea of which approaches might help. Boosting self-esteem is the best way to help with most teenage difficulties, including eating problems, because people who value themselves are most likely to take good care of themselves.

Psychological problems are very common in the teenage years, with around 25% of teenagers describing difficulties at some point and around 7–10% of them having moderate to severe problems. These problems are of more concern if they are frequent and intense and if they persist, although most teenage problems will gradually subside with support and understanding from family and friends.

One survey looked at how psychological problems affecting teenagers have changed over three generations of 15-year-olds, in 1974, 1986 and 1999. It showed that roughly one in five teenagers have behaviour problems such as lying, stealing, aggression, anxiety and depression. There was no change over time in aggressive behaviour, fighting or bullying or in the rate of hyperactivity, but the chance of emotional problems shot up after 1986. The study found that this increase couldn't be explained simply by an increased rate of divorce or single-parent families because the same proportion of two-parent households were reporting these problems. It's a society problem.

Teenagers today are under much more pressure than in years gone by. They are targeted by the hugely powerful advertising industry, there is information overload with scare stories about every last facet of life, and the education system is now horribly target-led, which piles on further pressure. Many teenagers are wealthier, so have access to designer gear, alcohol, cigarettes and drugs, none of which makes life simpler – indeed they complicate things. Even the teenagers who are strapped for cash are aware of much greater materialistic pressures to wear the right things and follow the right trends.

Money doesn't buy happiness, it buys choice, and this makes life more complex. Even though money may make life richer and more fulfilling in one way, having more choice creates anxieties about how money is spent and makes people more aware of, rather than less bothered about, what they do and don't have.

Most teenagers, whilst possibly experimenting here and there, will cope with pressures from peers, teachers and family, but some find life more of a struggle. Factors that increase the chance of difficulties during the teenage years, particularly aggression and experimenting with taking risks, include:

- coming from a separated family or where there is a lot of family discord
- parents who have had psychological problems themselves, including depression
- families who tend to use punishments and threats to keep their kids in line, rather than using positive rewards and encouragement
- children who have always had a 'difficult temperament', i.e. they have always tended to vent their feelings freely, been prone to irritability and had a negative outlook on things.

Anxiety problems and some eating problems are commoner where:

- there has been parental over-concern and a tendency to over-protection
- the young person has been helped to avoid fearful and difficult situations altogether
- certain stressful events have had a big impact on the young person
- the young person sets him or herself high standards and has tended to be a high achiever.

Why do teenagers start drinking and smoking?

Health education starts early these days, with many schools offering broad-based information to juniors about the dangers of smoking, drinking alcohol and using drugs.

Some important facts that children may be taught about alcohol include:

- Drinking large amounts (called bingeing) can be dangerous for young people because their bodies, especially the liver, are not yet mature enough to break down alcohol adequately, so it can have more effect and sometimes lead to alcohol poisoning.
- Mixing drinks can be more risky than sticking to one type of alcohol.
- Drinking alcohol and taking drugs together is very dangerous. It may increase the chance of a serious drug overdose.
- Young people are more likely to be involved in accidents or fights when drunk. This can lead to a criminal record, which may seriously affect the young person's future.
- Drinking regularly and heavily can lead to many health problems, including liver and stomach disease and alcohol addiction.

Some of the facts about smoking include:

- By age 20, 80% of smokers wish they had never started, but find it very difficult to give up.
- Nicotine is highly addictive; many young people who try occasional cigarettes will be smoking regularly within a year of their first cigarette.
- When nicotine from the last cigarette leaves the body (which only takes two hours), a smoker will feel irritable, restless and hungrier. This is withdrawal and the symptoms disappear when another cigarette is smoked. But only for another hour or two . . .
- Cigarettes never 'taste good' – people just get used to how foul they are because they are so effective at relieving the withdrawal feelings from the previous cigarette.
- For someone on 20 a day, that means 7300 cigarettes a year, which at roughly £4.50 a packet will cost about £1650 each year. Where does that sort of money come from?

So why then do those utterly convinced and knowledgeable ten-year-olds grow into teenagers who are likely to try the lot? Box 2.2 provides some statistics.

Box 2.2 Some statistics on smoking and alcohol

Smoking

- Smoking is commoner in teenage girls than boys, with 11% of 11–15 year-old girls smoking at least once a week, compared to 9% of boys. But by 16–20 years of age this changes round, with roughly 30% of males smoking compared to 26% of females.
- At age 11, only 1% of children smoke at least once a week, but by 15 years of age roughly 23% do.

- In 2001, 40% of 12–13 year-olds and 60% of 14–15 year-olds had tried smoking.

Alcohol

- Alcohol consumption starts soon after age 11 for many children, with a quarter of 11–15 year-olds likely to have had an alcoholic drink in the last week.
- There has been an increase in teenage weekly alcohol consumption in the last decade; 11–15 year-olds were drinking roughly 5.3 units per week in 1990, but this increased to 10.5 units per week by 2002.
- 1000 youngsters are admitted to hospital with alcohol poisoning requiring emergency treatment in the UK each year.
- Medically recommended limits for *adults* are 14 units per week for women and 21 units per week for men. In 1997, amongst 16–24 year-olds, 33% of males were drinking over 21 units per week, with 9% drinking over 50 units per week; 22% of females were drinking over 14 units weekly and 5% over 35 units.

There are many reasons why young people ignore health messages and take risks

One of the strongest reasons for risk taking – such as drinking to excess, smoking or even using drugs – is that it is a clear statement that the person no longer considers him or herself a child. Young people feel that they are autonomous, which means that they feel independent of other people and that they can weigh things up for themselves.

Another reason is that young people hear good things about risky activities and this makes them curious. They may have heard that smoking can calm nerves or help with weight loss and that alcohol gives a good buzz. When they first try these things they discover that they enjoy the short-term effects and that nothing terrible happens as a result. This can make the scare tactics that are often used to put people off seem irrelevant. Old age and the illnesses that might be commoner as a result of smoking seem a very long way off – long enough to be worried about some other day. For alcohol, especially, many young people see parents and family enjoying a drink, which leads them to see drinking as normal adult behaviour. As they are growing into their adult selves, it is understandable that many teenagers try alcohol as part of this process.

Many teenagers go through phases of just wanting to break the rules. Risk taking will often start after a family argument or in response to a stressful event or build-up of pressure. If the teenager can get some relief by using a substance which in addition to its calming effect will annoy parents and may give kudos amongst friends, then it may feel like a risk worth taking.

Most smokers are well aware of the risks and find shock tactics make little difference to whether they continue because it seems unlikely that the risks will apply to them. Almost every activity in life carries some degree of risk, but we don't let that stop us crossing roads, going for a swim or travelling by plane. Because we tend to ignore or minimise these daily risks, young people (and many adults) apply the same approach to the risks of smoking or drinking alcohol, even though those risks are far higher. For teenagers, in particular, increasing the price of cigarettes has more effect than educational measures on reducing smoking.

Young people and drugs

It is worth remembering that for most young people illegal drug use is not a part of normal life and that most people who try drugs do not continue using them.

There has been a big increase in the number of young people using 'recreational drugs', where drugs are taken at a club or party. Cannabis is the most commonly used drug among 11–25 year-olds, and it is estimated that around 4% of 16–25 year-olds have used ecstasy in the last three months. Only a very small proportion of people who ever take drugs will become 'problem users'. Very occasional use of these drugs is not likely to lead to dependence, but using them weekly or most weeks will increase the chance of the person getting hooked.

If there are concerns about a young person and drugs and alcohol, further information and support are available through the organisations listed in Appendix 2.

Young people and contraception

Sexual health is important to young people. The majority will have their first sexual encounter in the teenage years, but this is a time when it can be most difficult to get the right advice and support.

Risky or unprotected sex is commoner if young people have had little education about contraception and relationships. Giving them advice and access to contraception services does not mean they will be more or less likely to have sex, but it increases the chances that they will choose safe sex and have a relationship that they feel happy with.

There are various barriers that make it difficult for teenagers to get the right help:

- For many teenagers, fear of a parent being informed or finding a supply of contraception is a big barrier to using services.
- Inconvenient surgery or clinic hours can also make it difficult.
- Where healthcare is funded via insurance, such as in the United States (US), a parent may be required to sign insurance forms, so that the teenager is put off even trying to seek help because a parent would need to be involved.

Many young people assume that parents will automatically disapprove or interfere with a relationship if they try to discuss sexual matters. In addition, they feel that these things are private and personal and they do not wish them to be shared with the usual family gossip. Hence the family that has, until now, been the main source of advice and support no longer seems the place to turn to.

Although friends may be supportive and sometimes well informed, they may be short of the right facts or knowledge to sort out their friends' problems.

As there has been a big change in approach over the last generation, with much greater openness about sexual matters, many parents could overcome some of these difficulties by informing their teenager of their own views. In the UK, in particular, parents have been effectively excluded from taking any part in teenage sex education. However, this approach is unhelpful, and basic communication about opinions and values can help teenagers through this worrying phase of adolescence.

For parents who would prefer their potentially sexually active teenager to use effective contraception, they should make this clear and give simple guidance about how to sort this out. Parents don't need to get more involved if they don't wish to; it is the permission that makes the difference.

It is worth remembering that many early sexual experiences are not always welcomed, but some teenagers find it difficult to reject unwanted advances and may feel pressurised into having sex when they would have preferred to wait. This can create emotional turmoil, particularly if the teenager is unsure who to talk to. Teenagers will benefit from knowing what parental support they can expect if they find themselves in this sort of scenario, particularly if their parent has previously expressed strong disapproval of early sex.

For parents who feel uncomfortable bringing up the subject, it may be easiest to start with leaflets about relationships, contraception and sexual health. These are available from clinics and surgeries and in some schools. Information is also available on the internet – see Appendix 2 for further details.

Why do some teenagers turn to bullying others?

Bullying remains a part of life for many teenagers. In a large study called 'Bullying in Britain' by Young Voice, an organisation set up to find out young people's views, they discovered some of the reasons why some teenagers resort to making other people's lives miserable.

A half of male bullies and a quarter of female bullies had themselves been threatened with violence at school. The majority of the bullying teenagers in the survey had suffered either name calling (93%) or racism (81%).

Girl bullies were around three times more likely to try drugs in order to get some release from tension and depression.

Around a third of both male and female bullies had experienced violence from adults. Because they had been made to do things due to the threat of violence from others, they learned to use the same type of threats to get what they wanted themselves.

Young people need pride in their own identity

It is crucial to understand how fundamental self-esteem is to caring for ourselves in order to help teenagers make good choices. Just focusing on superficial symptoms will only give temporary improvements if low confidence and low self-esteem persist. Whether the concern is an eating problem, anger outbursts, depressive symptoms or rebellious and risky behaviour, the starting point should be to understand why the problems arose and then to tackle the underlying causes.

A common factor in young people is anxiety about their changing bodies alongside a greater awareness of the challenges of the wider world, which leads to lack of confidence in the adult identity that they are building. Creating a sense of pride in this new identity is a positive way to progress.

A study of the Pima Indians of Arizona looked at the effect of pride on health. These people tend to have high levels of obesity and diabetes and a study was developed to give advice on nutrition and exercise. There were two groups: the first was given standard healthy living advice and the second was given the same advice but with additional regular discussions from local leaders about Pima culture and history.

After 12 months the first group had made no progress and had in fact become slightly less healthy. The second group showed improvements in weight and diabetic tests. It appeared that their increased pride in their culture and community helped them to feel that their own health was worth looking after, and that their increased self-esteem improved their self-control.

Another example of the odd effect of self-esteem on health is the finding that actors who win an Oscar have a four-year longer life expectancy than those who are nominated but do not win. Not only do these actors know that they count – they know that other people think so too. Of course, handing out Oscars to teenagers is not a feasible way of improving their health, but focusing on self-esteem is.

There are many ways to boost self-esteem. Listed below are some of the principles that need to be applied in order for self-esteem to be generated:

- The reward received for work done should fit the effort that was put in. Working hard and receiving no recognition can be soul-destroying. Some people have to work tremendously hard just to earn the bare minimum of income and this has been shown to be demoralising and linked to worse health.
- People need to feel in control over their circumstances. Being confronted with a problem to which there is neither solution nor escape is a recipe for despair. Bullying is a good example of not feeling in control. It is usually a reflection of the bully's own problems, which the victim is not in control of. If there is no way of avoiding the bully – perhaps they are in the same class at school, or the bully is their employer – then the victim will have no feeling of control or way of escape. This then erodes self-esteem and makes them feel hopeless.
- Pride in ourselves should be cherished and encouraged. Injuring pride, for example when painstaking work is rubbished or when someone scoffs at a change in our appearance, is a good way to destroy self-esteem.

Emotional intelligence

Emotional intelligence, or EQ, is a way of summing up how emotions govern our lives. Are we in control of our emotions or do our emotions take control of us?

Those people who have good emotional health are in control of their thoughts, feelings and behaviour. The fact that they feel good about themselves gives them inner strength, which helps them to have good relationships with other people, including their family and teachers. It also enables them to have self-awareness and self-control, and to weigh up the pros and cons of a choice without rushing into snap decisions for superficial reasons.

Good emotional health allows people to value and care for themselves, which increases their ability to avoid unnecessary risks. By not copying the risk-taking behaviour of their peers (such as trying a cigarette) they do not feel left out, but glad that they can see beyond the pressure to try what their friends are doing.

When emotional health is poor, the person feels low and worthless. This increases the chance of risk taking for several reasons:

- When something is worthless, people don't bother to look after it – no one worries about throwing out rubbish. If people feel worthless then they will not be bothered about harming themselves and taking big risks will not seem to matter.
- When feeling very low, a person will clutch to things that give short-term relief. Feeling low makes it hard to think about the future, but temporary relief becomes important, so drinking alcohol or trying drugs can feel like a good short-term solution to problems.
- When people feel low, they have no confidence in their own opinions and may find it hard to make or stick to decisions. This can make it easy for other people to bully or take advantage.
- Low self-esteem makes it hard to weigh up values, so that materialistic gains may be rated too highly, which can lead to stealing; and short-term pleasure can override safety, which can lead to drug use or sexual experimentation.
- Low emotional health can result in a person rebelling against their current unhappy lifestyle and seeking approval and friendship from new people. This may lead to getting in with a 'bad crowd' who are more likely to encourage risk taking, and it may mean losing old friends.

Emotional overload

Some young people feel unsure of whether they are suffering from good or poor emotional health as they swing up and down with every passing comment. This is sometimes a symptom of emotional overload and can happen in response to good things as well as difficulties. It is a common reaction to too much going on or an accumulation of life-events (such as moving house, joining a new club, changing schools, getting a pet, parental upsets or physical illness).

Emotional overload can be reduced by some simple steps, which include:

- sharing concerns and talking with family and friends
- getting fresh air, exercise and adequate sleep
- having concerns listened to by others, rather than just being given more advice
- breaking problems down into smaller elements and finding several strategies to a problem, rather than putting all hope on one single solution
- being given guidance about the best person to talk to about a problem
- getting some positive feedback about progress, rather than finding that parents seem to criticise and focus on current problems.

'Sticks and stones may break my bones, but names can never hurt me . . .'

The commonest triggers for name-calling are weight and appearance. In a survey of almost 5000 US adolescents, 30% of girls and 25% of boys were being teased about their weight. This teasing resulted in low self-esteem plus low satisfaction with their body and high depressive symptoms, including suicidal thoughts. Because these symptoms were so common, it has led to the idea of teaching skills to enable young people to deal with 'harmful speech'. This does not mean equipping teenagers with a batch of snappy one-liners that would leave the bully reeling, but an approach that helps minimise the impact of hearing hurtful things (*see* Box 2.3).

Box 2.3 Dealing with harmful speech

- Recognise that other people, whilst being entitled to their own opinion, may not be right.
- No one has the right to say hurtful things without legitimate reason. (People who care about a person may discuss things that are upsetting if it is done constructively and to help.) Name-calling is usually a reflection of the bully's own inadequacies and need to appear tough.
- Challenge (silently, rather than out loud to the bully) the facts of what the bully is saying. Common insults include using animal names such as cow or pig, or making out that being overweight means being smelly or even stupid. These are all illogical insults because everyone is human, personal hygiene has nothing to do with body size but is related to whether people wash, and body shape tells nothing about what goes on in people's heads.
- If the bully is hitting a raw nerve because there are already concerns about weight, then remember that this is something that is already well known, but it remains none of the bully's business.
- Use hurtful speech to your own advantage. It can teach who to avoid wasting time with and who not to trust.
- Practise positive self-talk. Try to replace negative thoughts with either neutral or positive ones. For example, 'My life is terrible' can become 'I may be going through a tough time right now, but I am working on the problems which means life can improve'.
- Rehearse and practise situations that cause stress. People may find it helpful to practise holding their head up high and walking on without saying anything. Or build confidence in stating feelings, which should be expressed in a polite and firm way rather than by being overly aggressive or passive.
- Find a good stress-busting routine to help deal with hurtful speech. This will usually include sharing unhappiness with a family member or a friend, but may include kicking a football, hitting a punch bag or writing thoughts down.

- Building a network of friends who can be trusted and called on is a very good way to cope. People may have to offer support to others for them to start trusting first (perhaps to someone else who is being bullied too, for example), but that's how friendships often form.

Summary points

- The journey from childhood to becoming an adult means that teenagers start to distance themselves from their families and begin to make their own choices.
- Becoming more distant sometimes involves being rude or rebellious, and testing out what happens if they do the wrong thing.
- Emotions have a big impact on whether a teenager starts smoking, tries alcohol or experiments with drugs, as well as affecting eating patterns.
- Teenagers are more likely to say no to risky behaviour if they feel good about themselves and have good emotional health and self-esteem.
- Teenagers can be taught to combat bullying and name-calling by learning to deal with hurtful speech.

Chapter 3

Parents are no longer in charge of teenage decisions

Most teenage choices will be made when parents are not around, but parents can still contribute towards the decision-making process. Any parenting approach may have opposite effects to those intended and young people may abandon healthy habits due to peer pressure. Young people can be invited to have a say in domestic matters that previously happened without their input.

Secrecy is normal

With the onset of puberty, an invisible thorny hedge grows up between teenagers and their parents. Even in the most relaxed and sharing of households there are some things that teenagers just don't want to share. Privacy and secrecy are normal teenage requirements because the changes both physically and emotionally are scary and, by their very nature, induce a reduction in confidence. Low confidence makes it difficult to share worries – might a parent laugh? Might a parent be dismissive? Perhaps the changes are abnormal? Teenagers care what their parents think and feel unsure what reaction the changes will generate.

The teenage years are not secretive and distancing just because of lack of confidence; it is a time when teenagers prepare themselves emotionally for leaving home and becoming adults. This means making their own decisions and learning from mistakes. By becoming secretive, the teenager is getting some practice at dealing with problems – vital for the progression to adulthood – although one of the most important lessons learned is that they do not have to deal with everything on their own; sometimes they can and will ask for help.

Just because parents are no longer in charge doesn't mean that they are redundant. This section looks at many ways that parents can influence and help their child without needing to be in control.

Who else is now influencing the teenage mind?

Adolescence sees the dawning of self-awareness and this brings about constant comparisons with others of the same age. Teenagers are acutely aware of their own and other people's bodies, clothing, possessions, behaviour and relationships. One of the biggest fears around this time is of failing to be like their friends or not being able to do what their friends are doing. Most teenagers start to question the meaning of life, their identity and what their role in life may be, as well as feeling anxious about how they will cope. A teenager's personality becomes a major factor that governs behaviour – even though personality is evident from an early age, it really starts to have an impact on the decision-making process throughout the teenage years. Friends' opinions begin to matter far more than a parent's views, with peer pressure becoming highly significant. But even more, teenagers are susceptible to advertising pressures, media images and celebrity trends. They might not like to think so, but teenagers, just like adults, follow trends like well-heeled sheep!

Some of the rebellion of these years relates to the realisation that other families do things differently and that routines are not set in stone. It is normal to question why other friends get away with behaviours that are frowned upon at home and to double-check how rigid home rules are. Many young people experience resentment from noticing that some friends are better off, more attractive or more accomplished. For some people this provides the inspiration to improve their own lot, but for others it can blunt motivation because they perceive that life is not fair.

These increasing influences ensure that teenagers do not become mini versions of their parents. Just because the family has always done things a certain way doesn't mean that each teenager will automatically follow suit.

Any parenting approach can backfire

There is a wide variety of parenting types ranging from domineering control freaks right through to unconcerned, overly laid-back parents. Whilst most parents fall some way between the two, depending on the issue, it helps to know what effects these extremes have on young people.

When parents are rigid and inflexible, young people either lose all confidence in their own judgement, becoming shy and indecisive, or they react with aggressive defiance, exploring exactly how much trouble and effort it will take to stamp their own authority on their choices and take control themselves. Young people who experience conflict in one area are likely to test other boundaries too, and so arguments over one issue can easily spread to arguments about most things, leading to communication breakdown and rebellion.

At the other extreme, a very laid-back parent who never passes comment may generate a different set of problems. Although laid-back families are likely to avoid the degree of confrontation and conflict that rigid families may experience, parents need to take a stand over certain issues so that young people have a fixed starting point from which to work out their own approach. Teenagers do not have all the answers and rather than having to find out everything through trial and error, many young people are glad of some guidance. A parent who stands back and says nothing may miss opportunities to help their child, who meanwhile will resort to others for advice, thereby running the risk of being led astray. If teenagers feel that a parent's indifference means they are not worth caring about, it will damage self-esteem and increase the chance of risk taking, because young people remain sensitive to family approval even if their body language says otherwise.

All parents, including those who are just as caring as they are flexible, may experience a rebellious phase of some sort because the pressures of adolescence are complex and it is normal to make a few mistakes along the way.

The majority of parents take a mix and match approach – being lenient over some issues and strict over others, whilst often feeling unsure about what is best.

Many young people go through a difficult stage when they have to make important choices, such as deciding on a course that will affect their whole future. Parents may find it difficult not to let their own hopes and ambitions enter into the decision-making process, adding further worry, pressure and indecision to the young person's lot. The parenting approach will need to be sensitive to both a young person's desire to be independent and their lack of experience in order to minimise conflict at these stressful times.

Domestic issues may be a cause of conflict

The very nature of still living at home can trigger teenager frustration over not being in control of daily routines. Young people may find this frustration hard to pinpoint or put into words, so that it emerges as teenage angst and rebellion, reflecting the quandary of being neither a grown-up nor a child. Household routines may begin to feel boring, safe and predictable whereas the young person now craves excitement, variety and new chances.

Teenagers may see parents as uncool or dim-witted, old or out of touch, resulting in reactionary and volatile outbursts because these new emotions are unfamiliar and hard to contain. Whatever approaches a parent takes, there's a good chance a teenager will object.

The early teenage years are often a time when young people abandon some of the healthy habits and views that they were brought up with. This may be a temporary phase, particularly if parental reaction is measured and reserved, so that faddy diets, bizarre dress sense, experimenting with smoking or drinking to excess can be short-lived phases that the teenager feels happy to drop once the novelty wears off. If they feel trapped and unhappy, whether due to parental reaction or to problems outside home, these visible lifestyle changes may persist as a signal of inner despondency, illustrating the desire to appear grown-up by making clear statements that they are different from the rest of the family.

However, that doesn't mean that parents are now redundant, merely the providers of a free hotel to be outrageously abused. Many parents are able to stay friends with their teenagers throughout; some teenagers never need to rebel. Others are so enchanting, funny and kind that even the downs have their lighter side, and their natural generosity of spirit carries them through the pitfalls of the teenage years unscathed.

Couldn't we just let teenagers get on without interference?

Why do parents get so bothered about whether teenagers clean their rooms, dump dodgy boy- or girlfriends or consume an occasional mouthful of limp lettuce? Couldn't they be left to their own devices if they think they know what they want? Most parents struggle with the balance of allowing teenagers to grow up in their own way whilst trying to keep them safe and healthy along the way. A teenager's lack of adult experiences is one reason for keeping an eye out, but also parents remember mistakes they once made and which they don't want their loved one to repeat.

The excitement and liberty of adult choice do not come free. The teenage years are like an apprenticeship, where teenagers learn to manage pocket money, wages or an allowance, discover that having fun may involve taking risks, that work is usually a requirement in order to make ends meet, and that emotions can knock you sideways. Untidy bedrooms mean that important things get lost, turning up late means letting other people down, taking risks means taking a chance of getting hurt. There is no easy-to-read teenage handbook to the laws of the land, they pick it up as they go along, sometimes by experiencing brushes with the police but usually because parents and teachers are there to point out the difference between right and wrong.

By taking the trouble to give views and insist on certain standards and behaviours, a parent is showing that the teenage apprentice is valued and has the opportunity to make mistakes and amends within a relatively safe setting. Keeping quiet means young people must find the information from other, possibly less reliable, sources.

How can parents influence teenagers without appearing to interfere?

When direct advice goes unheeded or creates ructions and defiance, parents can use other methods to help young people stay on track.

Choose the best timing when giving advice

Even though teenagers are reactive and volatile some of the time, there will be other times when they are happy to listen. Lecturing at the time of a dispute is guaranteed to be as welcome as a cold curry on top of a hangover. Parents can state their opinions at the time and show their disappointment if trust has been abused, but further discussion should be saved until everyone has calmed down and parents have considered exactly what they want to say. 'We'll talk about this later' will show that problems are not to be brushed aside, even if discussing them at the time is not appropriate.

Planning a time when the issue is to be discussed is a way of showing that the issue is important, that the parent is prepared to put it on their priority list and will give the young person time to think about the issue.

Choosing the location where an important discussion takes place is also worth thinking about; chatting over a drink in the garden conveys very different body language from standing threateningly in the young person's bedroom doorway to prevent escape. If the matter is delicate or embarrassing then discussing it in the car is an option. The young person will not be able to walk away but will be saved from uncomfortable eye contact due to the need to keep eyes on the road.

For planned discussions on difficult topics, such as worrying risk-taking behaviour, tell the young person what to expect at the start of the discussion. For example, a parent might say that firstly they would like the young person to listen to their views, and then the parent will listen to what the young person would like to say. The parent could announce from the outset that they want to avoid argument and that if the discussion becomes heated then it should be put off for a calmer time once more.

When communication is very difficult, it can help to involve a third person to act as mediator. For this to be successful, the mediator should be impartial rather than an ally of either the parent or the young person. Sometimes a teacher, a relative or even the family doctor can fill this role.

When confrontation looms, try not to get angry

Many of the trials of adolescence are predictable, happening to the majority of young people to some degree or other, which means parents can plan in advance how they might react if they discover their child was blind drunk, or has had unprotected sex or tried drugs. If parents are caught unawares and find themselves losing their temper and entering a slanging-match, it will confirm the teenager's expectation that:

- parents are out of touch
- the conspiracy theory is true – 'everyone hates me and no one ever listens'
- rules are worth breaking if that is the only way they can lead their own life.

Parents should try hard to avoid threatening with punishments as this can generate resentment and ruin a good relationship. If a young person has been trying to act like an adult, then work on the responsibilities that come along with adulthood.

Make a point of showing respect

Teenagers feel hard done by at the best of times. Try not to belittle efforts or brush off worries as this can add to the sense of 'no one listens to me'. Knocking on bedroom doors, asking opinions on daily decisions and listening to their views on media topics can show that their general opinions are valued, giving more chance of a reasoned discussion at times of conflict.

Remind teenagers of the biblical line 'Do unto others as you would have done to yourself'. Respect is a two-way thing that pays great dividends in the long run, but is less effective when it only appears grudgingly.

Avoid forcing young people into changing their minds

Backing a teenager into a corner will achieve the same as backing anyone else into a corner – either resentful submission with loss of face and self-esteem, or defiant refusal to comply. By making too big a deal over an issue, a teenager may feel forced into sticking to a rebellious course just because they cannot now face backing down and looking weak.

Foster a sense of pride in young people

Encouraging young people to take pride in themselves and in being part of a family or in belonging to clubs or teams will encourage a sense of responsibility and value. This positive approach can reduce the impact of sibling rivalry if one child in the family seems to shine more than another, in the same way that the goal scorer of a team is not the only one that matters – each team member contributes in a different way. The whole team can enjoy the glory because that is what being in a team means.

Teach teenagers to be cautious about accepting other people's views

Just because a new friend is good at one thing doesn't mean he or she is the fount of all knowledge. Whilst it is good to put trust in friends and family, it is also good to be sceptical of advice if the source is not credible. For example, it would be reasonable to take the chemistry teacher's word when he teaches chemistry, but it might be helpful to know why he also teaches the ballet class before following his instructions. If it turns out that he attended the Royal Ballet School before doing his chemistry degree, then all is well and good, but if he simply drew the short straw due to staff shortage, and in fact is only qualified to teach chemistry, then it is another matter.

This matter of credibility is also important when absorbing advertising claims. Celebrities such as sports stars have a living to make, which may mean getting their income from advertising junk food or expensive kit. Marketing executives are very well aware that famous faces linked to a product can make a huge difference to its popularity. However, the fact that the celebrity is good at football does not mean that the product he is now marketing (and earning a handsome income from) is either healthy, good value or necessary. Some celebrities take great care that their image should only be linked to what they feel are worthy products, whereas others are happy to take any work that will pay the bills, regardless of the merits of the product.

Encourage young people to consider a variety of options

Personality counts for a lot when making decisions; some people chop and change their mind a thousand times whereas others make snap decisions on the spot. For those people prone to impulse, it can help to remind them of the varied choices on offer and of any goals they may have wanted to achieve. Equally, for those people who find it difficult to make decisions, reminding them of their ultimate goals can help decision making become more efficient.

Some examples of how a parent might comment include:

- 'Didn't you tell me you were saving to buy a different thing?'
- 'Weren't you keen to get fit? More computer games might make that harder.'
- 'It's up to you, but I thought you usually valued doing things in a different way to this.'
- 'Try it that way if you think that's best, but think about changing your mind if it doesn't work out.'

Discuss 'risk swapping' to reduce the impact of risky behaviour

If a teenager has already begun to experiment with a potentially dangerous behaviour, then rather than alienating him or her with a terse lecture advocating total avoidance, discuss ways to reduce the dangers of the behaviour. Young people are not stupid and may be interested in 'risk swapping' to a less hazardous pursuit so long as it is still fun and helps with the quest to appear cool. Explore safer ways to achieve the good experiences they crave without the need to take such risks.

Activities such as smoking or getting drunk are usually popular because the good things about them seem to outweigh the bad – for example, young people associate getting drunk with having a good time rather than with alcoholic liver disease. However, young people are at risk of alcohol poisoning, accidents and getting involved in fights when drunk, so reducing the risks of alcohol might involve drinking in moderation, which can achieve all the positive effects of alcohol without the bad effects that come from bingeing. Suggest lower strength alcoholic drinks and to not drink too quickly. Recommend sticking to one type of drink only when out, rather than trying a variety. Suggest starchy foods before going out to avoid drinking on an empty stomach.

If smoking has been tried in order to look cool in front of mates, suggest alternatives such as changing hairstyle or clothes, body piercing or even a tattoo, which are all less risky and potentially more promising in making a statement than smoking with its high risk of nicotine addiction. If the relaxation effect of smoking is used as an excuse for trying it, suggest starting t'ai chi, which is far less addictive.

Tell young people when they have made good choices and that they are welcome to sound out ideas before putting them into practice

Because little children are used to parents taking charge, it may not be clear to young people when the transition to making their own choices comes about. Parents can explain that they would like to continue offering their views but will begin to leave final decisions to their teenager. Clarifying this approach can help some young people feel happier to listen because they have been given the authority to ignore the advice if they wish. By being treated in a more adult way, many young people will respond by listening more and respecting their new position of personal responsibility, so rising to the challenge of acting in a grown-up way, rather than continuing to act like a belligerent child.

Even when a parent's views have been scorned or dismissed as being those of an old fuddy-duddy, any praise offered will be valued and welcomed, even if young people do not say so at the time. The more young people discuss varied, controversial and difficult issues together with the family so that everyone's views are known, the less they will need to go to peers and other role models to shape their view of the world.

Make it easier for young people to make good choices

The inertia of youth often means that young people will choose the easiest rather than the best option. If teenagers express an interest in eating healthily, stock fewer of the usual crisps and chocolates that would tempt them off course and increase the healthier foods in the house. If they suggest a fitness drive, then find easy ways to keep motivation going, perhaps by copying the example and doing a bit together or by fitting in small bouts of exercise by parking further away from destinations and fitting in a walk. If necessary, use incentives and rewards such as extra pocket money to keep new routines going.

Clarify aims if a young person starts a new healthy eating plan or fitness regime

Many people, whatever their age, are impatient for improvements when trying a new lifestyle. If a young person is expecting miracles then, realistically, disappointment will be round the corner. In order to keep healthy trends going a person will need motivation, so it is helpful to clarify what aspect will provide motivation, particularly if the young person is planning big changes. If he or she is relying on significant weight loss to provide motivation, the impetus will rapidly falter if weight reduction is slower than expected. However, if the aim of a health drive is to enjoy healthy food, motivation will increase as more healthy foods become familiar and hence more popular.

If a young person sets him or herself too big a challenge, which doesn't work out, then the resulting failure will damage motivation and reduce enthusiasm to try again at a later date. It is better to plan gradual changes with small attainable goals that can be built on with each small success. Young people may need to change their initial aims significantly from exuberant optimism to realistic stepwise changes in order to make progress.

Commitment to both healthy eating and increased fitness will be greater if young people realise they are valuable for their own sake rather than simply to change outward appearances or to lose weight. Eating more healthily gives many benefits even if weight doesn't alter, and fitness is vital for inner health and for the way people feel rather than for how they look. Focusing on reducing body weight creates a short-term goal, which is not good for improving longer-term health. Using a car analogy: it is better to maintain the engine so it runs well than to fuss over the paintwork. The Top Teen Health Plan takes a detailed look at goal setting and motivation.

A parent's job is to put safety high on the agenda

Always check out how young people are getting home and forbid them to get into a car when the driver has been drinking. Make sure they know they can always phone home, whatever the hour, in an emergency or if transport home has become a problem. The 'taxi fare' can always be negotiated the next day. Look out for signs of risk taking in young people – it may signal inner distress rather than curiosity about the wider world.

Summary points

- Although parents are no longer in charge of all teenage decisions, they can still influence their teenager in many ways and stay friends in the process.
- The teenage years can be seen as an apprenticeship for adulthood, where the responsibilities as well as the freedom of being your own boss are to be experienced.
- Other role models such as friends, sporting heroes and pop stars or celebrities may begin to have more influence than parents. Make sure young people learn to treat their messages and advice with scepticism, as they will not always have the young person's best interests at heart.
- Because teenage rebellion doesn't fit well with making safe choices, it is a parent's job to keep safety on the agenda. This involves talking about risky behaviours, encouraging 'risk swapping' and giving permission to get help if the teenager is in difficulty.
- Be aware that risk taking does not always stem from teenage curiosity, but may signal inner unhappiness or loss of self-esteem.

Chapter 4

The role of the food industry and government policy

The first three chapters have looked at different influences on how young people choose to eat, ranging from food provision and availability to advertising, peer pressure, family routines, nutritional knowledge, personal motivation and interest in eating. It is far from a level playing field when trying to decide what makes up a healthy diet. This chapter takes a closer look at some of the external factors that govern the way young people eat.

Knowledge of healthy facts doesn't necessarily mean they are put into practice

Many people have a good idea about what makes up a healthy diet, but still do not put this knowledge into daily practice. Surprisingly few people study nutritional labels, tot up how many portions of fruit or vegetables they have eaten that day, or worry about the salt content of what they are eating.

Despite many attempts to educate the population with health education campaigns, schools programmes and improved food labelling, people are continuing to become less healthy, with increasing rates of obesity and illnesses related to poor lifestyle. Leaving healthy choices down to each person is currently not working.

Looking at an individual's risk of obesity, there are two major causes at play: the *genetic tendency* of the individual to be slim or overweight, which is largely beyond influence, and the *'obesogenic environment'*, which means outside reasons why people tend to put on excess weight. It reflects whether healthy foods are cheaper or more expensive than unhealthy items, how easily available they are in practice and how much pressure there is from peers, advertising and marketing to buy things.

A further factor that adds into this obesogenic environment is the skill needed to prepare healthy food. Now that cooking skills are rarely taught in schools, pre-packaged meals are widely and cheaply available, and eating out is considered a regular norm there has been a big shift away from eating plain, home-cooked foods on ordinary days to eating rich foods far too often.

Simply telling the population to eat healthily is not going to work unless the environment helps people to do this with ease.

What role does the food industry play in making healthy choices?

The food industry as a whole does a fantastic job of bringing affordable, hygienic food to the masses, whilst catering for every conceivable taste and requirement. It provides employment for a considerable proportion of the workforce; it generates a huge amount of income for the government through taxation and helps to keep the population happy and well fed. As a consequence of these important issues, the food industry as a whole is very powerful, being able to influence government policy and organisations that set nutritional standards.

However, the food industry is made up of a huge number of individual components – small businesses, big businesses, retail chains, and independent farmers and food manufacturers – who all have individual pressures to make a profit, cut corners and reduce costs, and who may feel ultimately more responsible to shareholders in their company than to the consumers who eat their products. At the end of the day, a business aims to stay in business by making a profit rather than feeling that the health of the nation is their direct concern.

So, whilst the food industry as a whole has a huge collective responsibility towards the nation's health, this responsibility does not filter down clearly to individual companies. This is where the government comes in, regulating the food industry by insisting on minimum standards, good hygiene and accurate labelling of food. A very simplistic theory is that the food industry provides everything that might be needed and the government provides the regulations and advice on what to eat and when. Individuals simply need to take note of the advice and apply restraint. In practice, however, things are never that simple.

Regulating the food industry creates all sorts of dilemmas

At first glance, it might seem obvious that unhealthy food should be discouraged whilst healthy food is promoted, but the practicalities are a far cry from this.

Who is really responsible for how people eat?

The ongoing debates about the current obesity epidemic have involved a pass-the-parcel approach to who is responsible, with each major party blaming someone else (*see* Figure 4.1). In truth, any party that has some influence on how people eat will therefore have some responsibility too, but no one group takes overall liability (*see* Figure 4.2).

When looking at the role of the food industry, it is not simply the food manufacturer that has a vested interest in good sales. Also involved are the advertisers of the product, perhaps film makers making television advertisements; people who maintain the factory such as cleaners; shops that sell the product; banks that keep the business afloat by lending money; telephone, heating, lighting, computer service workers; delivery men, and so on. The list goes on and on, and shows that one food manufacturer has many pressures to keep in business and make a profit. The health of the nation is way down on the priority list; keeping in business is the main concern.

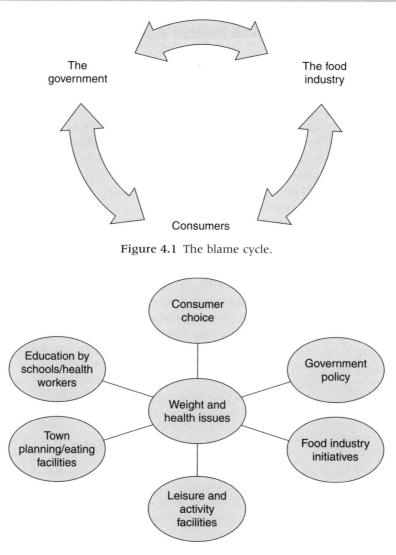

Figure 4.1 The blame cycle.

Figure 4.2 Who has responsibility for how people eat?

Some large companies have begun to take their responsibility towards the public's health more seriously – for example, some have made an effort to reduce salt levels or the targeting of young children with unhealthy foods – but these initiatives are not yet widespread. Other companies have made small attempts to improve their image with 'healthy initiatives' because they have been scared into making improvements by the threat of litigation. Some fast-food chains have made token gestures, phasing out their 'super-sizing' policy (where larger portions were offered for minimal increase in price) and offering fruit in an attempt to appear more health-friendly, even if the mainstay of their products remains nutritionally poor and is still heavily targeted at young people.

Selling only basic food might be cheap, but would be unprofitable and unpopular

Taking away the convenience of processed and pre-packaged foods and going back to selling far more raw ingredients for people to cook at home might give health benefits, but would be highly unpopular due to the type of lives people now live, with little spare time for elaborate cooking and food preparation. As the nation has become wealthier, people are prepared to pay for someone else to do their cooking for them, whether by eating out or purchasing ready-prepared items to eat at home. The food industry feels it is providing what people want and the population soon objects when it is subjected to too much of a 'nanny state'.

Producing rich, unhealthy foods is a good way to employ people and generate wealth

Sending people out to work in the food industry encourages a cycle of wealth creation. Instead of staying at home and preparing their own food, families earn a wage that allows them to spend money not only on food, but on other aspects of life too. The government wants as many people to be employed as possible, which means creating jobs rather than limiting them by discouraging products. It is in the paradoxical position of wanting to create a flourishing manufacturing industry (of both foods and luxury goods), but which then encourages gluttony and inactivity, so that health initiatives are required to counteract the resulting harm. Currently, the balance of these two factors has moved too far in the direction of poor lifestyles.

Who has the right to say what is healthy and what is not?

This is tricky because, as *The Balance of Good Health* shows, it is not that any particular food is bad, it is the balance of the overall diet that counts. Having a small amount of rich, fatty, salty or sugary food is no problem if the rest of the diet is well balanced. Just because a manufacturer produces a rich, fattening product doesn't mean that they intend everyone to eat it excessively; blame does not fall entirely at the manufacturer's feet. One could argue that the local town planners are just as much at fault for giving planning permission for fast-food outlets in their locality as the food manufacturers themselves.

Putting guidelines in place is all very well, but only if people follow them. Nutritional guidelines drawn up by official bodies are often disputed by those companies that are in danger of losing out because of the guidelines. For example, the soft drinks industry has contested the evidence that demonstrates a link between sugary drinks and obesity. It has tried to discredit the evidence used to show the link and has disputed the way it is interpreted, whilst suggesting alternative reasons for the obesity epidemic, as illustrated in the blame cycle (*see* Figure 4.1).

The tobacco industry took the same approach over evidence on the dangers of smoking, so that the dangers of tobacco remained hidden for far longer than they should have done. Even today, the tobacco industry tries very hard to perpetuate some of the myths about smoking, whilst attempting to discredit research that confirms the dangers of both smoking and passive smoking.

The food industry lobbies hard when new guidance is being produced to make sure its interests are not harmed, and it uses all sorts of approaches to buy influence over committees that decide on national advice. This results in guidance that is often watered down or woolly enough to allow interpretation in different ways, or has loopholes that allow unhealthy practice to continue.

Food availability may make healthy eating advice hard to follow

No one forces people to eat junk food. But equally, if no healthy alternative is available then people do not have much choice. This concept is called 'the food desert', where healthy foods are either too expensive or not easily obtainable. Reasons for this include difficulties in reaching out-of-town supermarkets, which tend to be cheaper than small shops, plus many high streets, shopping malls, convention centres, etc. have only fast-food outlets. The government does not control the prices charged by shops or what they choose to sell; this is left to market forces, meaning that shops are able to charge what they can get away with, bearing in mind the prices that other shops nearby are charging, and are free to stock whatever they feel their customers wish to buy.

It is impossible to legislate over portion size and frequency of consumption, which are just as important as a food's nutritional value

All food that is sold must comply with health and safety guidelines, so that it is not poisonous or dangerous when eaten as intended. However, it is impossible to legislate over quantities or portion sizes of foods that are safe in moderation but harmful in excess. There is no guide on chocolate biscuit packets to say how much a portion should be. The king-size chocolate bars in every garage forecourt are not illegal, even if one bar would best be shared amongst a whole family! Even though small snack-size confectionery bars are available, they come in bags of 25 or even 50, which encourages people to take several, so removing the benefits of small portions.

Products are rarely standardised, making legislation over their content difficult

When trying to create helpful 'rules' about the fat, sugar or salt content of a food item, it is not possible to give standard guidelines because food is so variable. For example, there is no widely accepted and standardised version of cottage pie or spaghetti Bolognese, so food manufacturers are free to make up their own recipes. This leads to huge variation in salt, sugar and fat content in similar products. For example, McCain's Cheese and Tomato Micro Pizza has nearly four times as much salt as the Pizza Express version and Tesco's Hot Chicken Tikka Masala without rice has more than double the fat than Asda's. One supermarket's quiche may have double the salt of another brand.

Whilst there is plenty of debate about reducing salt, fat and sugar in foods, little progress is being made, with changes being left to individual manufacturers at present. If people wish to know which products are healthiest, this currently means studying food labels to compare products.

Further information about measures being taken to curb the salt, sugar and fat in processed foods is available from www.which.co.uk.

Would a 'fat tax' help control products that are high in trans or saturated fats?

A 'fat tax' would make life more difficult for lower-income families, whilst it would have little impact on a wealthier family. Instead, incentives and price reductions for healthy foods such as fruit and vegetables would be more beneficial. This would encourage the purchase of nutritious foods that would displace some of the less healthy things from the family diet. However, fresh produce is already the least profitable area of food manufacture and so there is little incentive to make this area even less commercially viable. In countries where food companies are trying to increase their investment, it has been shown that for every $100 invested in fruit and vegetable production, over $1000 is being invested in soft drinks and confectionery.

Focusing too much on unhealthy eating ignores the role of inactivity in the current obesity epidemic

Whilst the quality and quantity of food consumed will have a significant effect on a person's weight and health, exercise and activity will have equal impact. Initiatives to improve the nation's eating habits must be accompanied by measures to encourage fitness and activity in order for them to be effective. Too much emphasis on controlling weight through dieting and restrictive eating makes people neurotic or obsessed with food, making successful weight control even harder. The food industry is likely to be more positive about food regulations and initiatives if they form part of a plan to improve overall lifestyle, rather than an attempt to lay blame at its feet.

What advertising and marketing tactics does the food industry use?

One of the reasons why so many people struggle to control their weight is because they are led to believe that they already eat a healthy diet. The knowledge that they are eating well but still carry too much weight leaves people feeling frustrated and confused. What else can they do?

This section looks at some common marketing tactics used by the food industry that create the impression of a healthy diet and encourage people to eat too much of the wrong thing. Understanding more about these tactics can help people resist the hard sell.

Pricing tactics

BOGOFs (Buy One, Get One Free), value packs, family packs and '10% extra' offers are rife on every shop shelf. Convincing the buyer that the product is good value overrides any question of whether the product was needed in the first place or is nutritionally healthy. The manufacturer, whilst making a smaller profit per item, will ultimately sell more, perhaps take away custom from a competitor, get the consumer familiar with the product and generate the impression that the company offers good value. These offers entice people to buy products that they might otherwise not buy at all.

Other pricing tactics are used to bolster a brand's image, for example creating a 'high-quality' image by pricing things highly and using glamorous packaging. End-of-season sales are also highly effective at encouraging people to buy 'bargains' – often items that are totally unwanted but seem too good to ignore.

Creating the right image or brand identity

Getting a product's image right means that people will want to buy it regardless of whether it is good value, necessary, nice or healthy. Hence manufacturers go to great lengths to create an image or identity for a product and decide who the target group is and how best to tap into that market. If a product is linked to images of success, happiness, social acceptance and positive emotions then it will do better than a similar product that has no image attached.

Various images are successfully used:

- Sexy glamour: for alco-pops and other alcoholic drinks, rich confectionery and desserts. Drinking an exotic rum and coke will not really make men fall at your feet or transport you to a palm-fringed beach, despite the image created by the ads.
- Wholesome goodness: used to make processed meals appear healthy and suitable for the family, regardless of actual nutrition.
- Sporting prowess: high-sugar soft drinks and snacks are often linked to images of improved sporting performance, even though they can lead to obesity which would in fact reduce performance.
- Nostalgic memories: foods from the past are revamped to suggest they are free from modern contamination and contain goodness from a bygone era.
- Hi-tech superiority: modified foods are given supposed 'health-giving' ingredients, such as 'bio' dairy products and probiotics, to combat the ills of modern life.
- Child entertainment: linking a product to cartoon, film or television characters is a highly effective way to make it popular. The popularity of the character is used to 'wash over' the product, even though the yoghurt or cereal inside may be identical to other cheaper brands on the shelf.

Brand awareness

Why do certain companies hog the 'brand leader' position? Do different brands of cola, for example, really taste that different? Brand leaders guard their position fiercely with aggressive marketing and huge advertising budgets. One technique is that of flooding – putting the company logo onto as many surfaces as possible. Therefore cola companies put their logo on pencil cases, beach towels, sports wear and clothing, buildings and advertising hoardings. They sponsor big events so the logo is seen by spectators and, more importantly, appears on television. By the time the logo is ingrained in the national consciousness, shops are happy to give prime shelf space to the familiar brand and consumers pick it up because they recognise it. Brand leaders are not necessarily the best; they are the most actively marketed.

Product placement

This involves displaying branded products, despite the product having nothing to do with what the audience came to watch. Examples are TV shows and films that always show happy people eating specific foods or drinking particular drinks. The film *Toy Story* made an art form of this, generating huge sales for all the toys featured in the film. James Bond films have become a shop window for German cars. Even though no direct reference is made to the product itself, the frequent appearances in positive or impressive settings place the product in a good light.

Hidden compliments

Making a consumer feel smart and in control is a secret way to control the choice they make. People do not like to be pushed into a choice, preferring to feel they have come to an independent decision. If an advertisement butters up viewers, making them feel superior to people who have chosen a competing product, then they will feel more favourably inclined towards the advertised one.

Age-specific advertising

Advertising is highly sophisticated, tapping in to specific groups in ever more inventive ways. Many adults never see the advertising targeted at young people via mobile phones, video games, teen websites and magazines, so that a youth culture is created which promotes specific products and trends. Because the whole culture is unknown to people outside that age group, the mystique this creates increases the allure of the associated products.

Payments and gifts to schools

Because of pressures on funding for schools, most schools accept some help from outside. Some companies provide financial support in return for advertising their products, promoting the idea that both the company and the school are in a win–win situation. But it is the children in the schools who lose out because of yet more exposure to minimally regulated advertising. Endorsement of a product by a state school suggests state approval, giving the impression that these products are healthier than they really are.

Examples include swimming badges and certificates funded by sugary breakfast cereal manufacturers or books and school equipment emblazoned with a confectionery company's logo. Vending machines in schools is another area where young people are targeted with unhealthy products because the school generates income from sales. It is hard for a school to give a consistent message on healthy eating and lifestyle when the chocolate vending machine in the corridor is busy paying for classroom basics.

Fortunately, in the UK new mandatory nutritional standards for school meals and vending machines are currently being drawn up with a planned phased introduction of these standards by 2009. This should help schools to implement healthier whole-school food and nutrition policies.

Advertising by the consumer

This is the cheekiest tactic of all, but is so commonplace that no one notices. Every time people leave a shop with a carrier bag bearing the name of the shop, they are doing the shop's advertising. Some shops realised early on that luxury carrier bags, whilst more expensive, would be used more than once, creating more effective advertising plus a luxury brand image. However, this has now become a speciality with people clamouring to pay high prices for branded goods. Wearing a t-shirt bearing a trendy shop's logo may make the wearer feel cool, but he or she has paid handsomely in order to do the company's advertising for them.

Brand loyalty

The ultimate goal of any company is to achieve brand loyalty, meaning that customers would rather go without if their preferred brand was not available and would be prepared to search for and insist on their favourite product or trek high and low to visit their preferred shop. By insisting on a particular type of baked beans, flavour of tea or make of trainers, people add to the positive image of the product in question.

In addition to flooding the company logo, companies use various tactics to create brand loyalty so that consumers stick with a familiar product rather than try something new. Supermarkets and big shops have loyalty cards that give small bonuses for regular use. Collecting a series of free gifts inside the packaging encourages multiple purchases. Money-off coupons tie people in to the same brand.

Brand loyalty is also increased by product endorsements from celebrities or big events such as the Olympic Games. If a revered sporting hero drinks a certain drink or eats a particular type of crisps, the chances are the fans will follow suit. Paying celebrities to endorse products is huge business and is a major way by which sports stars and other famous faces make their money. However, most big names do this for the money rather than because they have a deep-seated belief in the product itself.

What is the government doing to improve the health of young people?

With so many competing pressures on the choices made by young people, it is unsurprising that the government has, as yet, made few inroads into the current obesity epidemic. It is not for a want of trying, however, with many positive health initiatives in action and more planned for the future.

The World Health Organization has summarised helpful approaches to preventing obesity, as shown in Box 4.1.

Box 4.1 World Health Organization summary of helpful approaches to preventing obesity

Individuals should try to:

- uphold an active lifestyle
- limit television viewing
- increase their intake of fruit and vegetables
- restrict pre-packaged snack foods that are energy-dense and poor in micronutrients
- restrict their consumption of sugar-sweetened soft drinks.

Political measures should focus on the following:

- encourage physical activity in schools and in communities
- limit the exposure of young children to heavy marketing of junk foods
- provide information and skills to allow healthy food choices.

The government is actively putting in place initiatives to tackle some of these areas, although there is plenty of room for further improvements. Some examples include:

- National Healthy School Standard Programme. This is a programme that all schools are encouraged to follow, which takes a whole-school approach to improving school culture. It promotes healthy eating (by encouraging healthy school meals in addition to nutritional education), physical activity, sex and drugs education, physical safety and emotional health and well-being.
- Game Plan. The government's strategy, published in December 2002, spells out sport and physical activity objectives. It involves local authorities, the education sector, the voluntary sector (sports clubs and national governing bodies of sport) and the private sector to increase access and participation in sport generally. Sport England is the organisation responsible for delivering the government's sporting objectives and is committed to creating opportunities for people to start, take part and succeed in sport. They deliver funding and invest in a range of sporting projects, including the Active England fund. Further information is available at www.sportengland.org.
- Minimum nutritional standards in schools were reinstated in 2001 after having been scrapped in the 1970s. School meals have come under close scrutiny following the ground-breaking work of the TV chef Jamie Oliver. Improvements to school meal funding and training are now in hand, with the School Meals Review Panel drawing up workable recommendations now that the government has recognised the importance of healthy school meals.
- Free fruit schemes for younger children now operate in most schools.

What issues would benefit from further action to improve the health of young people?

- As yet, the UK government has not put in place any restriction on advertising to children, leaving the food industry to regulate itself. This is a concern because currently food advertising accounts for around half of all advertising broadcast during children's TV viewing times, and three-quarters of these adverts promote high-calorie, low-nutrient foods. It is estimated that an American child watches as many as 40 000 television adverts per year, and British children are not far behind.

- It is common practice for official organisations to receive high-profile sponsorship by the food industry, even though official government advice is to avoid links with companies that promote unhealthy products. These food companies gain credibility in addition to advertising by being seen to be endorsed by official organisations. For example, the Football Association accepts funding for its community projects from McDonald's, thus helping the company to target the youth market. It is particularly cynical for sports organisers to accept funding and hence promote a company when that sport's top athletes would not eat the food.

- Cooking skills are no longer taught in UK schools. The national curriculum may include a certain amount of theory underlying nutrition and hygiene within design and technology lessons, but cookery skills are unlikely to be taught apart from during optional after-school cookery club settings. However, young people are likely to be taught how to design packaging or how a conveyor belt in a food factory might work, because food manufacturers sponsor design and technology lessons and therefore influence their content. Food manufacturers perceive more benefit from children learning about the processing of foods, rather than showing them how to fend for themselves using basic ingredients.

- The UK government highlighted the need for action on vending machines in schools and on school sponsorship by companies associated with unhealthy foods in a report in 2004. Workable solutions are currently being drawn up although individual schools have shown initial scepticism about restricting the availability of preferred snacks. Schools may find it difficult to change either because they are dependent on the income from sponsorship and vending machines or because they are tied into long contracts with these companies. However, there have been recent improvements to vending technology, such that machines that dispense healthy foods are now available. With government support and pressure from the public, there is now a strong possibility that healthy snacks in schools will become a reality, whilst still generating income for schools. Further information is available from the Health Education Trust at www.healthedtrust.com.

Summary points

- The environment plays a significant part in whether people eat well. A good diet requires ready access to good food, which is difficult if there are only fast food outlets to hand.
- No one single factor is responsible for poor health or obesity; there is always a combination of factors at play. Improving health means tackling all the factors rather than shifting the blame onto someone else.
- Individual food manufactures feel the health of the nation is not their direct concern and so push products that may lead to health problems because they need to balance food provision with making a profit.
- Many marketing tactics are used, which may involve making a product look healthier than it really is or appear such good value or so fantastic that its nutritional content seems irrelevant. Tuning in to these tactics can make it easier to resist the hard sell.

Section 2

Nutrition

Chapter 5

Nutritional basics for young people

This chapter looks at the building blocks of the diet and at the specific nutritional needs of young people.

Fat facts

Fat has its uses

Despite a national obsession with eating low-fat foods, fat is an essential part of the diet, especially for people who are still growing. It provides energy, insulation to keep the body warm, padding to sit on and is an essential part of many cells in the body, allowing them to function. In addition, some vitamins can only be absorbed into the body when combined with fat, such as vitamins A, D, E and K.

Fat is very energy-dense, which means a small amount contains a lot of calories – around twice as many per gram as carbohydrate or protein. Therefore one spoonful of fat will contain the same calories as two spoonfuls of either carbohydrate or protein. This is good news for people who have a small appetite because a high-fat diet provides lots of energy without having to eat a lot.

Without fat in the diet, many foods would taste unpleasant. Fat adds a different type of moisture to a food than water and it is often fat that gives a food its creamy 'mouth-feel' or enjoyable texture. Unfortunately, this is a major reason why so many people struggle with their weight – fat in combination with other ingredients tastes great and this can lead to overeating.

Understand why low-fat eating is recommended

After the early years, when a high-fat diet is suitable, young people should be encouraged to enjoy lower-fat foods so that no more than 30% of the calories in the diet come from fat. Most of this fat will be found in dairy products and in some of the protein-containing foods, but some will come from cakes, biscuits and confectionery.

Too much fat is a problem for a variety of reasons:

• Fat is far more energy-dense than protein and carbohydrate, making it easy to overeat because fat triggers the sense of fullness more slowly than both protein and carbohydrate.

Type of food	Calories per gram of food
Protein	4
Fat	9
Carbohydrates	4

- People are not very good at adjusting for a fatty meal whilst eating, but can do so over the course of the day. This can be explained by using an example.

  If two identical plates of spaghetti Bolognese were prepared, but the first was high in fat with plenty of oil in the sauce whilst the second used extra-lean mince and virtually no oil in the sauce, it would be difficult to tell the two meals apart even though one contained more calories than the other. People would be likely to eat a similar quantity of either recipe, leading to different calorie intakes. If people were used to registering how hungry or full they felt, they would balance the fattier meal by eating a bit less later on, because they would feel less hungry. But those people brought up to clear their plate, regardless of hunger, would find it harder to adjust for the richer meal, putting them at risk of overeating over the day.

- Too much fat in the diet can push out the healthier items. If people fill up first on fried foods and snacks, there will be less room and less desire for the healthy parts of the diet, such as wholegrain carbohydrate foods, fruit and vegetables. If a meal begins with low-fat foods and fresh produce, whilst the richer items are reserved for the end of the meal, there is a greater chance of healthy basics being eaten, and because this will take the edge off the appetite there will be less risk of overeating richer foods later in the meal.

- Although hibernating animals need to fatten themselves up for winter, humans have ready supplies of food all year round and are better off leaving their energy stores in kitchen cupboards than tucked around their waists. Carrying too much fat through adulthood has been linked to a whole range of illnesses, as listed in Box 5.1. Diabetes is the likeliest weight-related condition to cause problems. In overweight women, where body mass index (BMI) is between 25 and 30, the chance of diabetes increases by five times. But by the time BMI creeps over 35 (which is in the obese range) then the risk of diabetes increases by a staggering 93 times. The picture is very similar for men too.

Box 5.1 Illnesses and conditions associated with overweight and obesity

- Diabetes
- High blood pressure
- Stroke
- Heart attack
- Heart failure
- Blood clotting tendency
- Raised cholesterol level
- Gallstones
- Some cancers (of the breast, womb and pancreas)
- Reduced fertility
- Osteoarthritis symptoms
- Breathing problems, in particular whilst asleep
- Liver problems
- Depression

Some fats are better than others

If up to 30% of the diet is to be made up of fat, does it matter what sort of fat is eaten? The answer is yes. There are two main types of fat: saturated (usually hard at room temperature) and unsaturated (usually liquid at room temperature). Saturated fats raise cholesterol and increase the risks of heart disease and cancer. Unsaturated fats can lower cholesterol, which can reduce the chance of heart disease. Examples of which fats are found in different foods are given in Table 5.1.

Table 5.1 Types of fat and common foods that contain them

Type of fat	Found in
Saturated fats (try to limit)	Visible fat on meat, processed meats, dairy products, lard and some margarines
– Vegetable fat or palm or coconut fat, also known as 'tree lard'!	Pies, pastry, biscuits, cakes and processed foods
– Hydrogenated vegetable oil or fat	Cakes, confectionery, ice-cream, pies, cereal bars, crisps and many other products
– Trans fats	These are formed in the manufacture of hydrogenated fat and worsen heart disease risks further
Unsaturated fats (healthier, because they can improve heart disease risks by improving cholesterol level)	Usually from plants
– Monounsaturated fat	Olive oil, nuts, seeds, avocados, rape seed oil
– Polyunsaturated fat	Vegetable oils, such as sunflower oil and vegetable oil spreads, oily fish, nuts
– Omega 3 and 6 oils	Omega-3 enriched eggs, oily fish, nuts and seeds, soya beans and vegetable oils

How can families choose lower-fat foods without taking a calculator and textbook around the supermarket?

There are some easy concepts to follow to make lower-fat eating straightforward.

- The list of ingredients can give a rough idea of how much fat a food contains. Ingredients are listed in order of proportion, so the main ones will be listed first. If a fatty ingredient is one of the first two or three items, it is likely to be a higher-fat food. If it is listed at the end of a long list or not at all, the fat content should be very low. Watch out for processed meats though, as they use fatty meat or untrimmed meat rather than lean, so even though the ingredients will list meat, the fat content may still be high.
- Watch out for alternative words used to describe fat on food labels: butter, buttermilk, dripping, lard, milk fat, peanut butter or oil, vegetable oil or fat, any word that ends in 'glycerides'.
- Reserve processed foods such as pies, burgers, sausages and batter-coated meats or fish to once or twice a week only. Avoid the trap of varying the weekly diet with different processed foods each day, or this will result in a high-fat diet. Choose lean meats (or trim excess fat off fattier cuts), stews and try vegetarian options on occasion.
- Choose lower-fat dairy products, such as semi-skimmed or skimmed milk and low fat yoghurts.

Skimmed milk	0.6g fat per pint
Semi-skimmed milk	9g fat per pint
Full-fat milk	22g fat per pint

- Change cooking methods. Try steaming, boiling, grilling, poaching or microwaving food, rather than frying or roasting. Deep-frying, in particular, results in a very high fat content because the food becomes soaked in oil.
- Try 'dry-roasting' or a 'dry-fry', which is frying with next to no oil. If some oil is really needed then oil sprays are available that give a fine mist rather than the amount used when pouring from a bottle. Alternatively, put a small amount of oil on some kitchen roll to smear thinly over the pan's surface *before* heating.
- Make use of the natural oil that is within the food already when frying or roasting. If a recipe calls for onions to be fried first in a little oil and for meat to be added second, by reversing this order the onions can be fried in the oil that comes out of the meat when it is sealed, so that no extra is needed. Alternatively, after using a little oil to begin with, any oil that is not absorbed into the ingredients can be poured away or skimmed off later during the cooking process.
- If there are concerns about being overweight, then reduce all types of fat – saturated and unsaturated – as both are equally full of calories or energy.
- Be sceptical about 'low fat' claims on packaging: this information is sometimes used to make a product sound healthier than it really is. If in doubt, check out its food label and think about where the item fits on *The Balance of Good Health* plate. Remember that '80% fat-free' actually means that 20% of the food *is* fat.
- Use the guide below to judge the fat content that is listed on the food label. If the amount is in between the figures shown, then it will be a moderately high-fat food.

High-fat food	Low-fat food
20g fat or more per 100g	3g fat or less per 100g
5g saturates or more per 100g	1g saturates or less per 100g

Make sense of 'sugars'

Everyone thinks of 'sugar' as the sweet granules that are sprinkled on desserts. However, sugar means roughly the same as carbohydrate, so sometimes these terms are interchanged. There are various types of carbohydrates, ranging from simple sugars – ones that taste sweet and dissolve easily – to complex carbohydrates or starch. After they have been eaten, the body breaks down all carbohydrates into glucose, which is the main carbohydrate within the body.

Complex carbohydrates are more useful to the body than simple sugars. Glucose on its own is a bit like a lost worker without any tools – the worker might be vaguely useful but isn't organised or well equipped enough to be really helpful. Unrefined complex carbohydrates, in which glucose molecules are linked together in long chains, are like whole armies of workers all grouped together. Not only are they organised but they come with tools and equipment too – which are fibre, vitamins and minerals. Complex carbohydrates provide essential nutrients in addition to their steady slow release of energy, whereas simple sugars provide only a rapid surge of energy without additional nutrients, which is why they are sometimes called 'empty calories'.

Simple sugars

These occur naturally in food, for example in fruit, some vegetables, cereal grains and milk, and can also be added to food, when they are termed extrinsic or added sugars. As they provide energy but little else, they do not contribute much to a balanced diet.

Limit the amount of added sugars in the overall diet because they are a cause of tooth decay and also because they are often combined with fat, making them unsuitable for frequent consumption. On food labels they will be listed as 'carbohydrates (of which sugars)'.

Many different words are used on packaging to mean sugar, such as brown sugar, cane sugar, dextrose, fruit sugar, glucose, honey, molasses, syrup and treacle.

> A high-sugar food will have at least 10g sugars per 100g.
>
> A low-sugar food will have less than 2g sugars per 100g.

Complex carbohydrates

These provide a healthy way to fill up without consuming excessive energy, whilst bringing along other essential nutrients too, such as minerals and vitamins. There are three different types of complex carbohydrate to be aware of: unrefined carbohydrates, refined or processed carbohydrates, and fibre (see Table 5.2).

Table 5.2 Types of carbohydrate

Type of carbohydrate	Found in	Essential nutrients they contain
Unrefined carbohydrates	Wholegrain cereals	Fibre
	Wholemeal or granary flour	Protein
	Brown rice	Vitamins B and E
	Potatoes	Minerals: zinc, copper and iron
	Wholewheat pasta	Antioxidants
	Lentils and other pulses	Phytonutrients
	Fruit and vegetables	
Refined or processed carbohydrates	White flour, hence in white bread, pastry, cakes, sugary breakfast cereals	Small amounts of fibre
		Small amounts of vitamins and minerals
Fibre (also known as non-starch polysaccharides or NSP)	Fruit and vegetables, especially coconut	Roughage that helps the gut to work smoothly
	Wholegrain cereals and flour	Helps to keep moisture within the gut, which keeps motions soft
	Bran-enriched cereals	
	Beans and other pulses	
	Nuts	

Unrefined carbohydrates

These tend to be eaten in much the same form that they were harvested, so that very few of their nutrients have been lost in processing by the time they are eaten. They are the healthiest form of carbohydrate because in addition to plenty of fibre, they contain protein, vitamins B and E, minerals (such as zinc, copper and iron), antioxidants and phytonutrients. These last two are substances that help body cells to resist damage from pollutants and toxins. Unrefined carbohydrates have a low glycaemic index, or GI, which means they are broken down and absorbed slowly in the gut, so they are able to keep hunger at bay for longer than refined carbohydrates or simple sugars.

Refined or processed carbohydrates

Examples include white flour and bread, cakes and low-fibre breakfast cereals. Not only do these carbohydrates lose many nutrients in the refining process, they are often combined with added sugar and fat, resulting in tempting and tasty foods that upset the balance of a good diet. The body is able to absorb them quickly into the bloodstream (which is shown by a high glycaemic index), giving a rapid surge in blood sugar but then an equally rapid fall again, so that hunger may not be staved off for long. Where possible they should be swapped for wholegrain options.

Fibre

The body is unable to digest dietary fibre, so instead of providing energy, it helps the gut to work by increasing bulk in the bowel and by stimulating the gut walls.

Many foods contain fibre, especially wholegrain foods, but some contain particularly high amounts, such as fresh or desiccated coconut, high-bran breakfast cereals, baked beans, red kidney beans and other pulses. Choosing plenty of wholegrain foods and fresh produce should ensure that the diet contains plenty of fibre without necessarily needing to eat high-bran breakfast cereals. However, some people have trouble with constipation despite eating a range of healthy foods, in which case a high-fibre breakfast cereal can be a simple way to overcome the problem. It can also improve stomach symptoms in the short term whilst experimenting to see which other foods will achieve the same improvement. Because extra fibre can cure abdominal pains, it could be described as a 'healing' food, where a high-fibre breakfast cereal, for example, acts as a dose of medicine.

How much fibre should young people eat?

The advice for adults is to eat around 18 grams of fibre each day, but this amount varies between individuals. Some people eat far more and others eat less; the 'right' amount depends on the ease with which a person's digestive system works. If this is causing problems then more fibre is usually a good idea.

For young people, the 'right' amount varies in much the same way, but it is also recommended they eat around 18 grams per day. Some need more fibre than others, but many young people hardly eat any fibre at all. If they strain when visiting the loo or suffer colicky stomach pains then the fibre in their diet is inadequate. There is a surprising number of people who have always suffered discomfort from their bowels, but because it has been a lifelong problem they believe that this pattern is normal. Just because family tendencies have suggested that a weekly motion is the norm does not mean that this is healthy: small changes to the general diet can make a big difference to a person's regular habits.

It is worth developing a taste for, or at least tolerance of, higher-fibre foods so that if additional fibre is needed, the change will not be a problem. Table 5.3 lists good sources of dietary fibre and also some examples of lower-fibre foods (marked with an asterisk) for comparison.

Table 5.3 Dietary fibre guide for common foods

Food		Average portion size	Grams of fibre per portion
Breakfast cereals:	High-bran cereal	30 g (or 1 small bowl)	8.1
	Bran Flakes		4.5
	Malted wheat/Shreddies		3.6
	Weetabix	2	4.0
	Corn Flakes*		0.9
	Rice Crispies*		0.45
Bread:	Wholemeal	2 slices (47 g)	3.5
	Brown		2.8
	White		1.8
Vegetables:	Peas	3 tablespoons or 80 g	3.6
	Broccoli		1.8
	Carrots		2.0
	Runner beans		2.5
Fruit:	Satsumas	2 (100 g)	1.3
	Apple	1 (150 g)	3.0
	Banana	1 (120 g)	3.7
	Peach	1 (120 g)	1.8
Potatoes:	Jacket	180 g	4.9
	Boiled	180 g	2.2
Rice, boiled:	Brown	180 g	1.4
	White*	180 g	0.2
Beans and pulses:	Baked beans	200 g (half can)	7.4
	Red kidney beans	3 tablespoons	7.7
	Red lentils	3 tablespoons	2.2

* Lower-fibre foods for comparison.

Protein puzzles

Humans need an assortment of different proteins for good health and the secret, as ever, lies in eating a varied diet so that all individual protein building blocks (otherwise known as amino acids) are consumed. There is nothing particularly special about protein that comes from meat – most proteins ultimately come from plants. All the protein in a nice juicy steak was obtained from grass in the cow's diet. Vegetarians should have no problem in finding all the proteins that are needed to keep them healthy, as long as they eat a varied diet.

If excessive protein is eaten it does not produce extra muscle. The amount of muscle bulk created depends on how much muscles are used and exercised, plus the effects of hormones (such as insulin and growth hormone), rather than how much protein is eaten. Any extra protein that is not used up in building muscles, making hormones or cell repair will be burned as fuel or laid down as fat. Humans do not store extra protein in the way that excess fat is stored.

If young people are still growing and especially if they are taking part in high levels of exercise, they will need a higher proportion of protein than adults and should aim to eat about 1 gram per kilogram of body weight each day. This means that a person weighing 60 kg (the weight of an average 16-year-old boy) should eat about 60 grams of protein from several different sources each day (*see* Table 5.4). Adults will get by on around 0.75 grams per kilogram of body weight.

Table 5.4 Sources of protein

Example of a day's diet containing at least 60 grams of protein	*Grams of protein*
One quarter-pounder beef burger	17g
80g pasta (uncooked weight)	10g
Two servings of milk, 200 ml each	13g
Five portions of fruit and vegetables (400g), such as peas, carrots, apple, satsumas, orange juice	Around 7g
Wholemeal cheddar cheese sandwich	12g
Low-fat fruit yoghurt, 150g	6g
Total	65g

How can people be sure they are eating sufficient protein?

Proteins are in all sorts of foods, as shown in Table 5.5, so if the family diet is reasonably varied then it will provide different sources of protein. There are 20 different amino acids, which can be chemically joined together in long chains in a huge variety of ways to make different types of protein. Humans can manufacture some but not all of these building blocks, which means that the ones that can't be made are essential in the diet. This is why a varied diet is so important – some protein foods are good for some of the building blocks but not others. A varied diet will ensure they are all eaten one way or the other.

Take a look at the list of foods in Table 5.5 to see how much of their energy is in the form of protein.

As this varied list shows, protein is present in many foods that are not usually considered to be a source of protein, such as pasta. If a person eats large amounts of pasta then this will provide a fair amount of protein. Some vegetables are surprisingly high in protein, such as broccoli and peas. Be aware that some good sources of protein also contain high levels of fat too, such as full-fat cheese, whereas choosing a reduced-fat cheese means much more protein per mouthful.

In many communities traditional food combinations have developed which help to balance essential proteins by combining plant and animal proteins, especially milk, which contains almost all of the proteins that humans require. These combinations mean that any of the essential building blocks not found in one ingredient will appear in the other. Some examples are beans on toast, macaroni cheese, rice pudding, breakfast cereal with milk, lentil curry with rice, tortillas and beans.

Table 5.5 Percentage of energy from protein-containing foods

Protein-containing foods	% of energy from protein
Tuna, tinned in brine	95
Baked cod	89
Roast chicken	75
Boiled ham slices	53
Broccoli	52
Cheddar cheese, reduced fat	48
Cauliflower, raw	42
Boiled egg	35
Peas	35
Red lentils, boiled	30
Semi-skimmed milk	29
Baked beans	25
Cheddar cheese, full fat	25
Yoghurt	20
Peanuts	17
Wholemeal bread	17
Pasta	15
White bread	14
Custard (carton)	11
Boiled potato	10
Carrots, boiled	10
Cornflakes	9
Boiled rice	8
Chocolate	6
Banana	5
Apple, eating	3

Five-a-day fruit and vegetables

Looking at *The Balance of Good Health*, a third of the daily diet should be in the form of fruit and vegetables, but that doesn't mean the nation must endure a lifetime of rabbit food! On the contrary, fruit and vegetables are highly versatile with many cheap varieties that can be easily incorporated into family meals and handy snacks.

Some food manufacturers and supermarkets are now labelling packaging with the '5 a day' logo (*see* Figure 5.1), which can help to show how many portions of fruit and vegetables a typical serving of the food contains. If the logo appears on a packet it confirms that at least one portion of fruit or vegetable is within and that it will contain no added salt, sugar or fat. If two of the little boxes are coloured in then that shows that one serving counts as two portions.

Figure 5.1 '5 a day'. Reproduced by kind permission of the Department of Health.

Why are fruit and vegetables so great?

Firstly, they are a very natural thing to eat. Humans evolved as 'grazing omnivores', which means our ancestors would eat anything edible that was available, whether meat or plant food. Unlike lions, for example, that gorge every few days on a meat kill, humans learned to grab any opportunity to eat anything vaguely palatable, such as berries, fruit, nuts and grains, in addition to meat. By evolving to make use of nutrients from very varied sources, humans became very adept at survival. Even though humans no longer graze particularly, instead following community habits by eating at set meal times, most are still usually omnivores. The essentials of the human diet are easiest to obtain by eating meat, cereal foods, and fruit and vegetables, rather than pinning all hopes on only one food group as lions do.

Secondly, fruit and vegetables are ideal for filling up healthily without any worry of eating too much. Looking again at *The Balance of Good Health*, if the fruit and vegetable segment is missed out, then other foods are eaten in greater amounts, which usually means eating more 'junk' foods so that calorie intake goes up. Putting fruit and veg back in means pushing some of the less healthy foods 'off the plate' (*see* Figure 5.2).

Thirdly, as already mentioned, fruit and vegetables are an excellent source of vitamins, minerals, fibre, antioxidants and phytonutrients. More fruit and veg means less heart disease and cancer.

How do fruit and vegetables fit into the five-a-day plan?

- Fruit and vegetables count towards each day's quota regardless of whether they are raw, frozen, cooked, chilled, canned or dried. Vegetables within a stew or takeaway count too.
- Even fruit that is past its best can be blended into a smoothie to count as a portion.

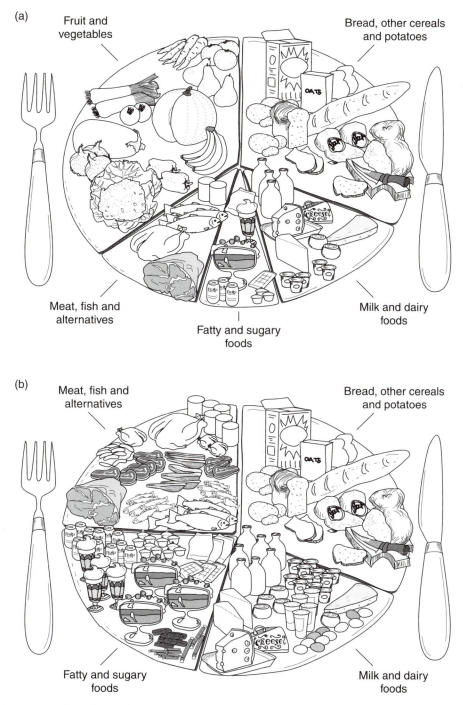

Figure 5.2 *The Balance of Good Health* with (a) fruit and vegetables and (b) without.

- Whilst it is best to have five portions of different produce, this is not essential and some servings will count as two portions, such as cauliflower cheese served as a main course.
- Some items only count as one portion, however much is served. An example is fruit juice, which counts as one portion even if several glasses are drunk, because part of the fruit is left behind during the juicing process, leaving it with very little fibre.
- Pulse vegetables and beans such as chickpeas, lentils and kidney beans also only count as one portion per day, regardless of amount, because whilst good for fibre, they are not so good for vitamins and minerals.
- Portion sizes of dried fruit such as raisins, apricots and dates are smaller than fresh portions because as they lose moisture during the drying process, the other sugars and nutrients become more concentrated. One spoonful rather than three counts as a portion, but only one portion counts each day.
- Potatoes do not count as fruit or veg at all because they are counted in the carbohydrate group along with rice, pasta and bread.

What about portion sizes for young people?

Although scientists have worked out formulas for ideal portion sizes for adults, there is no fixed amount that is correct for younger people. *The Balance of Good Health* shows that what matters is the proportion of mouthfuls that come from fruit and vegetables compared to other types of food, which should be about one-third for everybody. However, it can help to have a rough idea of average adult portion sizes to encourage sufficient intake and so that amounts for younger people can be scaled down where necessary. More importantly, if people are encouraged to enjoy fruit and vegetables, then this enjoyment will lead them to choose as much as they want – which might be far more than the minimum five-a-day recommended amounts. Forcing fruit or vegetables is pointless and may put people off for good.

Adult portions of fruit or vegetables are roughly 80 grams (or 3 ounces), which works out as about three tablespoons of chopped vegetables, a cereal bowlful of salad or one whole fruit such as a medium apple, orange or banana (*see* Tables 5.6 and 5.7). For younger people, the amount is reduced according to appetite: if a person eats roughly two-thirds the volume of food as an adult then the fruit and vegetable portions will also be roughly two-thirds.

Another way to work this is by thinking of a 'portion' as the amount that fits in the palm of the hand. Big hands: big portions. Smaller hands: smaller portions.

Tips for making fruit a success

It is very disappointing to choose a shiny green apple only to find it hard and bitter. A person's early experiences of unripe or impossible-to-peel fruit could make fruit in general seem like hard work. It is worth learning how to choose the right item from a selection so that fruit will be appealing:

- Fruit needs to be ripe in order for it to taste good. Peaches, nectarines, plums, strawberries, grapefruit and melon give off a sweet smell when they are ready for eating, whereas some fruits tend to give off their smell only when they are a

Table 5.6 Fruit portion sizes for adults

Fruit	Portion equivalent to 80g
Apple	1 medium apple
Apricot, dried* or fresh	3 whole apricots
Avocado	Half an avocado
Banana	1 medium banana
Blueberries	4 heaped tablespoons
Cherries	14 cherries
Cherries, canned	3 heaped tablespoons
Clementines, satsumas or tangerines	2 fruits
Currants*, raisins*, sultanas* or dried mixed fruit*	1 heaped tablespoon
Fig, fresh or dried*	2 figs
Fruit juice*	150 ml glass
Fruit salad, canned or fresh	3 heaped tablespoons
Fruit smoothie*	150 ml glass
Grapefruit, fresh	Half a grapefruit
Grapefruit segments	3 tablespoons or 8 segments
Grapes	1 handful
Kiwi fruit	2 kiwi fruit
Lychee, canned or fresh	6 lychees
Melon	1 x 5cm slice
Orange	1 medium orange
Peach	1 medium peach
Peach, canned or dried*	2 halves or 7 slices
Pear	1 whole fruit or two canned halves
Pineapple, canned	2 rings or 12 chunks
Pineapple, fresh	1 large slice
Plum	2 medium plums
Raspberries	2 handfuls
Rhubarb, cooked	2 heaped tablespoons
Strawberries	7 strawberries

* Counts as only one portion per day regardless of amount eaten.

bit over-ripe, such as kiwis, bananas and pineapple. All of these fruits, plus pears, can also be checked for ripeness by pressing very gently on the surface. If it yields slightly the fruit will be ripe, but if hard then it should be left for a few more days to ripen before trying again.
- Fruit is more likely to ripen well in the right season. For example, imported strawberries at Christmas are often a disappointment, looking far better than they taste, whereas they are far more enjoyable in the summer.

- Many fruits are now sold to 'ripen in the fruit bowl'. Once fruit has ripened in this way it can then be kept for longer by putting it in the fridge.
- Apples can be tricky to tell if ripe. If in doubt then leave apples in the fruit bowl at room temperature and they will ripen a little more. Apples that are getting old tend to lose their shine and may become slightly shrivelled, but the flesh inside is often even sweeter at this stage. Some varieties are more reliably sweet than others, so try several types and then stick to the ones that seem most tasty.
- It can be hard to tell if oranges will be sweet or rather tangy and bitter. In general, the smaller fruit such as clementines, satsumas and mandarin oranges are easier to peel and more reliably sweet. Larger oranges with thicker skins, whilst delicious, may require peeling with the help of a knife and leave fingers sticky, so that they are inconvenient when out and about.
- Many people are put off by unsightly blemishes, bruises or the presence of grubs in fruit. Get used to tolerating small blemishes by cutting out bruised areas of fruit, rather than wasting it all. Cut up imperfect fruit to make a fruit salad, adding several types, which can include dried or tinned fruit for interest and texture.
- Fruit that has been chopped up and put on the table is far more appealing than when left whole in the fruit bowl.

Hints on vegetables

- In addition to serving vegetables on their own, they can be thrown in with other foods such as cook-in sauces.
- Vegetables taste great when very lightly cooked so they are still crunchy, such as in a stir-fry. Adding herbs, garlic, Worcestershire sauce or some lemon juice gives them extra flavour.
- Do not underestimate raw vegetables. Boost a plain salad with sliced or grated carrot, small broccoli florets, sugar snap peas, a tin of sweet corn or frozen peas that have been allowed to thaw. Raw mushroom has an unusual texture and delicate flavour, as do baby corn cobs, which can be eaten raw, cooked or straight from the tin.
- Although potatoes don't count as vegetables because they fit into the starch category, swede or carrot added to mash will count. Root vegetables such as sweet potato, swede, turnips, carrots and parsnips all count as a vegetable portion if they are eaten in addition to (and do not normally replace) starchy staples such as potatoes, yam, cassava, rice or pasta.
- Leftover vegetables can be dry-fried the next day with a few fresh ingredients or a piece of bacon or chicken for an easy meal.
- If a recipe calls for onion, then leek can be used instead or in addition to increase vegetable portions.

Further ideas on using fruit and vegetables to improve the balance of family meals are given in Chapter 6.

Table 5.7 Vegetable portion sizes for adults

Vegetables	Portion equivalent to 80g
Artichoke	2 globe hearts
Asparagus, fresh	5 spears, or 7 if canned
Beans, dried then cooked – black eye*, butter*, cannelloni*, kidney*	3 tablespoons
Beans, French or runner	4 tablespoons
Beansprouts, fresh	2 handfuls
Broad beans	3 tablespoons
Broccoli	2 spears
Brussels sprouts	8 sprouts
Cabbage, shredded	3 tablespoons
Carrots	3 tablespoons
Cauliflower	8 florets
Celery	3 sticks
Chickpeas*	3 tablespoons
Courgettes	Half a large courgette
Cucumber	5 cm piece
Leeks	1 leek, white portion only
Lentils*	3 tablespoons
Lettuce or salad leaves, including fresh spinach, rocket	1 cereal bowl
Mangetout or sugar snap peas	1 handful
Mixed vegetables, frozen	3 tablespoons
Mushrooms	14 button, or 3–4 tablespoons sliced
Onion	1 medium onion
Parsnips	1 large parsnip
Peas, fresh, frozen or canned	3 tablespoons
Pepper	Half a pepper
Spinach, cooked	2 heaped tablespoons
Spring onion	8 onions
Swede, diced and cooked	3 tablespoons
Sweet corn	3 tablespoons canned or 1 cob
Tomato	1 medium or 7 cherry or 2 canned plum tomatoes
Tomato puree*	1 tablespoon

*Counts as only one portion per day regardless of amount eaten.

Vitamins and minerals

What are vitamins?

Vitamins are essential nutrients that the body needs in small amounts in order to work properly. There are two types of vitamins: fat-soluble and water-soluble. The body can store fat-soluble vitamins in the liver and in fat, which means that, whilst they are needed in the diet, they are not essential every day. However, water-soluble vitamins cannot be stored, which means that they need to be eaten daily.

All vitamins should be obtainable through a varied and balanced diet so that vitamin supplements are not a necessity. However, if a person has difficulty in eating sufficient fresh produce, has been ill or is involved in high levels of sport or exercise then a vitamin supplement may be a good idea. Discuss this with a pharmacist to obtain more information about available preparations. Do not exceed recommended doses because some vitamins can be harmful in excess. Giving a vitamin supplement does not take away the need for a balanced diet and will not make a diet of excess sugar or fat any healthier!

Many staple foods are fortified with additional vitamins and minerals, making it easier to obtain the right amounts. Examples include many types of breakfast cereals, certain types of flour, vegetable spreads and margarine.

Fat-soluble vitamins

Fat-soluble vitamins are found mainly in fatty foods such as animal fats (including butter and lard), vegetable oils, dairy foods, liver and oily fish (*see* Table 5.8). They are not destroyed by heating or cooking.

Table 5.8 Fat-soluble vitamins

Vitamin	Needed for	Found in
Vitamin A	Night vision, growth, immune system, antioxidant. Deficiency leads to night blindness.	Liver, eggs, oily fish, dairy products and fortified margarine. The body can also manufacture it from beta-carotene, found in yellow and green leafy vegetables such as spinach, carrots and red peppers, and yellow fruit such as mango, melon and apricots.
Vitamin D	Regulates calcium levels in the body and helps bone strength. Deficiency leads to rickets.	Most vitamin D is made in the skin using sunlight, but some is needed in the diet. Found in oily fish, liver, eggs, fortified foods such as margarine, breakfast cereals, bread and powdered milk.
Vitamin E	It is an antioxidant, which helps to protect cell membranes. Deficiency is rare.	Vegetable oils, leafy green vegetables, fruit, nuts and wholegrain cereals.
Vitamin K	Used in blood clotting and for bone strength. Deficiency rare, apart from bleeding disorder of newborn babies.	Leafy green vegetables, vegetable oils and cereals. Small amounts in meat and dairy foods. It is also produced by bacteria in the intestines. Vitamin K is usually given to newborn babies.

Because the body is able to store these types of vitamins it is also able to take on board too much, so that in excess they can actually lead to harm. It is therefore not advised to overdose on supplements. It is very unlikely that a person could overdose on these vitamins just by eating a balanced diet.

Water-soluble vitamins

The body is not able to store water-soluble vitamins so they need to be eaten frequently. If too much is eaten the body gets rid of any extra vitamins in the urine, so they are not harmful.

Water-soluble vitamins are found in fruit, vegetables and grains (*see* Table 5.9), but they can be destroyed by heat or by being exposed to the air. They can also be lost in the water used for cooking. Therefore the best way to serve these foods is raw, steamed or grilled rather than boiled.

Table 5.9 Water-soluble vitamins

Vitamin	*Needed for*	*Found in*
Vitamin B_6	Energy release from protein and carbohydrate and for blood manufacture. Deficiency can lead to anaemia.	Meat, fish, bread, eggs, wholegrain cereals, vegetables, soya beans, peanuts, milk, potatoes and some fortified breakfast cereals.
Vitamin B_{12}	Works with folic acid to make healthy red blood cells and for the nervous system. Deficiency leads to pernicious anaemia.	Only found in animal foods, especially meat, fish and dairy products, but not plant foods.
Vitamin C	Needed for iron absorption and for keeping cells healthy. Deficiency leads to scurvy.	Most fruit and vegetables, especially broccoli, Brussels sprouts, peppers, kiwi and oranges.
Folic acid	Healthy red blood cell formation. Essential during development of the spine in the fetus.	Broccoli, Brussels sprouts, chickpeas, peas, yeast, oranges and bananas plus many fortified cereals. 400 mcg supplements advised in early pregnancy.
Niacin	Energy release from food, and for healthy cells.	Meat, flour, eggs and milk.
Riboflavin	Energy release and metabolism.	Milk, meat, eggs, fortified breakfast cereal and rice.
Thiamin	Nerve function and for energy release. Deficiency leads to disease of the nervous system.	Dairy products, meat, fortified cereals and flour, fresh and dried fruit.

What are minerals?

Minerals are essential nutrients that are required in small amounts in the form they are found in food. They are found in varying amounts in a variety of foods such as meat, cereals (including cereal products such as bread), fish, milk and dairy foods, vegetables, fruit (especially dried fruit) and nuts. A varied and balanced diet will ensure that adequate minerals are taken in.

Some nutrients, particularly iron, are less well absorbed from foods with a high fibre content. Absorption can be improved by including fruit or fruit juice with each meal, because vitamin C aids absorption.

Minerals are used for building strong bones and teeth, controlling body fluids inside and outside cells, and turning food into energy.

A brief guide to essential minerals is given in Table 5.10. Calcium is discussed in more detail on page 75 opposite.

Table 5.10 Essential minerals

Essential mineral	Used for
Calcium	Strong bones and teeth and for blood clotting.
Iron	Fundamental part of haemoglobin, carrying oxygen in the blood.
Magnesium	Needed for bones and for cell walls.
Phosphorus	Required in bones.
Potassium	Essential for fluid control and nerve conduction.
Sodium	Essential for fluid control and blood volume.
Sulphur	Required for removing waste via the liver and for making protein.

What are trace elements?

Trace elements are also essential nutrients that the body needs, but in much smaller amounts than vitamins and minerals. They are found in small amounts in a variety of foods such as meat, fish, cereals, milk and dairy foods, vegetables and nuts. A few examples are given in Table 5.11.

Table 5.11 Trace elements

Trace element	Details
Copper	Important for early infant growth and development.
Fluoride	Needed for the enamel on teeth and will reduce tooth decay. Found in toothpaste and in the water supply in some areas.
Iodine	Used by the thyroid gland. Found in seafood and milk.
Zinc	Helps cell growth and wound healing.

Dairy products

There should be around three portions of dairy products, including milk, in the daily diet of all people, where one portion is about one-third of a pint (200 ml). The recommended equivalent of a pint of milk per day can be made up of milk to drink or on cereals, milk that is mixed in other foods and sauces, plus cheese, yoghurt or fromage frais (*see* Table 5.12).

Table 5.12 Examples of dairy products and portion sizes

Dairy product	Portion size
Milk, full-fat, semi or skimmed	200 ml or one-third of a pint
Cheese such as Cheddar, Brie, Edam, etc.	40g or a piece the size of a matchbox
Cottage cheese	1 large pot weighing 200g
Light cream cheese	80g or a serving the size of 2 matchboxes
Fromage frais	1 pot weighing 150g
Yoghurt, plain or flavoured	1 pot weighing 150g

Low fat or full fat?

Milk and dairy products are an excellent source of protein, providing almost all of the essential proteins that are needed in the diet. However, people often feel confused about whether dairy products are healthy because, despite being a good source of calcium and protein, some contain high levels of fat. Therefore some adults reduce their intake to help reduce their weight. However, low- or reduced-fat dairy products are widely available these days and so can form a healthy part of anyone's diet.

Even though it is fine for young children to eat full-fat dairy products (because fat is an important source of energy for 'small eaters'), as a person gets older and eats larger volumes of food they should move on to lower-fat products unless he/she requires extra energy, such as when doing high levels of sport.

Encouragingly, low-fat dairy products have just as much calcium as full-fat versions and may have higher amounts of protein per gram.

Why calcium?

Calcium is needed for growing bones and for the formation of teeth, but is also essential for blood to be able to clot. Even if a teenager has stopped growing in height, the bones themselves continue to be moulded and strengthened for quite a few more years, meaning that high levels of calcium are needed in the diet in order to lay down this 'peak bone mass'. It is not until the early twenties that full bone strength is reached, so a diet that is short of calcium during the teenage years may leave a person with weaker bones, giving an increased risk of osteoporosis in later life, which in turn can lead to fractures.

Full bone strength is also influenced by:

- exercise, especially weight-bearing exercise such as walking and running
- body weight – being underweight is linked to weaker bones, particularly in

females because the hormone oestrogen is involved in bone formation and it is suppressed in women who are underweight
- vitamin D – calcium cannot be absorbed without vitamin D. Although vitamin D is made in the skin using sunlight, the sun is not strong enough during winter months, meaning that it is also needed in the diet
- excess alcohol and smoking – both can reduce the amount of calcium taken into growing bones, resulting in lower peak bone mass.

Some people are sensitive to dairy products

Occasionally, a person may appear to be sensitive to dairy products, which is usually shown by marked eczema or severe asthma, or may be linked to excess wind and diarrhoea symptoms. If there is a suspicion that dairy products are worsening some aspect of health then this should be discussed further with a family doctor or dietician, to ensure that a diet without dairy products will still provide all the essentials that a growing person needs.

There is further information about dairy-free eating in Chapter 9 in the section on vegetarian and vegan eating.

Food additives and E-numbers

The whole issue of food additives, particularly in foods targeted at children and young people, is complex and confusing. This short section aims to explore some of the arguments for and against, find some reassurance for those people who find additives hard to avoid and provide sources of further information for anyone who wishes to find out more.

What are E-numbers?

E-numbers form the European classification that is used to identify all additives that go into foods. All of these additives undergo testing to ensure they are safe for people to eat (but not everyone agrees with the conclusions of some of these safety committees).

Table 5.13 lists the different types of additives commonly used and what they are used for.

Some E-numbers are natural ingredients such as salt, but others are synthetic and have been created to improve the convenience factor and attractiveness of food. Studies have shown that the more a food is advertised, the more likely it will contain high amounts of additives. Also, foods with a high fat and/or sugar content are far more likely to contain lots of additives than healthier low-fat, salt and sugar foods.

E-numbers *per se* are not poisonous or toxic, but there are concerns about their overuse in food manufacturing because they make unhealthy food more attractive and they are often used to cover up nutritionally poor basic ingredients by adding in artificial flavouring that has not come from the food itself. An example is chicken nuggets made from mechanically reclaimed meat. Without flavourings and additives these nuggets would be inedible.

It is of even more concern that targeting these types of foods specifically at children and young people helps them to develop a 'taste' for nutritionally poor foods from early on.

Table 5.13 Food additives

Additive category	Reason for use
Preservatives	Stop micro-organisms from making food go off.
Antioxidants	Prevent oils and fats from going rancid.
Gelling agents and stabilisers	Create the desired texture and consistency of foods such as ice cream, yoghurt and salad dressings.
Emulsifiers	Help fats and oils to combine with water within food such as chocolate.
Flavouring agents	Help create the right flavour, especially in soft drinks, soups and sauces.
Colours	Recreate colours in processed foods that have been altered or lost during processing.
Intense sweeteners	Provide sweetness with fewer or no calories.
Acids	Help create the sharpness of certain flavours.

There is frequently poor labelling of foods so that the amount of additives is not clear. Some manufacturers list E-numbers themselves and others list the full name of the ingredient so that it may not be clear that the item listed is a food additive.

Table 5.14 lists some of the advantages and disadvantages of food additives.

Table 5.14 Advantages and disadvantages of food additives

Advantages of additives	Disadvantages of additives
Must pass a safety assessment, carried out in many different countries, which is usually reviewed if new information comes to light.	Powerful food organisations are sometimes able to sway the interpretation of safety studies to allow additives to be approved.
They prolong the shelf-life and food quality and reduce the risks of food poisoning.	They are used to make poor ingredients appear better by improving colour and flavour artificially.
They make many foods more appealing.	They can make poor foods more appealing.
They can reduce the cost and improve accessibility of foods by prolonging shelf-life.	They make nutritionally poorer foods more accessible and cheaper due to longer shelf-life.

The problem with salt

Salt has been used as a preservative for centuries but it is now more widely used as flavouring in foods. The first problem is that high salt intake is directly linked to high blood pressure, which in turn causes hardening of blood vessels due to a condition called 'atheroma', where blood vessel walls become clogged and narrowed. This is a major cause of heart attacks and stroke. Other factors also add to this risk, such as smoking, being overweight and having raised cholesterol, but high blood pressure is the most significant factor. However, it is, encouragingly, the factor that is probably easiest to improve.

The second problem is that a high-salt diet makes people thirsty and this increased thirst has led to higher demand for fizzy, sugary drinks. This in turn has contributed to the weight problems faced by so many of today's population.

The food industry have had good reason to add as much salt as possible, as explained in Figure 5.3:

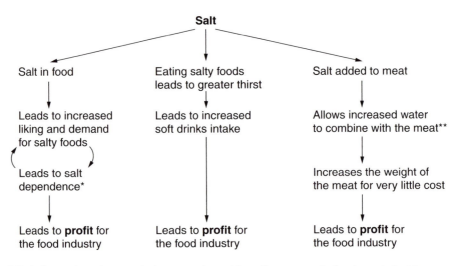

*'Salt dependence' means being accustomed to eating very salty foods such that less salty things taste bland and unacceptable.

**Water is frequently added to meat often in combination with a gel. For example, attempts to fry standard bacon will produce a pan full of scummy water, which is why manufacturers recommend grilling rather than frying.

Figure 5.3 Why the food industry uses salt. Adapted from *Obesity and the Role of Dietary Salt* by Professor GA MacGregor.

Three quarters of our daily salt is found in ready prepared or processed foods with only a quarter being added at the table. There is now a major campaign to help people eat less salt, which is leading to food manufacturers reducing salt in processed food. However, not all manufacturers have taken up this initiative so it is important to read labels to be sure items contain reduced salt.

Box 5.2 Salt intake

- Adults and children over 11 should eat no more than 6 grams of salt per day.*
- To work out whether a food is high or low in salt take a look at the figure for salt (or sodium) per 100g:
  - a *high*-salt food contains 1.25g salt or more per 100g (or 0.5g sodium or more per 100g).
  - a *low*-salt food contains 0.25g salt or less per 100g (or 0.1g sodium or less per 100g).

*Younger children should eat even less than this amount.

The Food Standards Agency has a good 'salt calculator' to help work out how much salt a food contains – see www.salt.gov.uk. The website also gives more ideas on moving to a lower salt diet.

It takes around one month to get used to a lower salt diet, so rather than going from excess to none, make gradual reductions to the amount used at home and begin to look for lower salt items in supermarkets, so giving a chance to gradually become accustomed to new flavours.

Controversial additives

It was not until the 1970s that scientists began to suspect a link between food additives and some health and behaviour problems. There has been extensive research into some areas, but because of the nature of symptoms, which are often non-specific and can be caused by several different factors, it can be very hard to prove that a food additive is the true cause of a problem. For example, despite anecdotal evidence (where one or two individuals feel sure that they can see a clear link) that an additive causes childhood behaviour problems, the link becomes much less clear when a large trial is organised, because all sorts of things influence child behaviour. This sort of trial does not confirm or refute the link – it is just not possible to be sure.

Tartrazine: E102

Tartrazine is a synthetic yellow food colouring used in many soft drinks, cakes, sweets, cereals, snacks and desserts. Despite reviews and government-funded surveys which have raised doubts, it is still approved and used widely in the UK, although it has been banned in Norway and Austria. It has been linked with rashes, asthma and hyperactivity in children, although the evidence for this is not clear-cut, as explained above. Food industry pressure has kept it on the approved list because it is such a useful additive.

Other additives that have been linked to hyperactivity in children are E110 (sunset yellow), E124 (ponceau 4 R), E122 (carmosine) and E211 (sodium benzoate). It has been suggested by respected sources that some 25% of temper tantrums in toddlers could be attributed to food additives, but once again it is hard to prove that one thing in particular is the cause when so many things can affect a child's behaviour.

Aspartame: E951

Aspartame is also known as NutraSweet and Canderel and is about 200 times sweeter than sugar. It is used in a huge variety of 'diet' or 'light' products, including fizzy drinks, to create calorie-free sweetness. It has been controversial because there have been claims that it can cause cancer, hair loss, depression, behaviour problems and epilepsy. However, it has been extensively studied by safety committees in America, Europe and other countries and has not been found to be harmful in normal daily intakes.

The lobbyists who support aspartame use claim that it reduces sugar intake and so should help to reduce diabetes, obesity and tooth decay. In practice, these benefits are as hard to prove as the claims that it causes harm. Whilst, at first glance, a calorie-free sweetener should achieve these aims, in practice both sugar and sugar-replacement foods encourage the development of a 'sweet tooth' and 'sweet teeth' tend to eat anything sweet on offer without always questioning the calories within.

A sweet tooth is not inherited, it is learned – and can be unlearned too. It only takes about two weeks to get used to sugar-free hot drinks or to move from full-fat to half-fat milk, whereas tolerating a low-salt diet can take a little longer. Hot drinks become far more enjoyable and thirst quenching when they contain less sugar. It is always preferable to find enjoyment in many varied things, including unsweetened drinks and water, rather than going along with the misconception that sweetness is the key to happiness.

Do additives affect young people as well as little children?

Whether there is any effect from additives on older people has not been established either, but it might be reasonable to question this if a young person is prone to temper outbursts, poor sleep pattern or lack of concentration for no obvious reason, particularly if these trends started long before puberty. There has been anecdotal evidence that school behaviour has improved following healthy school meal drives or when vending machines have been removed from school premises so that consumption of junk food has reduced.

In order to conduct a home exclusion trial that is of any value, behaviour should be monitored for a few weeks *before* the exclusion trial so that a baseline of the behaviour in question can be established. Then reduce or exclude as many additives as possible for a trial period of at least two weeks. Monitor if there is a noticeable change in, for example, frequency of outbursts, sleep pattern or ability to concentrate on a task. If there is a clear difference then it doesn't matter what the scientists say – stick to the improved foods and keep the problem foods off the menu as much as possible.

Table 5.15 lists some common problem foods, but there are many more processed foods that are brimming with additives – it is necessary to read food labels and develop a basic knowledge of additive-free items if the trial is to be a success. Wherever possible, prepare foods from scratch because then it will be clear what the food is made from.

Further information is available from The Food Commission and through the Hyperactive Children's Support Group (*see* Appendix 2 for further details).

Table 5.15 Common problem foods and good alternatives

Problem foods	Good alternatives
Fizzy drinks, squash	Water, dilute fruit juice, milk, tea without sugar
Fish fingers	Cod or salmon fillet, baked or steamed
Chicken nuggets	Stir-fried chicken strips or home-made nuggets of chicken breast dipped in beaten egg and breadcrumbs
Burgers	Home-made burgers from lean ground beef or a thin strip of frying steak
Flavoured crisps	Ready salted crisps
Yellow custard	Colour-free varieties or choose plain yoghurt with a little added sugar instead

---

Summary points

- Young people should aim to eat a diet that contains no more than 30% fat.
- Young people should try to eat *more* unsaturated fats and oils and *less* hard or saturated fat, especially 'trans' and hydrogenated fat.
- A healthy diet should contain *more* wholegrain, unrefined carbohydrates and *less* refined carbohydrates, such as white flour, which are often combined with high levels of fat and sugar. This will ensure the diet contains essential nutrients, such as fibre, vitamins and minerals.
- Young people should eat around 1 gram of protein per kilogram of body weight.
- A variety of different protein building blocks are needed, which can easily be obtained by eating varied combinations of both animal and plant proteins.
- Increasing intake of fruit and vegetables is the best way to improve the diet because they contain lots of essential micronutrients such as fibre, vitamins and minerals.
- Fruit and vegetables reduce the risk of serious illnesses throughout life and can help with maintaining a healthy weight by pushing richer ingredients 'off the plate'.
- Essential vitamins, minerals and trace elements are obtainable through a well-balanced diet, so supplements are only needed if the diet is poor, during illness or for high levels of sport.
- The body cannot store water-soluble vitamins so they are needed daily. Fat-soluble vitamins can accumulate so should not be taken in excess.
- Low-fat dairy products are just as good a source of calcium as full-fat ones.
- Plenty of calcium is required in order to achieve peak bone mass by the early twenties.
- Be confident that some additives are beneficial, whilst taking steps to cut out poor foods that require colourants or flavourings to make them palatable.
- Although aspartame may replace sugar in many products, it can lead to the development of a 'sweet tooth', so that overall more sugary products are eaten.

Chapter 6

The Top Teen Health Plan family guide

Young people gradually take control of their lifestyle during the years between childhood and adulthood, ready for full independence when they leave home. For those interested in improving their health there is much support and help that families can offer, without forcing their views or overriding the young person's own efforts to change things. The more those healthy initiatives have family support, the more likely they will persist and become normal and routine.

This chapter looks at a variety of ways for families to improve eating structures and to put young people more easily in charge of how they eat. It takes an in-depth look at getting hunger under control, plus ways to become wise to the heavy advertising and marketing now directed at young people. It ends with a brief reminder of important teenage nutritional needs.

Who is in charge?

> 'You can lead a horse to water, but you can't make it drink.'

This old adage sums up people and choice. To make good choices a person needs to feel in charge of the choice being made. Despite a parent's best efforts, young people will only make significant improvements to an unhealthy lifestyle if they want to, and so these transitional years are the time to get them involved in decision making. This doesn't mean putting them in sole charge of household meals, but it means sharing the decisions and incorporating their requests and ideas.

Teenagers have been used to having meals plonked down in front of them: it is time to ask for feedback about family meals and to encourage discussion about nutrition, including what would be chosen if a parent wasn't there to cook (*see* Table 6.1).

There are varied ways for young people to take charge

A significant reason why so many adults have weight problems is due to having little control over how and what they eat. Bad habits may be learned in childhood and then continue into adulthood because eating patterns have become fixed. Giving a teenager a good sense of control over eating patterns is excellent preparation for adulthood. There are various ways of doing this.

Portion sizes

Portion sizes should reflect how hungry the person feels, rather than how easily the food divides amongst the family. This means asking people how much they want, rather than making assumptions. Young people could serve themselves.

Table 6.1 Approaches to involve young people in eating well

Approaches to involve young people in eating well	Example of the approach
Give choices over daily foods and cooking techniques.	What fruit and vegetables would the teenager like to eat this week? Steamed or stir-fried?
Use a teenager's own interest in being healthy.	Does the teenager have ideas on a healthy alternative to chips or burgers?
Discuss the link with sports performance and nutrition.	Young people who do regular exercise need plenty of protein, calcium and iron for top performance.
Encourage some independence.	Would the teenager like to learn to cook some basic recipes, such as pasta with sauce or a simple 'cook-in sauce' curry and rice?
Is there interest in leaving old habits behind?	Are there any items that the teenager would be happy to leave off the weekly shop?
Would money increase motivation?	What about saving money by taking a home-prepared snack or meal, such as sandwiches, rather than stopping off for junk food?

A growing child who is served large portions because 'he's a growing lad' will get used to large portion sizes. Unless portion sizes reduce at the end of a growth spurt, why wouldn't that child assume that it is normal to have huge platefuls and to feel bloated at the end of meals? It is preferable for all people to be encouraged to follow true appetite, even if that means eating far less when not growing or being active.

Second helpings

There is nothing wrong with second helpings if the overall balance of the meal is still healthy. Indeed, offering second helpings can be a useful way to reduce portion sizes – no one need object to smaller portions at the outset if further food is available if still hungry. Breaking up the meal like this is one way to slow down the meal and give an opportunity to think about fullness, because for many people this needs conscious thought: 'Do I really want a second helping or am I now starting to feel full? Have I saved a bit of room for dessert?'

Cooking quantities

In busy households, it is understandable that the quantity of food prepared may seem unimportant. The usual motto is that too much is better than too little, because you can always finish things off later, whereas it is a pain to have to cook more. This can, however, put pressure on the family to eat more than they really want, because of the tendency not to waste food and to plonk extra spoonfuls onto any plate that looks emptiest. Some families find it difficult to change cooking quantities when someone in the household leaves home – if the same weight of potatoes or pasta is cooked then the chances are the remaining family will clear up the extra.

Pre-packaged portion sizes

How often do we cook a whole packet of something – not the amount we really want, but the amount the food manufacturer wanted to sell us? Supermarkets try to sell a variety of portions of fresh meat, but some items tend to come in predictable quantities, such as packs of eight sausages – too many if there are only two of you at home, and the wrong number for a family of five.

Ready meals are another example of losing control over portion size. There is huge variation in the calorie content of ready meals – some seem meagre and are aimed at the 'dieting market', whereas others look tempting and contain abundant calories. Without painstaking study of the nutritional information box, the purchaser will not know how energy-dense the food is, giving the chance of still feeling hungry at the end of a dieter's meal or having eaten too much at the end of a tempting meal. The tendency when eating an individual carton is to eat the lot – control has been entirely given over to the food manufacturer and your own appetite is not in charge. Where possible, it is better to choose foods that allow more control over portion sizing, for example jars with a lid so that some of the portion can be put in the fridge before heating what is needed.

Extra-large packets

The trouble with extra-large packets is that they tend to be better value in terms of cost, but only if you still eat the amount you might have eaten if you had purchased a normal-size pack. If buying in bulk means eating in bulk too, then you have not made a cost saving at all, but merely provided false justification for overeating. Special offers in supermarkets are another thing to be wary of – there is no point falling for excellent-value items that you wouldn't usually buy if they are going to cause problems with unnecessary temptation. It is cheaper not to buy special offers at all if they are not what you want or need.

Family factors

How often are teenagers overruled when going for a healthy choice or small portion, instead being encouraged to eat more or different things? It is odd that so many adults get an enormous sense of pleasure from seeing their family eat well and enjoying food; it can feel like a sign of love towards and from younger children, which can become a difficult emotion to leave behind. This can mean that parents continue to encourage teenagers to eat long after the 'fussy eater' early years have passed, with the result that some teenagers feel it is easier to overeat than to disappoint a parent.

How confident would a teenager be in saying no to a home-cooked dinner, even though they had already eaten a cooked meal at the canteen at college and stopped at the snack shop on the way home? Changes in catering facilities when teenagers swap to a new school or college or start work mean that family meal structures may need to change too.

Families can often sabotage attempts to eat healthily in the belief that the youngster does not know what is best. Many parents feel far more worried about the risk of anorexia than the presence of overweight or obesity and so try to minimise any attempts their teenager might make to consume fewer calories. If a teenager is showing concerns about their weight, try to establish the facts before overruling attempts to change. Further details on checking out weight are given in The Top Teen Health Plan (*see* p. 173).

Easy availability

Some young people have particular factors that make it difficult for them to take control of their eating. For example, it might be more convenient for a parent who works at a butcher's shop to serve fry-ups and roast dinners than to explore salads, pasta and other lower-calorie foods. What if a parent works for a chocolate factory? It would seem churlish not to bring home regular supplies of cheap misshapes. If one parent does a heavy manual job that requires a full cooked breakfast every morning, this might be served to the rest of the household too – but do they have the same sort of energy requirements if they are studying quietly at school all day?

Limited knowledge

Some parents feel it is fine to let their family eat whatever they want and make no attempt to limit access to packets of crisps, sugary drinks and bars of chocolate. This is only satisfactory if each person has sufficient knowledge to make a reasoned choice about the pros and cons of eating lots of rich or high-fat/sugar foods. However, without guidance young people do not automatically know that some things are best eaten in moderation. Everyone knows that eating too much can be a problem, but how much is too much?

Food advertising gives a one-sided view of a product's benefits, so balanced nutritional information is needed to put across the other side and to explain how a varied diet is required for good health. Children and young people grow to like things that are tasty, rich and familiar. Ready access to these foods without any guidance can lead to harm due to eating in excess without restraint. The Food Frequency Framework (*see* Chapter 7) provides guidance about eating rich foods appropriately, so that young people can feel confident about when they have had enough.

Understand hunger and how to get it under control

How hungry people feel depends on what food is available

Appetite is not simply governed by the need to replace the calories used since the last meal, but varies according to what food is available. If surrounded by an array of tempting and delicious foods, hunger will feel greater than if there is little more than dry bread and mouldy cheese on offer. In the same way, hunger is more likely to be triggered by a small mid-morning snack than by eating nothing and not thinking about food at all. Once people start nibbling it can be hard to stop.

The motivation to eat depends on the quality and tastiness of the food on offer plus how much effort it takes to get it, rather than whether people are carrying sufficient fat stores already. Humans evolved as 'opportunistic eaters', meaning that they are able to store food whenever it is available as well as to manage for a good while when food is short. If food is there, people will eat. Unfortunately, when food is plentiful, storing excess fat leads to health problems and, in today's society, to emotional problems too.

In order to overcome the tendency to be tempted by too many treats, it is important to be careful about shopping. People will be far less tempted to overeat plain foods than a cupboard full of treats. Buying treats and then expecting the family to show restraint is a tall order.

Tune in to the 'hunger-blocking mechanism'

The 'hunger-blocking mechanism' is like a switch – or sensation – that tells us when we've eaten enough. Hunger doesn't fade as soon as people start eating. Putting food in our mouths actually stimulates hunger – one mouthful of a biscuit usually makes us want to eat the whole thing. Eventually, the arrival of sufficient food in the stomach acts to block hunger, but this mechanism takes a while to kick in because it has to register the energy density of what has been eaten as well as how full the stomach feels. Eating quickly increases the risk of overeating because excess food can be consumed before the 'hunger-blocking mechanism' has time to act. We can also easily override how full we feel if there is something really tasty on offer – the enjoyment of the food can outweigh the discomfort of feeling bloated.

Many children are taught to ignore their 'hunger-blocking mechanism' by being encouraged or even forced to clear their plate. If this sounds familiar then it is time to change tack and encourage the family to tune in to inner fullness cues instead. Give permission to leave food if feeling full. At the same time, put people in charge of how much goes on their plate by asking how much they want or allowing them to serve themselves.

The 'hunger-blocking mechanism' can be harnessed to guide when to stop eating by considering the following:

- Slow down meals. This includes cutting up food into smaller mouthfuls and chewing more thoroughly. Eating together and sharing conversation is another way to slow down the eating process.
- Reduce portion sizes. Some surprising research has shown that people tend to eat the same number of mouthfuls of a portion, regardless of its size. For example, if you are served a huge slice of cake you are likely to eat large mouthfuls. If you are given a much smaller piece of cake, the chances are that you will take smaller mouthfuls, so that the overall number of mouthfuls is similar for both slices. In other words, a large portion tends to be eaten more quickly than a small portion. On the same theme, we tend to eat rich puddings such as chocolate mousse with a small teaspoon, whereas a bowl of rice pudding, which tends to come as a larger portion, would usually be eaten with a dessertspoon. If we have been conditioned to expect roughly ten spoonfuls of any dessert, then serving smaller portions perhaps with smaller spoons may be perfectly acceptable or pass unnoticed because the expectation of a 'normal'-sized dessert has been met.
- Include bulky foods, such as those high in fibre, which act to fill up the stomach more effectively than foods that are energy-dense, such as those high in fat.
- It may help to eat more 'slow-release' foods, which take longer to digest, such as wholegrain foods, starchy foods and a higher-protein diet, as a way of

keeping hunger at bay for longer. Looking at the glycaemic index (GI) may help to work out which foods are 'slow-release' (*see* Chapter 9, p. 130).

- Beginning the meal with a starter is a good way to take the edge off an appetite and to give the 'hunger-blocking mechanism' time to kick in.
- Either post a menu so that people know how much room to save for the next course, or make ordinary meals follow a familiar pattern so that the family knows what to expect.
- The 'hunger-blocking mechanism' will only work if people listen to it and obey what it is saying. So rather than asking if anyone wants more to eat towards the end of a meal, ask if people are feeling full instead. Unless people think about whether they are full during a meal, other factors will guide how much is eaten, such as: has all the food disappeared? Did it taste nice? Will the cook be upset if no one wants second helpings?

Hunger is greater if we are not sure what to expect

Why does a main evening meal tend to be larger than breakfast? It is simply a cultural thing for most people – we expect it to be so and hence it seems right. People would feel hungry and disappointed if they were hoping for a juicy roast dinner with all the trimmings, but could only find a cheese sandwich. But if they were looking for a cheese sandwich, then it would fit the bill perfectly.

This is a very important aspect in gaining control over appetite. By establishing good, regular and predictable mealtime expectations, hunger will be less of a problem. People feel far hungrier if they never know what type of food to expect, whereas hunger carries less impact if meals follow a predictable pattern. For example, if lunch consists of a sandwich and a piece of fruit plus a small biscuit each day then, even if the fillings and fruit vary, it will always provide roughly the same volume of food and people will get used to expecting that amount every day. The same would apply if lunch meant a bowl of soup and a roll or a small bowl of pasta – varying the type of soup or sauce wouldn't matter. But varying between a huge plate of sausage, egg and chips to a few crackers with a stick of celery would confuse expectations and generate a greater sense of hunger.

Being as consistent as possible about portion sizes and structure of meals will help to combat hunger. Of course, mealtime structures can be left behind when on holiday or for celebrations and more lenient structures might be fine at weekends, but stick to predictable structures for ordinary meals (*see* Table 6.2). These can reduce the tendency to eat everything in sight if a person is confronted with a fridge full of food that is supposed to last the week.

Arrange the daily timetable to take advantage of distraction to reduce the impact of hunger

Many people know that they eat far more when they are bored and that hunger can disappear if they are busy or distracted. Eating is enjoyable and can work very well as a boredom cure. However, eating is not the only way to overcome boredom, but it can take a bit of will-power and organisation to think of something more constructive in those hungry moments leading up to a meal.

Time meals for when the family seems most hungry – change mealtimes around if there is a daily discussion about snacking at the wrong time. Or serve

Table 6.2 Suggestions for weekday meal structures

Breakfast	Lunch	Evening meal
Bowl of cereal with milk	Sandwich, fruit and small biscuit	Main course followed by dessert
Or toast and marmalade		
Or fruit with yoghurt	Or small bowl of pasta or noodles with salad, then fruit	
Cooked breakfast for people doing manual jobs or hard exercise	Or soup and a roll	

the dessert first in place of a starter if this is simple to prepare and the rest of the meal is not yet ready. Serving sliced fruit or a plate of salad as a starter is a useful way to encourage the whole family to increase their quota of fresh produce, because hunger at this time increases the chance of eating foods that might otherwise be less popular.

Involve young people in food preparation or cooking – this can alleviate boredom as well as increase interest in healthy foods. Some young people get into a routine of doing homework or sport or music practice in the time leading up to a meal, which is a constructive way to distract them from hunger.

Discourage any strong association between exercising and eating so that activities do not automatically need to be rewarded with food. Remember: 'healthy exercise – healthy snack'.

Untangle hunger from other sensations and emotions

Hunger has become a bit of a dirty word – politically incorrect! Almost every dieting regime promises weight loss without having to feel hungry. But what is wrong with feeling hungry now and again? The reason it generates such panic is that it gets mixed up with other emotions.

If people have been eating to stem boredom, find comfort and provide some excitement in life, this can mean that their subconscious mind starts to misread the sensation of hunger as indicating boredom, loneliness and an empty life. At the end of a bad day, feelings of unhappiness become jumbled together, resulting in the person feeling very hungry.

Eating at the first stomach rumble is a way of blocking out those fears, of somehow pushing those factors out of the way by trying to ensure that hunger is controlled. What is more, the more unhappy life becomes the hungrier one feels, because hunger has become a clear and simple signal of inner unhappiness. Although eating is nice, do not allow the joy of eating to be the only thing that combats the worries of the day. Otherwise, when life gets really tough, ever-increasing amounts of food will be needed to block out the misery, leading to binge eating and gross obesity. This psychological muddle can become very complex and can lead to eating problems throughout life if the sensation of hunger is not untangled from these other emotions.

The solution to this scenario requires more than a simple quick fix because it involves changing the way people think and feel at a subconscious level. It can be done by treating the emotional problems that underlie an eating problem and by relearning techniques for coping with stress, loneliness and boredom. This may involve looking for and treating depression or anxiety.

One technique that has been shown to work for these types of psychological 'muddles' is *cognitive behaviour therapy*, where a psychologist teaches ways of identifying negative thoughts that are associated with the problem behaviour – in this situation overeating – and learning to challenge and distract these thoughts and to confront the real underlying issues. If anyone feels concerned about abnormal hunger and is eating in response to emotional problems, discuss this with a family doctor and, if severe, request further help from a psychologist or an eating disorder clinic.

If the tendency to eat in response to worries is recent, then start by untangling the sensation of hunger by talking about general worries and dealing with problems at face value, focusing on building and maintaining self-esteem, and by finding healthy ways to deal with hunger. Remember that hunger is a normal sensation, a bit like the fuel gauge in a car. When the tank is getting low it is not an emergency, just time to think about the next fuel stop and managing until then. Use distraction by getting busy, perhaps rearranging mealtimes and choosing healthy snacks in between meals to help put the sensation of hunger back in perspective.

Get real about the effects of advertising and gimmicky eating regimes

Many people with weight problems think that they eat a fairly healthy diet and feel mystified over what is wrong with the way they eat. If adults struggle to get their facts straight, then it must be even harder for young people to have a clear idea of what makes up a healthy diet. This section takes a look at some common factors and misconceptions that can lead people into thinking their diets are healthier than they really are.

Advertising directed at children and young people

There is current debate about limiting the amount of food advertising directed at children, but less focus on the heavy marketing directed at young people. Children are naturally trusting and so tend to believe messages that they see. If advertising didn't work, it wouldn't be splattered on every visible surface of the modern world. However, an inexperienced child cannot be expected to accurately weigh up the pros and cons of a product when a team of marketing executives have spent months perfecting their sales pitch. Marketing executives want their product to sell well, regardless of whether it is healthy or not – its ultimate effect on the person who buys it is not their concern, but the sales figures are. This means making products look exciting, cool, trendy, tasty, fun and healthy, even if they aren't. These executives always end their defence of their marketing strategies by saying that people don't *have* to buy their products – that it is up to the consumer.

An excess of any one product on its own will not cause much problem, but children and young people are now bombarded with sophisticated marketing at every opportunity on television, on mobile phones, through sports and in schools, as big businesses sponsor many school programmes. Many adults struggle to make up their minds and cope with the hard sell that is sometimes used, but children and young people are even easier to confuse, mislead and tempt. Allowing unscrupulous and currently unlimited advertising aimed at susceptible groups is asking for trouble – and the obesity statistics show that that trouble has already arrived.

Although it is not the only factor contributing to the obesity epidemic, it is certainly a significant one. Everyone, whatever their age, should learn to be sceptical about marketing claims and advertising. Question and check out claims, including how healthy the product is, whether it is of good quality and whether it is good value.

Remember that the food industry only does the hard sell on things that give it lots of profit, rather than items that are good for the nation.

A calorie is a calorie

The vast array of dieting regimes and concepts has led to a huge amount of confusion over how food is converted into energy once inside us. There is plenty of pseudo-science around; for example some schools of thought suggest that eating a high-protein diet somehow alters metabolism, or that eating very high-fibre foods requires extra energy to burn up the food, leading to weight loss. The reason these approaches sometimes work is because the strong focus on one type of food means other foods are displaced or forbidden from the usual diet – not because miracles are afoot!

However hard we might try, we cannot escape from the simple fact that eating fat, carbohydrate, protein, fruit and vegetables or high-fibre foods means eating calories – they all contain calories. A person who needs 2000 kcal a day would be at the same risk of weight gain if they ate 3000 kcal per day of either healthy or unheathy foods. However, there is less temptation to overeat healthy foods because they contain fewer calories per mouthful, giving a greater chance of feeling full with fewer calories on board. They also contain lots of vitamins, minerals, fibre and antioxidants, which give other health benefits.

Whatever the claims of odd dieting regimes, the only way to lose weight is to eat fewer calories than required, and when aiming for weight maintenance, to eat roughly the same number of calories that are being used up. Any diet that works will be following this basic law, whatever claims it makes.

'Slimming foods' create a false sense of security

Studies have shown a tendency for people to be conned over dieting products, because they tend to eat larger portions of them. Somehow, eating a 99% fat-free item makes a larger portion feel justifiable, so that in the end the same amount of energy is consumed as for a standard product, which is why some dieting regimes don't seem to work. In addition, some food manufacturers push the low-fat concept whilst piling in extra sugar so that the calorie content remains high.

People overcompensate after exercising

After an energetic game, good swim, brisk walk or workout at the gym, the tendency is to reward the hard work with an edible treat. Sports stadiums and clubs know all about this tendency and provide tempting vending machines. However, it is very easy to eat far more calories than have just been used up, as shown by Table 7.6 in the next chapter.

Indeed, there are people who think exercise requires no personal effort and that pampering on a toning table, sitting in a Jacuzzi or having a massage in a gym will help fitness or promote weight loss. If these activities are followed by a 'post-exercise' snack then it is more likely they will lead to weight gain than reduction. Whenever possible, make the post-exercise snack fit in with the overall balance of the day's diet, rather than something extra. Make it healthy by taking fruit or a sandwich along, rather than resorting to overpriced confectionery from a vending machine. Arrange for exercise sessions to finish just before a meal or rearrange meals for those hungry times after sports.

Skipping meals

In the same way that low-fat or 'diet' foods mislead people into taking larger portions, there is the same tendency for deception after skipping a meal because people overcompensate at the next meal or with snacks. By skipping a meal the sensation of hunger builds up, which makes food seem even more attractive so that self-control goes right out of the window and restraint is lost. This results in much greater food consumption at the next opportunity. Sticking to a consistent meal strategy is a far better way to keep hunger under control and to avoid the tendency to overeat.

'Health-giving' foods and other confusing concepts

Marketing executives have had a field day with the concept of 'health-giving' foods, creating the impression that if certain foods are eaten illnesses may go away – that people can 'eat' themselves into health. Whilst it is true that a balanced diet can reduce the chance of many illnesses, there is no one specific ingredient that is required.

It is just as important to avoid too much of the unhealthy things as it is to consume 'health-giving' foods. Simply adding an apple, a bio-yoghurt drink or a vitamin-enriched cereal bar will not take away the excess fat, salt or sugar from a diet of chips, burgers, crisps and fizzy drinks.

The general public are now so confused as to what is good and what is not that almost any product can get away with some claim or other to improve health. For example, it is astonishing that a hard-boiled lollipop, made of pure sugar, with no nutritional value at all but a high potential to cause tooth decay, can claim that it is 100% fat-free as if it were in some way healthy! This is cynical marketing at its worst. The fact that a product contains or does not contain specific ingredients does not make it healthy, 'health-giving' or in any way essential. The secret always lies in the overall balance of the overall diet.

Labelling issues

Many common terms can be confusing or misleading. For example, what is meant by 'natural' ingredients, such as honey? What do the labels 'farm assured' or 'farm fresh' or 'butcher fresh' mean? The following section looks at some examples to see which terms are helpful and which are misleading.

Generally helpful or reliable labelling

- 'Organic' foods. This is a helpful term that refers to farming practice and the way the food is produced. An organic vegetable or cereal grain will have the same calorie content per 100 grams as a standard product, but the improved farming techniques will benefit the environment by using fewer artificial fertilisers. Organic farming is closely regulated and so the organic label is a reliable source of information about how the item was produced. Organic farming severely restricts the use of artificial chemical fertilisers and pesticides. Instead, organic farmers rely on developing a healthy, fertile soil and growing a mixture of crops. Animals are reared without the routine use of drugs, antibiotics and wormers common in intensive livestock farming.
- Food assurance schemes. These schemes are often accompanied by a red tractor logo. Food bearing this logo will have been produced on a farm that has been following a quality standards scheme, but it does not imply a nutritional advantage over other products.
- Free-range products. This term reflects the conditions under which the farm animal was kept and does not imply a nutritional advantage over a non-free-range product. If choosing free-range eggs, the chickens involved in the egg production will have had a better environment than battery chickens, but the nutritional value of each egg will be the same.
- 'Polyunsaturated' or 'monounsaturated' fat. These types of fat have been shown to lower blood cholesterol and therefore help reduce the risk of heart disease, hence products containing these fats are a good idea.
- 'Gluten-free'. For people who wish to avoid gluten in the diet, this label reliably states that a product is gluten-free.
- 'Lactose-free'. This shows that the product contains no milk sugar and so is suitable for someone with lactose intolerance. Some products are labelled 'reduced lactose', meaning that they contain low amounts rather than none. These products may suit people with milder symptoms who can tolerate small amounts.
- Allergy advice. From November 2005, new regulations are being introduced so that any product containing a possible allergen should be clearly labelled. Up to November 2005 there has been no legal requirement to do so, although many manufacturers have given this information. Some food labels say 'may contain nuts' or 'may contain seeds', which means that, although they are not deliberately added, there could be small traces. Allergy sufferers should avoid these products.

Potentially misleading or meaningless labelling

The following terms have not been clearly defined by law, so that some manufacturers have applied them in a confusing and possibly misleading way. Regulations are in the process of being tightened in respect of accurate food labelling, but these terms currently may lead to confusion about the product:

- 'Natural' ingredients. Consumers assume that a product labelled as 'natural' will have no artificial additives, but such foods may still contain permitted additives and colourings. 'Natural' does not mean healthy. Honey, which is often referred to as 'natural', is a type of sugar, but it has no particular power or benefit over other forms of sugar apart from its distinctive taste and texture; indeed, it is equally harmful to teeth and, if eaten in excess, will lead to the same weight problems as other sugars.
- 'Pure' should refer to a single ingredient to which nothing has been added, but can apply to some food combinations if each ingredient was originally in a pure form. The term has been used in misleading ways in the past.
- 'Fresh' should mean that the food has been recently prepared or harvested, but the term has been incorporated into many meaningless phrases such as 'ocean fresh', 'garden fresh' and 'oven fresh', which say nothing about the food apart from making it sound nice.
- The terms 'farmhouse', 'home-made', 'traditional', 'authentic' and 'original' are often used to give a product an emotive appeal, but they tell the customer nothing about the nutritional quality of the food. They can all be misleading.
- 'Value' or 'economy' labelling. These terms have no legal definition and so can be used to convey whatever the food manufacturer wishes. It could mean a poor product that is cheap or a reasonable product that has cheaper packaging than similar products. The only way to tell is to compare the nutritional information with other similar products.
- Live yoghurt is shrouded in mystifying health claims. Whilst yoghurt may form a reasonable part of a balanced diet, there is no convincing evidence that it will somehow enliven life or improve medical conditions.
- 'Lite' or 'light'. These terms suggest the product has a lower fat content than a standard product, but the law does not clarify actual fat content. This may give a misleading image of the quality of the food, particularly because some 'light' products have high sugar levels giving the same number of calories as a standard product.
- The fat content is the most confusing and commonest label of all. '75% fat-free' means that a quarter of the product is fat, not that it is low in fat. Indeed, as already described, choosing a low-fat product may subconsciously encourage eating larger portions of that food. Remember that some fat is healthy – it is not a poison, people just don't need too much. By focusing on getting the overall balance of other ingredients right, the impact of any fatty or dairy products will be less because they won't make up too much of the overall diet.

These endless and confusing marketing claims are damaging because they make it difficult to know what to believe, such that some people cease to take note of food labelling altogether; but reading every label would be very confusing and time-consuming and could lead to an almighty muddle. The way to cope with confusing labels is to get back to basics and ensure that the overall diet contains plenty of fresh produce, not too many treat items and a good balance of wholegrain cereals, protein-containing foods and dairy products, as outlined in Chapter 1. That way, the small variations in different products will be evened out without having to worry about too much small print.

A summary of the nutrients required for good teenage growth

Full nutritional guidance for young people is given in the Top Teen Health Plan at the end of this book, and ways to incorporate good nutrition into daily family meals are covered in Chapter 7 'The Food Frequency Framework', but a short summary is given here for easy reference.

The teenage growth spurt involves a rapid increase in the amount of bone, muscle and circulating blood around the body. This requires plenty of protein, vitamin D, calcium and iron, but a teenage nutrition survey in 2000 showed that many teenagers are short of these essentials. This can lead to long-term problems such as osteoporosis, diabetes, obesity, cholesterol problems and failing to reach one's expected adult height.

Calcium

Too little calcium results in weaker bones, which can also result in osteoporosis later in life. Teenagers should aim for 800 mg per day for girls and 1000 mg per day for boys. This can be found in three 200 ml glasses of milk a day plus a lump of cheese (45g) and a yoghurt (125g). (Note that full-fat, semi-skimmed and skimmed milk all have roughly the same calcium content.)

Vitamin D

This is also required for bone development because it helps the body to absorb calcium. Although it is found in the diet, it is also made by the skin when exposed to sunlight. During the winter, however, there is insufficient sunlight of the right wavelength for the skin to make enough and so it is needed in the diet. Fish oils and oily fish such as sardines and mackerel are good sources, as are egg yolk, liver and butter. It is added to margarines, low-fat spreads and some breakfast cereals by law in the UK.

Iron

Iron deficiency is common with over a quarter of 15–18 year-old girls having low iron stores and 9% being anaemic. Girls are at greater risk of anaemia due to blood loss during their periods.

Iron is essential for enabling blood to carry oxygen around the body and for helping the immune system and muscle development. It is found in red meat, green vegetables, baked beans, eggs, wholemeal bread and many breakfast cereals.

Whilst many other nutrients are also required they will appear in a well-balanced diet, particularly if a teenager is trying to eat foods that are rich in the above nutrients.

Summary points

- Young people can take charge of how they eat in simple and practical ways that include getting more involved in how the family eats and being more responsible for what goes on to their own plate.
- Hunger can be actively managed and minimised by tuning in to the 'hunger-blocking mechanism' by creating consistent mealtime structures and making use of distraction.
- Hunger can be confused with other emotions so that sadness, loneliness or boredom becomes misinterpreted as hunger. This leads to comfort eating and, in extremes, to binge eating.
- Check out common misconceptions that deceive people into thinking their diet is healthier than it really is.
- Young people require plenty of protein, calcium, vitamin D and iron in order to achieve a healthy adult frame, but many do not get enough of these nutrients.

Chapter 7

The Food Frequency Framework

Find out which family meals are fine for every day and which should either be put on the 'specials' list or be modified in order to become healthy daily meals. Work out which snacks fit the occasion and use portion size to stop fattening favourites from becoming a problem.

What is the Food Frequency Framework?

How often is it okay to eat cheesecake? Or waffles soaked in maple syrup? Or cookie-dough ice-cream? What about roast beef with Yorkshire puddings and all the trimmings? How about chicken nuggets or burgers? All of these common foods have their place, but many foods are not suitable for daily consumption, however tasty they may be.

The Food Frequency Framework shows how to decide which foods are suitable for everyday meals, which are better kept for once-weekly enjoyment and which are best reserved for special occasions or times when food is the centre of the feast. It also gives ideas on how to make family favourites healthy enough to be served frequently, if they are currently falling into one of the richer categories. Portion size is covered later in the chapter. Following the Food Frequency Framework will help more meals fit in with *The Balance of Good Health* (*see* Chapter 1).

Studies have shown that mealtime expectations are not that high and people are happy to eat healthy foods if they are familiar. People usually expect a meal at mealtimes, not an all-singing, all-dancing food extravaganza. Hence families will be content with a basic framework of family meals that are nutritious and healthy. Reserve rich and more elaborate foods for weekends or special occasions when it will be more appropriate to get extra pleasure from food. The more these ordinary meals fit in with *The Balance of Good Health*, the more freedom this gives to eat richly on special occasions. If the basic diet contains plenty of goodness, then the odd 'junk food day' won't matter.

Puddings are part of the meal, not an optional extra for good behaviour, and can be a way of adding in extra fruit, dairy or starchy ingredients. Puddings do not have to be overly sweet or sticky, especially on ordinary days, and should fit in with *The Balance of Good Health* just as much as the main course.

Fitting foods into the Framework

Table 7.1 shows what factors lead a food to be in one category or another.

Table 7.1 The factors that lead a food to be in one category or another

Celebration foods or rare treats	Once-weekly or weekend foods	Daily basics
Nutrition is simply not an issue.	There is a compromise between convenience or flavour and the food's nutritional value.	Nutrition is important and these foods all have some benefit within the diet.
May contain a high proportion of 'bad' fats such as saturated or trans fats.*	May be moderately high in fat or have some 'bad' fats.	Either low- or no-fat foods, or high in omega 3 and 6 oils or other unsaturated fats.
Expensive or require lots of time and effort to prepare. May be elaborately packaged.	Moderately expensive or fiddly to prepare. Alternately, its cost is offset by its convenience.	Plain ingredients that may be cheap†, with little in the way of fancy packaging.
Requires advanced cooking skills or is available ready prepared, but at a price.	Highly convenient foods that simply require heating up.	Requires basic cooking skills to prepare ingredients.
May be highly decorated or ornate.	May have some decorative features that make the food attractive.	Plain foods with little decoration.
May be high in additives and E-numbers.	May contain some additives and E-numbers.	Will have very few additives and E-numbers.
Usually highly processed ingredients, resulting in very low vitamin, mineral and fibre content.	May contain added vitamins and a little fibre, but their benefit offset by high sugar or fat content.	Unrefined foods containing complex carbohydrates and good levels of vitamins, minerals and fibre.
Do not fit into *The Balance of Good Health* – so keep for special occasions when it doesn't matter.	Can be modified or improved to fit *The Balance of Good Health*.	Fit very well into *The Balance of Good Health*.

* See Table 5.1 in Chapter 5 for details about different types of fat.

† Many basic ingredients are very cheap, although good sources of protein such as meat and fish tend to be more expensive, as do exotic fruits and vegetables.

From Table 7.1, it can be seen that there are five questions to ask about a food when deciding what it is suitable for:

- Is it cheap or expensive?
- Does it require elaborate preparation or is it easy to prepare?
- Is it a high fat and/or sugar food?
- Does it contain vitamins, minerals or some fibre?
- What about its novelty or enjoyment value?

The answers should help to place foods in the right category and so guide how often they can be served. Alternatively, a favourite food can be modified in order to become more nutritious, so that it becomes suitable for eating more frequently. The third way to improve the family diet is by reducing portion sizes of rich foods and padding out meals with more nutritious ingredients, so that they fit better with *The Balance of Good Health*.

Examples of how to fit savoury foods into the three categories

Table 7.2 gives some examples of common family foods, assessing a combination of flavour, convenience of preparation, nutrition, fat content and cost. It is by no means an absolute guide and many families may disagree with how some foods are positioned in the table. This doesn't matter because it is more important for families to decide on the position of their own family favourites, using the guide for ideas. But once decided then this should guide how often they eat those foods. Families should make some changes if they realise that most of their meals fit into the 'weekend foods' category. It is asking for trouble if a different 'weekend food' appears every day of the week apart from Sundays when a celebration food is chosen!

Table 7.2 Fitting savoury foods into the three frequency categories

Celebration or rare treat foods	Weekend foods	Daily basics
Roast with all the trimmings, rich sauces and heaps of stuffing	Simple roast dinner	Oven-baked lean meat with boiled or steamed vegetables
Rich picnic foods such as pork pies, pasties, sausage rolls, samosas, onion bhajis	Special breads with garlic or cheese toppings, white bread, stuffed naan	Wholemeal bread, rolls, sandwiches, herb bread, pitta bread, plain naan
High-fat sandwich fillers such as corned beef, salami, pâté, egg mayonnaise	Canned tuna in oil, premium potato salad or coleslaw*, hummus, full-fat cheese, fish paste	Canned tuna in brine, boiled ham, beef, chicken, cottage cheese, tomato salsa, potato salad or coleslaw with reduced-fat mayonnaise, reduced-fat cheese
Batter-coated foods, deep-fried foods	Sausages, burgers, fish fingers	Grilled lean meat and fish, home-made burgers or nuggets
Quiche, cheese omelette	Spanish omelette	Egg or reduced-fat cheese on toast
Deep-fried chips	Oven chips, roast potatoes	Jacket or boiled potatoes
Steak and kidney pudding*	Lasagne*, shepherd's pie*	Stewed steak with gravy
Crispy cod steaks in batter*	Fish steak in butter sauce*	Baked or poached cod with tomato sauce
Creamy pasta sauces, pesto sauce	Sun-dried tomato sauce	Sieved tomatoes, tomato and herb pasta sauce
Creamy curry sauces* or creamy cook-in sauce*	Tomato-based curries* or cook-in sauces*, vegetable curry*	Stir-fry meat and vegetables

*Refers to standard pre-packaged items rather than home-made varieties or diet-range products.

If too many weekend foods are currently on the week's list, they do not automatically have to be abandoned. The next section looks at ways of improving existing meals.

Tips for turning 'weekend foods' into 'daily basics'

There are three approaches that can help to introduce more nutrition and result in fewer undesirable ingredients in family meals:

- altering cooking techniques
- reducing portion sizes of richer items
- padding the meal with healthier items.

Alter cooking techniques

- An obvious way to reduce fat is to grill food rather than fry it. It is not simply that grilling avoids putting extra fat into food; it allows some of the fat already within to melt and drip out, whereas frying in oil tends to seal the surface of the food so that more of its own fat is kept inside.
- Avoid deep-frying anything. Chuck out or sell the deep fat fryer and do not be tempted to get another. Deep-frying completely soaks food in oil, leaving it literally dripping fat, which could double its calories.
- Invest in good non-stick pans so that food can be cooked with the bare minimum of oil. This sort of dry-frying or dry-roasting is a good alternative to traditional frying and is easy with a non-stick pan.
- When light- or dry-frying, apply very small amounts of oil using kitchen paper to wipe thinly over the pan's surface (before heating) or invest in an oil sprayer.
- Cook for longer at a lower temperature. If sausages, burgers or other grill items (such as nuggets, or fish in batter or breadcrumbs) are cooked in the top of a hot oven rather than under a grill then the slightly lower temperature will allow more fat to melt out of the meat before the food's surface becomes sealed. They may appear smaller than when fried because more fat will have been lost, but this will leave a higher proportion of nutritious protein behind.
- Reduce the amount of salt added to any foods when cooking. Add herbs and spices to keep food interesting, rather than salt.
- Use alternatives to sugar when preparing sweet things, such as dried or fresh fruit or fruit juice (see below).
- Exchange white flour in recipes for wholemeal flour or oats.
- Steam vegetables (and fish) instead of boiling to improve flavour and texture and to retain vitamins and minerals.

Reduce portion sizes of richer ingredients

Looking at *The Balance of Good Health*, around one-sixth of the daily diet will consist of richer foods with a higher fat or sugar content. Far from being banned, it is just a case of getting the proportions right. Rather than arguing with a reluctant family over how often a favourite food might appear, the alternative approach is to reduce the amount that is served on any occasion so that regular appearances will be less of a problem.

- The easiest way to make reductions is to prepare or buy less in the first place, rather than expect people to exercise restraint when food is ready and waiting.
- If large quantities are cheaper or on offer then divide appropriately and freeze in separate bags as soon as purchased so that only the required amount is defrosted when needed. Alternatively, cook it all but put the extra straight into the freezer for an easy meal another day.
- Rather than buying individual steak and mushroom pies, for example, which tend to have a lot of pastry for the amount of filling, buy one family pie that can be divided up into smaller but juicier portions.
- Stock up on plastic containers with lids, such as old ice-cream cartons, so that leftover food can easily be put in the fridge as soon as it has cooled, rather than be nibbled at the time.
- Try not to let food manufacturers decide on what quantities should be eaten – decide yourself. Watch out for items that are sold in the wrong amount for the family, such as packets of small cakes or bacon rashers. Choose an alternative brand or go to the deli-counter or a butcher so that the right quantities can be purchased.

These suggestions will not leave the family hungry because there will be other filling but healthy ingredients on the plate.

Pad meals with healthier ingredients

If families are not used to eating much in the way of fruit and vegetables, then padding out familiar meals is a good way to gradually introduce them. Rather than serving them as a separate portion, virtually all vegetables can be sliced up and added to stews, stir-fries and sauces. Some are best cooked a little first whereas others can be thrown in almost at the last minute. Many can be added uncooked to salads too. Commonplace examples are given in Box 7.1.

Box 7.1 Ideas for adding vegetable padding

Frozen peas, runner beans and broad beans – throw into stir-fries, cook-in sauces, stews and casseroles. They need only a minute or two to heat through and so can be last-minute additions.

Frozen spinach – perfect addition to curries and casseroles, tomato-based pasta sauces or even to parsley sauce.

Peppers, red, yellow or green – can be thrown into stir-fries, or light-fry with onion before adding to casseroles or cook-in sauces. Alternatively, stuff with minced meat and oven bake.

Carrots, swede, turnip, squash – add chunks to casseroles for a slow-cook, but if adding to cook-in sauces that require a shorter cooking time then cut into smaller slices to ensure they cook in time.

Mushrooms – can be added to virtually anything because they need next to no cooking, but can cope with a slow-cook too.

Leeks – go well with onion and can be used instead. Easy padding for slow-cook meals – just throw them in as the liquid is added.

Courgettes – ideal with tomato-based sauces or in stir-fries. Can be dry-fried with garlic and pepper as a delicious alternative.

Broccoli and cauliflower – easy addition to stir-fries and tomato-based sauces. Use small florets to ensure adequate cooking and the stalks can be sliced thinly and added too.

Cabbage – great in stir-fries or light-fried with bacon chunks. Alternatively, use blanched whole leaves to wrap up home-made meat balls, securing the 'parcels' with a wooden cocktail stick, before oven-baking.

Marrow – instead of Bolognese sauce with pasta, pour it over a marrow sliced lengthways and bake covered in foil then serve with pasta or rice.

Sweet corn – tinned sweet corn can be added to soups, stews, stir-fries, salads or sauces, or eaten straight from the tin.

Salad padding – the following can all be added to a plain salad as no cooking is required: peppers, spring onions, thinly sliced courgette, mushroom, broccoli, frozen peas, mange tout or sugar snap peas, sweet corn or baby corn cobs, whole young spinach leaves, grated or thinly sliced carrot, thinly sliced cabbage. To make a salad into more of a meal add cold rice, couscous, sliced potato or pasta so that it serves as a main meal.

Meal padding does not have to involve fruit and vegetables. Providing a plate of wholemeal bread or bread sticks alongside the meal is a good way to add more carbohydrate. Beginning with a starter is another way to take the edge off appetite and encourage either carbohydrate or fruit and vegetables to be eaten when appetite is usually at its greatest.

Home-made family favourites such as shepherd's pie can be made very healthy by using lean minced meat or by skimming off fat when the mince is first fried, before adding further ingredients. Many vegetables can be added to the meat for padding too. The potato topping can be mashed using a little light stock and sliced spring onion, rather than extra butter. If pastry pies have been popular, try the same filling but with lightly boiled then sliced potato as a topping instead. Alternatively, use the filling to cover a dish of boiled pasta to create a pasta-bake.

Making 'daily basics' easy

One reason why processed foods have become so popular is because they are quick and easy. With far less teaching of cooking skills in schools nowadays, some families are less confident about cooking traditional dishes and many other parents find they simply do not have enough time.

Daily basics do not necessarily need complex cooking; there are many ways to prepare basic ingredients with just as little effort as putting a pre-packaged tray into an oven or microwave. Some examples are listed in Box 7.2, but many more ideas are available in a wide variety of family cookbooks (*see* Appendix 2).

Box 7.2 Quick and easy daily basics

Jacket potatoes – take five minutes or so in a microwave or a more leisurely hour in the oven.

Boiled potatoes – don't bother peeling them to save time and to retain more nutrients.

Rice – takes around 10–15 minutes to boil. Or try risotto rice (also called Arborio rice) because it is easy to add vegetables, meat and stock during cooking to give a complete meal in itself.

Pasta – try pasta filled with meat or cheese stuffing such as tortellini or cannelloni for a more varied meal.

Couscous – the quickest of convenience foods: just pour boiling water over and wait five minutes! Pre-flavoured varieties are also available or add dry-fried vegetables.

Vegetables – try 'ready bags' of mixed vegetables, which can be simply heated in the microwave without any preparation at all. Alternatively, invest in a steamer so that vegetables can be easily steamed over other things on the hob.

Pitta bread or tortillas – fill with a quick stir-fry for a change.

Home-made chicken nuggets – make healthy home-made ones with strips of chicken breast brushed with beaten egg and dunked in breadcrumbs. Dry-fry or grill.

Home-made burgers – use lean minced beef, finely chopped onion and a beaten egg and squash into burger shapes. Dry-fry or bake at the top of a hot oven.

Help young people move away from a 'junk food' diet

Even though studies have shown that many young people enjoy healthy foods, there are many parents who find it difficult to get their family to accept newer, healthier foods and flavours, because they have already developed a strong liking for convenient processed foods.

The family diet can improve without causing upset by introducing change gradually and getting everyone involved in which healthier options are chosen. Bear in mind the following:

* Try not to cook separate meals for different members of the family. If there are twice the meals to cook then convenience foods will be more tempting due to the hassle of so much cooking.
* Use the general rule: if the cook wouldn't eat a food because it is poor quality, then don't serve it to the rest of the family either. Convenience foods have their place partly because they can be simple to serve, but also because some taste good. However, many foods targeted at young people are not only nutritionally poor, but taste awful too. If parents don't like them, don't teach the family to develop a liking for them by serving them often.

- To begin with, reduce portion sizes of 'junk' foods and pad with healthier items, rather than reduce how often a food is served, so that healthier foods become familiar. Experiment with different food combinations (for example, sausages with pasta and salad rather than always with chips) before gradually moving towards serving them less often.
- If healthy menus go down well, serve them often.
- Don't worry about the family getting bored with basic foods – people don't grumble about things that are taken for granted. (For example, many adults eat the same breakfast year in, year out from childhood.) People get bored if they are expecting fun but find the reality is less entertaining than expected. They don't get bored when doing routine things that were never likely to give a buzz in the first place. The family does not expect excitement at every meal, so gourmet dishes are not required on a daily basis.
- Create clear guidelines about when 'junk food' is okay such as 'Junk food is for journeys', when the convenience factor will be useful and an enjoyable rich snack may break up a long journey.
- Create healthy home-made versions of junk foods such as healthy burgers and chicken nuggets, as above.
- If the family is used to exciting meals, then find varied ways to make meals appealing without resorting to unhealthy ingredients. Novel ideas and themes can introduce just as much interest to a meal as rich foods and exploring a theme is a good way to get people involved in food. There are many approaches that can achieve this, as described in Box 7.3 and Table 7.3.

Box 7.3 Ideas for making ordinary meals special

- Sit down as a family whenever possible – don't let the television take over mealtime conversation and attention.
- Choose mealtime themes or variety night ideas, as listed in Table 7.3.
- Use candles or unusual table decorations.
- Use unusual implements, such as chopsticks, a fondue set or kebab skewers.
- Invite friends around for a meal.
- Eat in unusual settings, such as outside or a picnic in the car.
- Plan some topics to discuss before sitting down, such as holiday plans, new jokes or birthday party plans, so that the food on offer will not be the main focus of the meal.
- Avoid topics that may generate upset, such as progress with course work, personal appearance or bedroom tidiness.
- Encourage all the family to share worries so that the young person gets used to being treated as an equal, rather than as a child who is too young to understand.
- Include everyone in adult conversation. Bored people who feel excluded will either overeat or misbehave in an attempt to entertain themselves.

Table 7.3 Variety night ideas

Theme	Suggestions
Pick a colour night	Plan different ingredients for, say, red night, or yellow. Blue is probably the trickiest colour to theme a whole meal, but not impossible. Try www.5aday.com for ideas.
Cook your own tea night	Let everyone choose ingredients and teach them how to cook them.
Turf out the cupboards night	It's surprising what is lurking at the back of kitchen cupboards – you might find inspiration or some nasty surprises! Some things, such as dried fruit, can be put in a bowl to be eaten up, or soaked in hot water then added to yoghurt, whereas others will be best reserved for collage material!
Kebab night	Wooden skewers are cheap to buy, and can make roasted vegetables or pieces of meat seem quite different. They're a good idea for barbeques, and fruit kebabs are great too.
Odd combo night	This is a good way to introduce new combinations – why not have steak and strawberries or lamb chops with a dried apricot on top? The rest of the family might dream up any number of interesting combinations given the chance.
Suits-all soup	If everyone is suggesting a different thing for tea, why not try throwing all the suggestions into one big soup, casserole or dry-roast dish?
Shape night	Similar to pick a colour night, but ingredients must be a certain shape – long and thin, squashy or round. How about star shapes?
Alphabet night	As many ingredients as possible to start with a chosen letter – perhaps a name initial.
Build a pizza night	Start with plain pizza bases (available in supermarkets) and let the family experiment with toppings of their choice.
Food from abroad night	Choose a country and explore their dishes – you might try countries discusssed at school or places you have visited or would like to visit on holiday.

Schemes for sugary foods and snacks

Sugary foods are a normal part of most people's diets. The important thing is to make sure they do not make up too big a proportion of the overall diet, leaving little room for healthy ingredients and putting teeth at risk of decay.

Puddings

For puddings, the same three groups can be used to help guide how appropriate they are: celebration or rare treat foods, weekend foods and daily basics. Some examples are given in Table 7.4.

Breakfast cereals

Breakfast cereals can be thought of as either daily basics (unsweetened) or holiday/weekend choices (sugar-coated).

Table 7.4 Fitting sweet foods into the three frequency categories

Celebratory or rare treat foods	Once-weekly or weekend foods	Daily basics
Suet pudding, thick pastry pies with cream	Fruit crumble* with custard, sponge pudding with syrup	Fruit salads, plain and fruit yoghurt, poached pears, fruit compote
Crème brûlée	Fruit cheesecake	Egg custard
Profiteroles, choux buns filled with cream	Lemon meringue pie	Rice pudding
Speciality ice-cream with fudge sauce*	Banana split with chocolate sauce	Plain ice-cream
Festive or novelty cakes with thick icing, butter-cream or fresh cream	Sponge cakes with jam or chocolate filling, carrot cake	Tea breads, fruit scones, Chelsea buns, fruit cake
Bombay mix	Crisps, peanuts	Low-fat crackers and bread sticks

*Refers to standard pre-packaged items rather than home-made varieties or diet-range products.

Snacks and sweets

Snacks and sweets require a different way of assessing their suitability because they are eaten frequently and may form a significant part of the diet. There are three groups: sugar-buzz foods, stodgy sugars and safer sugars, which give an indication of what, if any, useful function they serve within the overall diet.

> A high-sugar food will have at least 10g sugars per 100g.
> A low-sugar food will have less than 2g sugars per 100g.

Sugar-buzz foods

These have a very high sugar content and indeed some are almost entirely sugar, with added colours and flavourings. Most have little filling power, virtually no nutritional value and are fantastic at rotting teeth. High-sugar breakfast cereals appear in this group because many contain over half of their carbohydrate as simple sugars. Even though all cereals are reasonably filling and the addition of milk gives good nutrition, sugary ones provide far more calories per bowlful, but are no more filling than non-sugared versions.

Sugar-buzz foods may taste nice, but they add very little to a balanced diet and should be eaten sparingly in order to avoid tooth decay.

Stodgy sugars

These sugary foods also contain lots of fat. They may be more filling than sugar-buzz foods, but tend to contain far more calories per mouthful and may be responsible for overweight problems in young people. If chocolate confectionery and similar stodgy sugars are popular, suggest small 'snack-sized' portions plus a healthy accompaniment such as fruit or a more filling sandwich at the same time, so that appetite can be satisfied without eating too much stodge.

Safer sugars

Sugars in this group have some nutritional value alongside their sweet flavour so that they fit more easily into *The Balance of Good Health*. They may provide vitamins and fibre; they may contain unrefined starchy carbohydrates in addition to the sugar content for slower release of energy; or they may contain dairy products or protein and hence contribute in some way to a balanced diet.

It is worth checking the packaging of any item that claims a health benefit (such as some cereal bars) to make sure it is not awash with added sugar.

Some examples of how foods fit into these categories are given in Table 7.5.

Table 7.5 Examples of sugar-buzz, stodgy sugars and safer sugars foods

Sugar-buzz foods	Stodgy sugars	Safer sugars
Boiled sweets, lollipops, chewy sweets, iced gems	Chocolate confectionery, chocolate-coated biscuits and cakes, plain biscuits	Raisins, nuts, seeds, fruit, cereal bars*, wholemeal scones
Sugar-coated breakfast cereals	Maple and pecan crunchy breakfast cereal, chocolate croissants, pancakes	Sandwiches, toasted tea-cakes, unsweetened cereals such as cornflakes, porridge, muesli
Meringues	Cheesecake, gateaux	Wholemeal fruit crumble and custard, baked apples, carrot cake, fruit muffins, rice pudding
Sorbets, jelly	Speciality ice-creams such as cookie-dough ice cream, or chocolate-coated ice-cream bars	Plain ice-cream, especially with fruit, yoghurt
Fizzy drinks, sports drinks (non-diet)	Milk shakes	Fruit juice, diluted squash, fruit smoothies, semi-skimmed milk

* Applies to lower-sugar versions only as some cereal bars are very high in sugar.

Which snack foods and when?

Wherever possible, choose safer sugars for snacks, which are the most nutritious, particularly when wondering what to put in the snack tin. Keep sugar-buzz foods to a minimum both in terms of portion sizes and frequency. Reserve fizzy or so-called sports drinks for an occasional treat when eating in pubs or restaurants or when there is no easy alternative, because they have significant calorie content and no filling power. They are also terrible for teeth due to their acidity as well as their sugar content. Diet versions are an option, but preferably encourage people to enjoy healthier drinks such as dilute fruit juice, unsweetened tea and coffee, milk and plain water.

If the next meal is a long way off then avoid sugar-buzz foods altogether because they give a rapid rise and fall in blood sugar, which will result in further hunger pangs in a short while. Choose a more filling snack, either from the safer sugars or a combination of a small portion of a stodgy sugar plus the benefit of a safer sugar for filling power.

This is particularly important after taking part in sports when people may feel very hungry. If stodgy sugars are an automatic assumption there is the risk of replenishing far more calories than have just been used up (*see* Table 7.6). A better way to replenish the energy used up in sports is with safer sugars, which tend to be starchy and lower-fat foods, plus plenty of dilute fluids or water, so that blood glucose is maintained without giving the rapid surge and fall that simple sugars give.

Table 7.6 Comparison of number of calories used up in various exercise activities with number of calories contained in some popular snacks

Activity (minutes)	Calories used up	Snack (grams)	Calories contained
Moderate cycling (30)	100	Mars bar (62.5g)	281
Moderate running (20)	148	Kit Kat chunky (55g)	290
Swimming (30)	130	Snickers (64.5g)	323
Table tennis (30)	160	Packet of crisps (34.5g)	181
Golf (60)	160	Lucozade energy original drink (380 ml)	277

Developing healthy snack rules

Devise household rules for snacks that are easy to stick to, so that young people are confident about suitable snacks to stave off hunger (*see* Box 7.4). The more confident they feel about choosing the right thing at the right time, the less likely they will be tempted by inappropriate foods when confronted with snack machines and a pocket full of loose change. Although it might be slightly more trouble to prepare slices of toast for hungry youngsters than to open the treat tin, it will encourage good habits and expectations.

Box 7.4 Healthy snack house rules

- No snacks in the half hour before a meal. (Consider a healthy starter instead.)
- Fruit is always a good choice.
- Do a 'take five' check before choosing rich snacks to see if fruit would be more suitable.
- No snacks during the first hour after a meal. Don't confuse hunger with boredom and try distraction instead of food.
- No snacks or sweet drinks after teeth have been cleaned at night.

For serious chocoholics who cannot bear the idea of being deprived of their chocolate 'fix', incorporate something chocolatey into meals, as the dessert, whilst ensuring that the rest of the meal is fairly well balanced. Vary the amount of chocolate and alternatives on offer so people get used to non-chocolate treats without feeling hard done by.

Breakfast reduces snacking later on

Some people refuse to eat breakfast, but tuck into food later in the morning. This first snack is, in effect, a meal and so should fit in with the overall nutritional needs of the day. Once again, if a stodgy snack is the preferred option then add a safer sugar alongside, in order to provide healthy ingredients in addition to fat and sugar.

Studies show young people are more likely to eat breakfast if everyone in the family sits down together for evening meals, and also that breakfast eaters are less likely to be overweight than those who skip it. A starchy start will reduce the likelihood of mid-morning snacking. Breakfast also provides an important opportunity to restock energy reserves that are used up overnight. This may explain why breakfast eaters are more alert mentally. For people who adamantly refuse breakfast, offer a meal replacement bar or a shake fortified with vitamins and minerals mid-morning. A carton of fruit juice or milk would also be preferable to a can of anything fizzy.

Summary points

- Decide whether family foods fit in to the daily basics category or whether they would be better kept for weekly treats or reserved for special occasions.
- Modify popular meals that are high in fat or sugar to fit in better with *The Balance of Good Health*.
- Reduce portion sizes of less healthy family favourites or rich treats that appear often.
- Use variety night ideas to make ordinary meals more interesting.
- Choose safe sugars for snacks because they contain some nutritional value, particularly if snacks make up a sizeable portion of the daily diet.
- Encourage young people to eat breakfast because it boosts mental alertness in addition to reducing unhealthy snacking later in the morning.

Chapter 8

Overcoming teenage inertia

Why do teenagers exercise less than younger children?

There is a whole series of factors that combine together to reduce the likelihood of exercise during the teenage years. Most teenagers do not get the recommended amount of an hour of moderate physical activity each day – only a third of girls and just under half of boys manage this. Table 8.1 gives some reasons why.

For those who don't retain an interest in sport and keep themselves fit, the good news is that many of these factors wear off with time, so that enthusiasm for health and fitness can re-emerge towards the end of the teenage years. It is good to establish as many healthy ground rules as possible so that young people are in a good position to take up healthy activities when enthusiasm returns.

Table 8.1 Reasons why teenagers do not get the recommended amount of daily exercise

Time pressures and outside interests	Young people may get heavily into schoolwork, a part-time job or sedentary hobbies such as computer games, leaving little time or interest for fitness.
Image	There is much greater pressure to look cool, get the image right and follow the right crowd than to keep fit.
Peer pressure	Friends who feel the same way are likely to encourage each other to give up team sports or exercise and choose other pastimes instead.
Laziness	As the exuberance of earlier childhood wears off, many young people go through phases of feeling short of energy and sluggish.
Anxiety and loss of confidence	Some young people feel threatened by the risk of failure or by being less successful at sports than their friends, leading to loss of confidence in joining in.
Pride	The likelihood of becoming sweaty or spoiling make-up or hairstyles may destroy interest in doing sports or swimming.
Bodily changes	The changes of puberty can lower confidence and raise self-awareness so that teenagers feel reluctant to change clothes in front of others or wear scant sportswear. The onset of periods for girls can feel like yet another barrier to enjoying exercise.
Hormones	Puberty brings about mood changes and loss of drive and enthusiasm.

Activity ground rules

We do many daily routines out of simple habit. People do not question the need to brush teeth or to wash hands after visiting the loo – they are such a basic part of life that they are not usually seen as optional, but as standard. This approach can be applied to some activities so that they become accepted routines for all the family, without question.

Parental example

Even though teenagers may tell their parents how old-fashioned, out of touch and uninspiring they are, the chances are that they will end up copying a few habits by the time they reach adulthood. Hence, positive parental example is an important investment in the long run. For example, if a parent is keen on golf, even though the teenager may not play at all during the teenage years, the chances are that they will pick up information about the game, see magazines and television coverage, hear the sport's celebrity gossip and have a few ideas about why it is enjoyable. By the time adulthood reveals a few empty-looking weekends then the more familiar the activity, the greater the chance they will give it a try, especially if there is a set of old clubs to borrow. A few lessons before puberty on how to hold a club would increase the chances of playing again even more.

Establish a minimum level of exercise or activity

Whilst some parents are glad of the peace and quiet of a teenager sleeping until lunchtime at weekends, it is worth keeping track of general routines and establishing a minimum level of activity for everyone. This does not have to be formal exercise or even exercise at all, but may be lifestyle options that are seen as non-negotiable normal behaviours in the household. Some examples are:

- going for a family stroll on certain occasions, such as Boxing Day
- playing crazy golf or going for a swim at least once when on holiday
- being dropped off at the end of driveways rather than at doorsteps
- walking to or from school, clubs or friends' houses when possible
- taking items upstairs rather than leaving them on the stairs for later
- helping to bring the shopping in
- running the same errands that were normal during the junior years, such as popping to the postbox or getting the parking ticket in the car park
- earning pocket money by doing household chores, rather than begging for handouts.

Each family will have its own set of activity ground rules and its own approaches to enforcing them. Most teenagers will go through a phase of feeling they can't be bothered, which may lead to heated conflict with parents. If they can avoid becoming inert slugs during the difficult spells then they will regain their energy levels more readily later on. Whilst some teenagers require serious bribery to sample fresh air and never really adopt the habit, many others go through only a short sluggish phase and find that encouragement from family, college and clubs reawakens their motivation.

Keep fitness and health on the agenda

By looking at why they are important as well as ways of making them achievable, activities will become more worthy of some effort. Look at the varied benefits of exercise and then ways to make taking part more straightforward (*see* Box 8.1).

Box 8.1 Benefits of getting some exercise

- Increased fitness makes people feel happier with themselves and boosts energy levels.
- Practising a sport can improve ability, which increases confidence as well as enjoyment from taking part.
- Getting some physical exercise during the day can help improve sleep by ensuring that the body is physically as well as mentally tired.
- Exercise can be a very sociable thing, which can broaden friendships and interests. A new relationship can get off to a better start if both people have a sport in common.
- Some forms of exercise can enrich life by giving reasons to travel, see more of the country and visit places on holiday.
- Some forms of exercise can be a way of earning money, for example by coaching younger children or by entering competitions.
- Many enjoyable jobs require a level of fitness and/or sporting knowledge or ability, so keeping a sport going may increase job opportunities.

Watch out for problem signs; young people should not exercise purely to lose weight, to punish themselves or to impress others. Be clear about the motivation to exercise and make sure that goals are both reasonable and achievable. Parents can be good role models in various ways, such as taking part themselves, ferrying the family around or by simply showing an interest in their youngster's preferred sport and progress.

Sort out where motivation is coming from

If something is great fun then it will not feel like an effort to take part. The problem is that, as people get older, life becomes busier and more pressured so that less important things get chopped off the bottom of the priority list. Exercise has to be really enjoyable to withstand the endless time pressures that most young people are under today. Sorting out where motivation is coming from can help in putting an exercise slot back into the week's routines.

Are goals realistic?

Which feels better? Aiming to do ten minutes of exercise but only achieving seven minutes or aiming to do five minutes of exercise but finding you achieved seven minutes? Achievable goals are vital in keeping motivation alive and starting with small targets that can be built upon is the best approach. A series of small steps is preferable to an early marathon because it is easier to sense success from making a start, but if it comes to nothing and fizzles out then it will not be a big deal either.

Answer the following questions to find out if goals are realistic and worthwhile:

- Where do you want to be in three months' time? In six months' time? In a year?
- How much free time do you have now that you could spend exercising?
- How many other activities compete for that free time? What about boy/girl friends, mates, working for exams, part-time jobs, sleep, watching TV and other hobbies? Are they worth giving less time to?
- What will increased exercise give you? More fun? Are you hoping it will make you slimmer? Fitter? Will it impress someone? Will it be a form of self-punishment? Will it make you feel more energetic and proud of yourself?
- Is that reward sufficient to keep the effort going?

How do these goals control motivation?

Motivation has three phases. First, the motivation to get started. This might be due to feeling fed up and low in energy so that taking charge and making some changes to routines seems like a good idea. Second, the motivation to continue. This will come from feeling more energetic and fitter, perhaps feeling proud of making a good start on healthy routines and finding enjoyment and fun in the new activities.

The third phase is the one to avoid! The motivation to stop. There will be plenty of pressure to stop new routines, particularly if:

- goals are short-term only. For example, if the aim was to lose 5 lb before a holiday then there will be little incentive to continue healthy eating and exercise routines once the holiday is over, which will mean that weight may be regained and health benefits lost once old habits resume
- goals are found to be unachievable, because this will give a sense of having been defeated. Examples are having insufficient time due to other pressures, or practical issues such as aiming to do more of a sport that is not available locally, such as skiing. Aiming to achieve weight loss in a short time is a common cause of people giving up new routines. Exercise can lead to gradual weight reduction, whereas having high expectations of rapid weight loss can lead to a sense of failure despite the activity being worthwhile
- goals are found to be not worthwhile. Setting out to impress someone who turns out to be a jerk, trying to punish oneself or trying to make use of expensive gym membership are all poor reasons to make a lot of effort. Indeed, they are more likely to make someone stop their new routines than to carry on with them.

Find practical ways for young people to be active

Clarify goals

Having looked at where motivation to change is coming from, write down a plan of action and be clear about the time-scale for change. Put exercise sessions in the diary or timetable or on the wall planner. Aim to take part in the chosen activity once a week for the next year, rather than aiming for three times a week for three weeks before copping out!

Think about transport or kit requirements so that these do not become a last-minute excuse to miss out sessions. Joining a club or team is an excellent way to boost motivation because the activity will feel more of a sociable pastime than a punishment.

If the aim is rapid weight loss after briefly breaking into a sweat then there is going to be disappointment. Exercise will improve fitness and good health, rather than result in weight loss. Even if the benefits are small in the short term they will still be worthwhile. The first benefit is often a simple feeling of pride in oneself and a sense of being a little bit more in control of life.

Devise ways to assess and reward progress

As weight loss is unhelpful as a sign of progress, it is important to have other ways of measuring this and keeping up enthusiasm, especially as small sustainable increases in exercise will not make a major difference to life in the short term.

Try an activity chart, such as a tick-box sheet with 'did I get breathless from some exercise today?', or a point system. Every five-minute block of exercise gains a point, for example using an exercise video, cycling, brisk walking or running, or time spent at a sports club. Add in bonus points for other activities such as running fast up and down the stairs – three trips up and down could score two points, a run around the block could score one, and so on. An unfit teenager should aim to score at least six points most days and build up to around 12 points as fitness improves.

Another option is to try a step-counter or pedometer, which measures each step taken throughout the day. Check out the average number of steps taken each day before changing exercise patterns in order to get an idea of how things are improving. The recommended number of steps is around 6000 for health, but 10 000 to achieve weight loss. The most efficient way for step counting to help health is to aim for an uninterrupted walk of 4000 to 6000 steps each day.

Encourage other people to join in with activities, particularly other people in the family. Being a trend-setter is a great way to feel good and the more people take part, the more encouragement there is to keep going. If one person is having a lazy day, a bit of chivvying from someone else can kick-start enthusiasm.

Avoid unhelpful rewards – such as junk food which is likely to undo any health benefits – and watch out if bribery from others has been a major reason to take part. As soon as the bribes stop, so will the exercise.

Encourage simple and social activities

The first improvement that most people notice when going on a health drive is their ability to make up excuses! 'It's raining', 'I haven't got the right trainers', 'It's the wrong time of the month', 'I pulled a muscle in my shoulder', 'I've only got an hour, which isn't long enough to get to the gym', 'I've just had tea', 'I feel too hungry', 'My favourite telly programme will be starting soon' – the list is endless. Go for activities that don't require much organisation, such as walking;

that are independent of the weather and can be fitted into busy schedules. Think of alternatives if a planned activity cannot take place. The more sociable the activity is, with friends and family doing the same thing, the more likely it is to be a success.

Summary points

- Young people do not become inactive due solely to laziness. Many factors push exercise off the priority list.
- Some activities can be incorporated into invisible daily or household routines so that young people get a minimum level of activity without being aware of it.
- Motivation is crucial to keeping new exercise routines going. Watch out for unhelpful factors that motivate people to stop rather than continue.
- Find healthy ways to assess and reward progress in order to boost enthusiasm.

Section 3

Weight and eating problems

Chapter 9

All about 'diets'

This chapter looks at the drawbacks of going on a diet. It gives sound advice for young people who have weight concerns and then takes a look at the pros and cons of many common dieting regimes to see if they are worth looking into or best avoided.

What is the difference between healthy eating and dieting?

Table 9.1 shows the sometimes subtle differences between eating healthily and dieting in order to change weight.

Table 9.1 The differences between eating healthily and dieting

Healthy eating pattern	Dieting eating pattern
Healthy eating focuses on putting the good things in.	Dieting focuses on cutting out 'bad' things.
Small weight changes from eating healthily are likely to be realistic and achievable goals for the long term.	Dieting is often linked to unrealistic goals that are both hard to achieve and even harder to maintain for long.
Eating a well-balanced diet means all essential nutrients will be there.	Missing meals or certain ingredients raises the risk of missing essential nutrients.
Understanding the basis of healthy eating with realistic goals reduces the chance of trying unhealthy weight loss regimes.	Dieting to lose weight may encourage potentially harmful practices such as missing meals, self-induced vomiting, laxative use or drug use to suppress appetite.
When healthy eating is enjoyed then there is no need for it to end because the enjoyment will ensure that it continues.	Psychologically, no one 'diets' or restricts themselves forever and so it usually only lasts for a finite time.
Eating healthily is a good goal in itself so need not be associated with a sense of failure if weight doesn't change.	Dieting focuses on a specific weight-related goal, which creates motivation problems if the goal is reached and a sense of failure if it is not reached.
Healthy eating is a safe recommendation even for people who have suffered an eating disorder because it focuses on putting good things into the diet.	Dieting can be a precursor of eating disorders, particularly if it feels like a form of punishment and eating generates feelings of guilt.
Studies show that gradual long-term healthy eating changes are more likely to be maintained and to bring about health benefits.	Studies show that faddy crash diets are rarely successful in the long term unless they tackle long-term eating patterns.

What do the statistics tell us?

A huge percentage of young people are already dieting, often when there is no need at all. In the 1997 Health Survey for England, 20% of normal-weight girls aged between 16 and 24 years thought they were too heavy. The survey also found that 45% of girls of desirable weight (body mass index [BMI] between 20 and 25) and 10% of underweight girls were trying to diet.

It is equally worrying that even more young people are failing to get the recommended levels of exercise each day. It is recommended that young people get an hour of some sort of exercise or physical activity each day, but at least 40% of boys and 60% of girls fail to meet these targets. By the age of 15, only a third of girls exercise enough, although boys do better.

It looks simple on paper: instead of trying to diet, which can be harmful, why don't young people increase their exercise, which would help?

Why does dieting tend to be unsuccessful?

Let's face it, if dieting worked then overweight and obesity rates would not be escalating: around 20% of UK adolescents are obese by the time they leave school (2004 statistics) and adult obesity statistics are even worse, despite the multitude of diets available and the persistence of many dieters. Three-quarters of the UK adult population are now overweight or obese, with 22% of adults in the obese range. There has been almost a 400% increase in obesity in the last 25 years.

Unfortunately, dieting promotes a variety of problems:

- Diets are usually short-term eating plans rather than lifelong eating habits. What happens at the end of the diet? Reverting back to old eating habits means gaining back any weight lost.
- Most diets rely on restraint – denying oneself some of the pleasures of eating in order to cut down on calories. Denying the pleasures in life means that the motivation to continue will become harder as time goes by. Who wants to feel as though they are missing out for the rest of their lives?
- Many diets focus on inappropriate goals, setting target weights that are hard to achieve and cannot be maintained, which then results in a sense of failure and loss of will-power.
- Most dieters will have experienced 'saboteurs' – relatives, friends or even complete strangers (such as the advertising industry and every shop with a selection of chocolates at the checkout) who try to lure the dieter off course by offering tempting snacks. This induces guilt and feelings of failure in the dieter rather than enjoyment of the food that they have given in to, which reduces will-power and self-control even more.
- Young people in particular have nutritional requirements that may not be met by faddy diets. For example, growing bones require plenty of calcium and so a diet that recommends restricting dairy products may put bone strength at risk.

Dieting today is very trendy, as is the current obsession with underweight supermodels and the concept of living a glamorous, celebrity-like lifestyle. These influences do not promote contentment with body image, but instead lead to increasing dissatisfaction with ourselves.

Young people can improve their health, appearance and their happiness by improving the balance of their diet, harnessing their inbuilt eating control mechanisms (such as the hunger switch), and by developing a sense of inner pride because this unlocks self-control. The Top Teen Health Plan looks into these aspects and enables young people to take control over their eating tendencies, without any need to go on a restrictive diet. Even if a person is significantly overweight, it is better to make gradual lifestyle changes, which may take years to generate ultimate rewards, than to try a short-term quick fix.

How suitable is weight reduction for teenagers who appear to have finished growing but are overweight?

Reaching one's final height does not mean that 'growth' has finished. Even though final height may be reached soon after puberty (this tends to be later for boys than girls), bones will continue to be strengthened for some years, such that they do not reach their peak bone mass until the early twenties. Muscles are built and strengthened throughout this time and, especially in girls, the body lays down stores of fat, vitamins and minerals such as iron in order to be ready for parenting. The diet is therefore very important to enable healthy growth and reduce the chance of some conditions in later life, such as osteoporosis and anaemia. Slowing down the rate of weight gain during the teenage years (*see* Figure 9.1a, b), rather than looking to lose weight, is the safest way to achieve a healthy weight for that person's height. The Top Teen Health Plan outlines healthy lifestyle changes that can gradually improve body mass index and reduce the chance of obesity without needing to go on a diet.

It is safe to encourage young people to eat in accordance with *The Balance of Good Health*, which may involve cutting back on fatty and sugary foods and hence may bring about weight reduction, but it is not recommended that they should reduce their intake of dairy products or protein-containing foods. Reduced-fat dairy or meat products are good alternatives to full-fat ones and fruit and vegetables should form a significant proportion of any diet.

Heading for a healthier diet and lifestyle in general is a great way to boost self-esteem and outlook for the future without focusing on weight. Avoid becoming fixated over measurements and numbers, but instead focus on feeling fit and in control.

Does the advice apply to someone who is already obese?

If a young person has already developed obesity, meaning that the body mass index is over 30, the above advice applies because good nutrition is equally essential. However, successful weight and health improvements will also require an in-depth look at causes of the weight problem, because obesity usually signals problems with overall lifestyle rather than just the diet.

Obesity is strongly linked to feeling dissatisfied with oneself, having low self-esteem and feeling guilty about eating. Unfortunately, these things are also strongly linked to poor motivation, which creates a vicious circle. The more overweight someone is, the harder it is to make healthy choices, meaning more guilt when overeating which generates further self-disgust and a sense of failure. It is much harder to make an effort when feeling like a failure.

(a)

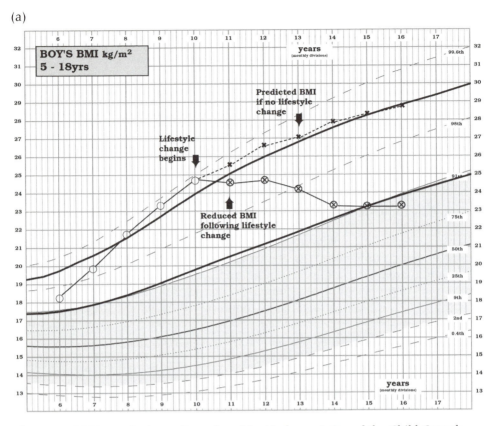

Figure 9.1 BMI growth charts. Reproduced by kind permission of the Child Growth Foundation. The two thick lines on the chart represent the International Obesity Task Force definitions for obesity (upper) and overweight (lower).

A good starting point is to boost self-esteem in areas not related to weight, in order to generate a strong sense of inner pride and value, before attempting to improve eating habits (*see* Box 9.1).

Box 9.1 Boosting self-esteem before improving eating habits

Melissa stopped going to school when she became obese.

By the age of 14, Melissa weighed almost 18 stone. Bullying from other school children was only one of her problems. She had to have her size 20 uniform made by a specialist store, but as the pressures grew and her confidence plummeted, comfort eating took over and her school attendance virtually stopped.

By the time she reached 15, Melissa had all but given up school, despite attempts by the school to stop the bullying. Just arriving at the school gates to collect lessons set by her teachers to do at home was enough to put Melissa into a cold sweat.

Eventually, Melissa was put in touch with a support group attached to a non-attenders unit for children who find it hard to attend school. Speaking

(b)

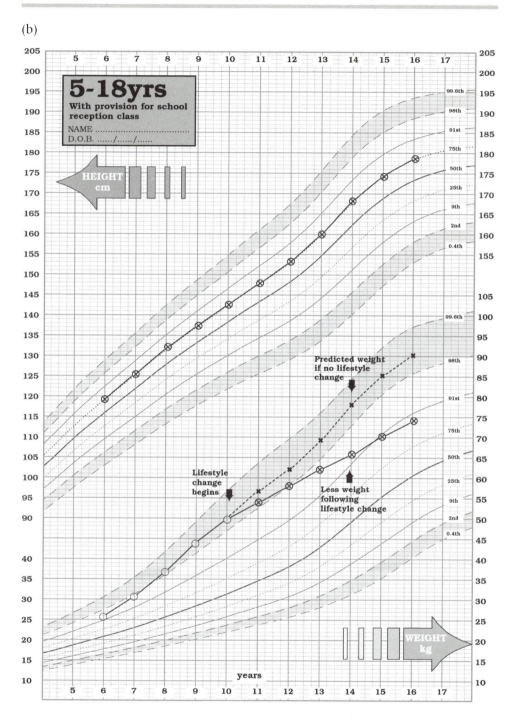

to other teenagers who were dealing with similar problems helped Melissa to begin to make progress, control her weight gain and make some plans for her future.

Looking back, Melissa could see the following factors had led to her weight problem:

- There was always ready availability of tempting foods and she would often keep her overweight mum company by sharing high-calorie treats.
- Her mum was unaware of how overweight Melissa had become until she noticed that she needed to buy clothes for a much older child in order to find things that would fit.
- Her parents' divorce, in addition to bullying at school, left her feeling miserable and low in confidence, which led to comfort eating.
- Her mum's attempts to go on a health drive led to Melissa stealing food, which then made her feel guilty and further eroded her self-esteem.
- When Melissa tried dieting, she was only interested in a 'quick fix' – which never happened. Her will-power was not strong enough to stick with any diet because food was essentially her only comfort, making dieting thoroughly miserable.
- She and her mum had many fights over school non-attendance, rather than over her weight or eating habits. This felt like a less painful problem to argue over; they both had a weight problem which neither of them felt confident about tackling.

It was only when Melissa met other people of the same age with similar problems that she was able to find some motivation to help herself. Knowing that her new friends would not judge her by her appearance was the starting point for rebuilding her self-esteem.

How much weight reduction should a young person aim for if advised to lose weight because of obesity?

Most studies have found that people struggle to maintain more than a 10% reduction of their starting weight for any length of time, so it is best to have a series of smaller goals that can be gradually built on if early goals are successful. Aiming for a 5–10% reduction in starting weight over a six-month period would be a realistic target. This should then be maintained for six months or longer before considering a further 5% reduction. The slower this process, the more likely it will be sustained, because rather than relying on restraint it is more likely to stem from an improved lifestyle such as walking more, drinking fewer fizzy drinks and snacking less in between meals.

It is important to find ways to remain committed to new routines even when there are setbacks, such as emotional crises or family upsets. Learning to cope with problems without resorting to old, comforting eating patterns is a major step to long-term success.

People *can* lose weight far more rapidly by crash dieting, but this leads to the yo-yo dieting cycle that many people struggle with throughout their lives, because rapid weight loss is frequently followed by equally rapid weight gain once more.

Going for a 'crash diet' approach means relying on a huge amount of restraint and denial of what are seen as the good things, in the hope that life will be much better at the end of it all. However, most people find that, whether fat or thin, life remains complicated, stressful and far from perfect. Family feuds, bullying bosses and financial worries will not vanish just because weight has reduced, so it is very important to have a realistic idea of what improvements a change in body shape might bring in order to avoid disappointment.

Almost all diets could work if, along the way, the person develops a love of healthy food, is glad to be without as much junk food and finds that increasing exercise opens up a whole new array of rewarding activities and people to socialise with. A study comparing four different dieting regimes, Atkins (high protein and fat, low carbohydrate), Ornish (very low fat), Weight Watchers (points system) and the Zone diet (balancing food groups), showed that all could lead to modest weight reduction, but that any success depended on the effort put into sticking with the diet rather than the type of diet tried. Overall success was low because so many people gave up, but for those people who stuck to their diet for a year, health benefits were noticeable.

How to spot a fad diet

There are endless diets now available, but not all are safe, logical or suitable for young people to follow. Indeed there are some bizarre eating plans based on all sorts of unscientific theories and whims, such that it can be tricky to know what a sensible eating plan is at all.

When assessing whether an eating plan is worthwhile, remember some simple facts:

- There are no miracles out there.
- A calorie is a calorie – you can only lose weight if you eat fewer calories than you use up.
- Boosting exercise will help any sensible eating plan.
- Will-power comes from liking oneself, not from being thin.

Fad diets are those that tend to offer short-term weight loss that is hard to maintain. They will often have certain things in common, such as they:

- promise dramatic weight loss in the first few weeks
- advise excluding a major food group or selection of foods
- recommend eating one particular food or a limited list of foods
- consist of complicated dieting 'rules'
- suggest complex science as to why the diet works better than others
- focus on unrealistic weight-loss goals associated with appearance rather than health benefits
- sound too good to be true.

[*Source*: Obesity and dieting. *Women's Health Medicine*. 1: 1 Nov 2004.]

The pre-diet check-list

Use the following check-list to make sure that any changes to lifestyle are well chosen, with realistic aims over a sensible time-scale.

1   What has triggered a desire to diet right now? Has there been some problem leading to concerns about weight or appearance? Are there any other ways to improve that problem without necessarily losing weight?
2   Is it appropriate to aim for weight loss or would it be better to stabilise weight if still growing?
3   Are changes planned for overall lifestyle, rather than just eating patterns?
4   Double-check whether normal household routines are causing problems, because changing routines may reduce the need to diet. This is discussed in The Top Teen Health Plan family guide (*see* p. 83).
5   Could the whole household get involved in improving general lifestyle, as this will make improvements easier to continue?
6   Is the target weight a healthy aim or rather overambitious? Remember that losing more than 10% of initial body weight will prove difficult to maintain in the long run unless the weight is lost very gradually.
7   Does the chosen eating plan get a good rating in the Safe Dieting Assessment Guide below? How will it fit in with the rest of the family?
8   What about having a chat with the family doctor before starting a new eating plan? Many diets suggest seeking medical advice at the outset and this would be a good idea if weight has been a cause of misery and very low self-esteem or if someone, such as a parent, feels that the weight loss target is unrealistic.

The Safe Dieting Assessment Guide

Use the guide shown in Table 9.2 to see whether different dieting approaches are suitable for young people. The key explains which aspects of each dieting regime are being examined.

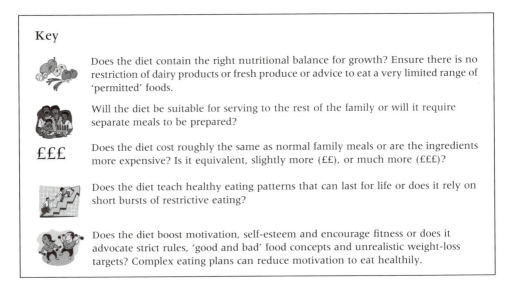

Key

Does the diet contain the right nutritional balance for growth? Ensure there is no restriction of dairy products or fresh produce or advice to eat a very limited range of 'permitted' foods.

Will the diet be suitable for serving to the rest of the family or will it require separate meals to be prepared?

£££   Does the diet cost roughly the same as normal family meals or are the ingredients more expensive? Is it equivalent, slightly more (££), or much more (£££)?

Does the diet teach healthy eating patterns that can last for life or does it rely on short bursts of restrictive eating?

Does the diet boost motivation, self-esteem and encourage fitness or does it advocate strict rules, 'good and bad' food concepts and unrealistic weight-loss targets? Complex eating plans can reduce motivation to eat healthily.

Table 9.2 The Safe Dieting Assessment Guide

	Well-balanced nutrition?	Suitable for the whole family?	Cost compared to usual meals? £££	Suitable as a lifelong guide?	Does it boost motivation and fitness?
High protein–low carbohydrate diets, e.g. Atkins	No	No	£££	Unlikely to be feasible – restrictive	Reduced, complex to follow
Very low-calorie diet	No	No	££	No	Reduced, relies heavily on restraint
Meal replacement milk shakes, e.g. Slimfast	No	No	££	No	Reduced, relies on restraint
Meal replacement soups, e.g. cabbage soup diet	No	No	Equivalent	No	Reduced, relies on restraint
Food combining	No	No	Equivalent	No	Reduced, complex to follow and relies heavily on restraint
Exercise video +/– diet	Depends on suggested diet	Yes, if diet is optional	Equivalent, cost of video	Yes	Improved (unless linked to a complex diet)
Low-fat eating	Yes, as long as low-fat dairy products included	Yes, but caution for under-fives	Equivalent	Yes	No effect
Points system diet, e.g. Weight Watchers	Yes	Yes	Equivalent	Yes	Yes, but may encourage too low a target weight making weight maintenance difficult
Very low-fat diet, e.g. Ornish diet	No	No	Equivalent	No – highly restrictive	Encourages exercise, but complex to follow and relies heavily on restraint
Glycaemic index guide	Yes	Yes	Equivalent	Yes	No effect
Vegetarian	Yes	Yes, with care	Equivalent	Yes	No effect
Vegan	No	No	Equivalent	Care required – highly restrictive	Reduced, complex to follow and highly restrictive
Top Teen Health Plan	Yes	Yes, but caution for under-fives	Equivalent	Yes	Improved

High protein–low carbohydrate diets

There are three popular 'high protein–low carbohydrate' diets: the Atkins diet, the South Beach diet and the Zone diet.

The Atkins diet advises high protein and high fat with a much reduced carbohydrate intake. *The South Beach diet* is also very restrictive, recommending high protein but low fat and low carbohydrate intake. *The Zone diet* is a highly complex system that aims to balance the protein, fat and carbohydrate content of each meal and snack with the intention of controlling insulin levels. It works out to be a high protein–moderate fat diet. It advises altering meal nutrient balance using protein or fish oil supplements, creating a highly artificial eating plan.

All three methods are restrictive diets that ban many common foods, in particular those containing processed and refined carbohydrates. They promise rapid initial weight loss by following strict rules and phases, and have become popular because the high protein content can help to control hunger. However, they are not designed nutritionally for healthy growth and their restrictive nature makes them too complex to fit in easily with normal family meals or healthy long-term eating patterns.

In addition, a very high-protein diet can put extra burden on the kidneys when breaking down the excess protein. If a person unknowingly had mild kidney problems, then the additional work could lead to kidney damage or kidney stones.

High-protein foods tend to be expensive and these eating plans do not fit in with a well-balanced diet that incorporates all the food groups. Limiting complex carbohydrates may result in too low fibre intake, which can lead to abdominal pain and constipation. In addition, some vitamins are found mainly in cereals and fresh produce, so limiting these foods may result in vitamin deficiency.

Reducing processed and refined carbohydrate foods (which are in many 'junk' foods) can improve a diet as long as they are replaced by unprocessed, wholegrain carbohydrates and fresh produce, rather than with fat or protein. This will keep the diet better balanced.

None of these dieting plans teaches the user to eat sensibly, but instead to follow strict rules, which can lead to feelings of guilt and failure if they are not strictly adhered to. Highly structured dieting regimes such as these do not fit in with the typical chaotic and unpredictable lifestyle of most young people or with practical family meal planning, particularly if there are other children in the household.

Very low-calorie diets

Very low-calorie diets are commercially available in the form of nutrient preparations for use as a total food substitute. They provide around 800 kcal a day and are *not* suitable for young people. In particular, they do not teach healthy eating habits, again relying on restraint and artificial eating patterns, so that weight gain is likely once normal meals are reintroduced.

Meal replacement diets

There are currently two different types of popular partial meal replacement diets, one using commercially available fortified milk shakes, and the other recommending a home-made vegetable soup instead of one or two ordinary meals. Both types recommend a standard evening meal after replacing earlier meals with the soup or milk shake.

Although the milk shakes are fortified with vitamins and minerals, this type of meal plan may not incorporate sufficient fresh produce in the diet, so that fibre and micronutrients may be lacking. The soup diet recommends a restrictive, low-fat meal plan that is also low in complex carbohydrates, which makes it unlikely to be sustainable in the long term.

The main drawback of both these dieting plans is that they focus on weight loss, rather than teaching healthy long-term eating patterns or showing the user where they were going wrong with their former eating patterns. Additionally, they do not fit in easily with family meal planning or a young person's hectic lifestyle.

Food combining

This concept advocates weight loss by carefully controlling the diet so that protein, fat and carbohydrate are eaten in very strict combinations and sequences. It requires very careful planning because, for example, a sandwich (carbohydrate) could not contain a protein filling such as cheese or ham but would need to have a carbohydrate filling such as salad. The next meal would then need to exclude carbohydrate, meaning that meat could not be eaten with potatoes, rice or pasta.

One reason that 'food combining' has helped some people to lose weight is that it bans foods that contain a combination of fat and carbohydrate, so cakes, chocolate, chips, crisps and biscuits are all forbidden! Any diet that cuts out all these foods is bound to help a few people, but is unlikely to be maintainable for any length of time. This diet does not teach healthy long-term eating habits that could apply to the whole household.

Exercise videos with or without dietary advice

There are multitudes available, some with complex restrictive meal suggestions (which should be used with caution, as explained above) and some advising on good common-sense low-fat eating that may well be suitable for the whole family. Exercise programmes or videos are even more effective if the whole family takes part. They can boost motivation and self-esteem and help people feel more confident, because fitness is a much healthier goal than weight loss.

Low-fat eating

Low-fat eating is both a healthy way to eat in the long term and can also help to reduce weight. There is no need to count calories in order to achieve a low-fat diet; instead read food labels, trim visible fat from cuts of meat and choose lower-fat products, especially dairy products. People develop a taste for most things once they are familiar, so it may mean persevering with low-fat foods for a while until used to their texture and taste – it takes about two weeks to get used to lower-fat milk or a new vegetable oil spread, for example. Once people are used to them they often find full-fat foods unpleasant.

Whilst the whole family can eat low-fat foods without a problem, children under five may need to eat more fat than the older members of the family because of their smaller appetite but high energy requirements. This can easily be achieved by, for example, adding additional butter or vegetable oil to a young child's portion of lower-fat family foods.

Points system diet

Weight Watchers is an example of an eating plan that uses a points system to guide the amount eaten each day. The diet recommends healthy, low-fat foods in general and gives guidance on activities too. However, it encourages significant weight reduction, which may sometimes become unmaintainable, leading to a yo-yo dieting pattern.

Very low-fat diet: the Ornish diet

The Ornish diet was designed to help reduce heart disease, advising a very low-fat intake of less than 10%. It encourages moderate exercise alongside dietary change. It is restrictive, advising no meat or fish, and does not take into account the fact that some monounsaturated and polyunsaturated oils have health benefits. Its rigid structure and narrow spectrum of permitted foods make it unsuitable for young people and unfeasible for family meals.

Glycaemic index

The glycaemic index (GI) is a recent term that has come into more common use and is now listed on some food labels. It refers to how quickly a carbohydrate is broken down and absorbed into the bloodstream. Foods with a low GI are preferable because they take longer to be digested and absorbed and can therefore keep hunger at bay more effectively than high GI foods.

High GI foods, such as pure sugar, are absorbed very quickly and efficiently, giving little control over hunger for any length of time, whereas eating a fibre-rich starchy food that has a low GI (such as a higher-fibre breakfast cereal with milk) is likely to keep hunger at bay far more successfully, because its energy is released into the bloodstream more slowly. Eventually all the carbohydrate will be absorbed, whatever the GI. It does not tell you about the calorie content of a food, but it gives an idea of how filling that food might feel.

The concept of GI foods can be confusing and it is not essential to understand it in order to eat healthily. Following *The Balance of Good Health* guide will ensure that the right balance of food is eaten without having to worry about the GI of an individual food, because it encourages wholegrain cereals and plenty of fresh produce.

People with diabetes may be recommended to pay attention to the glycaemic index, because it can help with controlling blood sugar. In addition, it can help to show which foods will be more filling if an overenthusiastic appetite is the problem.

Vegetarian diet

Throughout the world, vegetarianism is common and can be a very healthy way to eat. Between 6% and 12% of young people choose to become vegetarian, deciding not to eat meat or animal products with varying degrees of strictness.

It is important to get some good nutritional advice to make sure that vegetarian eating is well balanced and suitable for growth. Being vegetarian does not mean simply missing out meat and eating extra vegetables. It is important to eat other sources of protein to keep the overall diet well balanced, such as nuts and seeds, pulses (e.g. lentils, chickpeas or baked beans), eggs and soya products. It is also important to eat sufficient dairy products to provide calcium and vitamins. Low-fat dairy products will provide the same amount of calcium as full-fat ones.

Egg and dairy products provide almost all of the nutrients that would otherwise come from meat in the diet, and because there is strong emphasis on wholegrain cereals plus fruit and vegetables, vegetarian diets are usually rich in many useful nutrients. An American study showed that the diet of vegetarian teenagers contained better amounts of fruit and vegetables and lower amounts of saturated fats than meat-eating teenagers, which could well lead to a lower risk of heart disease and cancer if these eating habits continue throughout adult life.

There are different types of vegetarian diets

Vegetarian and vegan eating can be divided into four groups according to their effects on nutrition:

- red meat excluders – eat a normal diet apart from excluding red meat
- permissive vegetarians – avoid all meat but eat fish in addition to dairy products and eggs
- strict vegetarians – avoid all meat and fish, but eat dairy products and eggs
- vegans – avoid any products that come from animals, including all dairy products and eggs.

As long as the diet still follows the basic outline of *The Balance of Good Health*, with suitable non-meat alternatives, then all essential nutrients will be present. If meat proteins, eggs and dairy products are missing from the diet, then far more care is needed to provide suitable replacements for growing people.

Table 9.3 shows where different essential ingredients of the diet come from and how these fit with different degrees of vegetarian or vegan eating.

Why do people become vegetarian?

There is a variety of reasons why people choose to avoid meat or meat products. These include compassion for animals, dislike of the taste or texture of meat, peer pressure or a desired sense of independence, concern about food scares or for religious reasons. Children may follow the example of parents, particularly if they understand the issues behind the parents' decisions.

Many young people go through phases of disliking meat, which may mirror their growing awareness of farming practices or hearing off-putting information about how processed foods are made. These phases may not last, but care should be taken to ensure the diet contains adequate nutrition during the phase.

Table 9.3 Food groups and the essential nutrients they provide

					Essential protein	Fibre	Calcium	Iron	Vitamin C	Vitamin B$_{12}$	Vitamin D	Zinc	Folate
No exclusions to diet	Red meat excluders	Permissive vegetarian diet	Strict vegetarian diet	Vegan diet									
					Cereals*	+	+++	+	+	/	/	+	+	+
					Pulses	+	+++	+	+	/	/	/	/	+
					Nuts	++	++	+	+	/	/	/	/	+
					Fruit and veg	+	+	+	+	+++	/	/	/	+++
					Seeds	+	++	+	+	/	/	/	/	/
					Yeast extract	+	/	/	/	/	++	/	/	++
					Infant soya formula	++	/	++	++	+	+	+	+	+
					Eggs	+++	/	+	+	/	+	++	/	/
					Milk and dairy products	+++	/	+++	/	/	+	++	+	/
					Fish	+++	/	++	++	/	++	+++	++	/
					White meat	+++	/	/	++	/	++	/	++	/
					Red meat	+++	/	/	+++	/	++	/	+++	+

/ = nil present or trace only.
+ = small amounts present. Would need to eat large daily amounts in order to gain enough of the nutrient.
++ = moderate amounts present. Needs to feature in the daily diet in order to provide an adequate supply of the nutrient.
+++ = excellent source of the nutrient.
* = some cereals are fortified with additional nutrients. Check packaging of individual foods for further details. Lower-fibre products are available.

Making a vegetarian diet healthy and successful

As Table 9.3 shows, most of the essential nutrients are present in a wide variety of foods, and so varied eating is the key to a successful vegetarian diet. Because vegetarian sources of protein are often bulky and contain high amounts of fibre, there is a risk of filling up before taking in enough calories. Also, the high fibre content can make it harder for the gut to absorb iron and calcium from other foods. To ensure this is not a problem, the diet should contain plenty of nuts and lower-fibre cereals with not too much reliance on fruit and vegetables. The diet can be boosted with extra fat to increase the number of calories per mouthful if necessary. It is not advised to increase energy intake by providing excess sugar, because sugar tends to be nutrient-poor in addition to being linked to tooth decay.

Vegetarian sources of protein tend to contain fewer of the different protein building blocks, or amino acids. To overcome this, combine different sources of proteins together, such as cereals and pulses, so that each source provides a few of the essentials. Examples are baked beans on toast, pitta bread and hummus, lentil stew and rice.

Further advice can be obtained from the Vegetarian Society at www.vegsoc.org. More information about organic food and farming is available at the Henry Doubleday Foundation, www.hdra.org.uk, and The Soil Association, www.soilassociation.org. Further information about sustainable fish stocks and safe fishing practices can be found at www.fishonline.org.

Vegan diet

Vegan eating takes vegetarianism a stage further, where no animal products are eaten in any form. Humans did not evolve as vegans and so this diet results in nutritional deficiencies unless dietary supplements are taken. In order to comply with vegan principles, fastidious attention to this highly restrictive diet is needed.

Because vegan diets are highly restrictive, with no animal products consumed at all, advice should be sought from a dietician if a young person is considering becoming a vegan. It is likely that vitamin supplements will be advised because certain nutrients, in particular vitamin B_{12} and vitamin D, are difficult to obtain from a strict vegan diet. The European Prospective Investigation into Cancer and Nutrition study found that 30% of vegans in the UK were severely deficient in vitamin B_{12}, which can lead to permanent nerve damage.

Because vegan eating involves banning many foods on principle, it can make planning the diet complex and time-consuming, which may add to a young person's worries rather than improving their sense of control in life. Many young people are highly sensitive to wanting to 'fit in' at school and with friends, making the very limited vegan diet an additional complication in life. If vegan parents are keen for their family to follow suit, introduce the principles gradually and invite young people to follow suit as they get older through their own choice, rather than force restrictive practices that can lead to nutritional deficiencies.

Although well-balanced nutrition is possible from a vegan diet, it will require fine attention to detail, which may not be practical in a busy family setting or disorganised eating environment.

Further information is available through the Vegan Society at www.vegansociety.com.

The Top Teen Health Plan

The Top Teen Health Plan is a way of assessing the strengths and weaknesses of current eating habits before deciding what, if any, changes are necessary. In addition to completing a food diary, it takes a look at a person's self-esteem and motivation to make good choices, so that small but significant changes can be adopted with little trouble but long-term impact.

The Plan encourages people to eat according to *The Balance of Good Health* eating guide, so ensuring good nutrition that is suitable for the whole family (those over five years of age), and it encourages between 30 minutes and an hour of physical activity most days. By aiming to make small increases to the average food diary score, a person can choose which aspects of their diet and lifestyle they wish to concentrate on. It highlights increasing the good bits of the diet rather than cutting out the bad, but puts an even stronger emphasis on self-value and feeling good inside, so that making healthy choices feels relevant and achievable.

Summary points

- There is a significant difference between healthy eating and dieting in order to change weight. Dieting is rarely maintained in the long term whereas healthy eating is an ideal and achievable lifelong aim.
- Many young people try dieting even when their weight *is* appropriate for their height. Most young people get less than the recommended levels of activity.
- 'Growth' does not stop once a person's final height is reached. Bone, muscles and body fat stores continue to be laid down well into the twenties.
- Successful weight loss in overweight people requires motivation to keep up lifestyle changes in the long term. Motivation comes from a sense of self-worth, value and personal pride, but vanishes if a person feels like a failure.
- Fad diets are all the rage, but are unsuitable for young people due to nutritional concerns, complex rules, inappropriate short-term goals and a focus on artificial eating patterns that do not fit in with teenage pressures or family life.

Chapter 10

Eating disorders

Introduction

Eating disorders have become commoner in recent decades, but are still far less common than overweight problems. They have attracted much media attention, in part due to high-profile coverage of famous sufferers such as Diana, Princess of Wales and a series of pop stars, actresses and supermodels. This has led to a high level of concern in the general public, although people actually remain at far greater risk of suffering ill health from obesity.

Eating disorders arise when abnormal eating is triggered by emotional upset. The abnormal eating pattern is really a symptom of an underlying psychological problem and recovery usually requires exploration of this, rather than forcing a change in the way the person eats.

The different types of eating disorder

There are three different types of eating disorder, as shown in Table 10.1. Dieting has been included to show how it compares with eating disorders; most people who diet do not have an eating disorder.

Anorexia nervosa

Anorexia nervosa literally translates as 'nervous loss of appetite'. However, this is a misleading term because anorexics feel just as hungry as everyone else. Instead, they find ways of overcoming their appetite in their attempts to lose weight. Fear of weight gain and how to control weight become the focus of an anorexic's life, but at a high cost.

> Anorexia nervosa is a serious illness – a doctor should be consulted if there is any suspicion that it is developing.

The following information will explain more about anorexia, but it is not intended as a means of diagnosing the condition or trying to treat it because this should always be done through a specialist. Further support can be obtained through a family doctor and information about support groups is included in Appendix 2.

Table 10.1 Types of eating disorder

Type of eating disorder	Description	Female:male ratio	Percentage of population affected
Anorexia nervosa	Weight loss due to extreme dieting, self-induced vomiting or purging, and excessive exercise, leading to underweight which can be life-threatening.	9:1	0.4%
Bulimia nervosa	Binge-eating episodes followed by self-induced vomiting or purging and preoccupation with food. Weight may be normal or overweight and it may follow on from anorexia. Often a hidden condition where the family is relieved that anorexia seems to have stopped, without realising it has changed to bulimia.	30:1	1–1.5%
Binge-eating disorder	Binge-eating episodes, at least weekly, which are *not* followed by actions to compensate for the food intake. It often leads to obesity, which may be extreme.	Unknown	May be around 4–5% of population
Dieting	Changes to normal eating patterns with the intention of reducing weight.	1.5:1	35%

Who is prone to anorexia?

Although dieting is very common amongst young people, it does not necessarily signify an eating disorder. Just because someone is trying to diet does not mean an eating disorder is around the corner.

If a person is developing an eating disorder then eating and dieting will be linked to depressed emotions and low mood; there will be significant dissatisfaction with body size and/or shape, preoccupation with exercise and feelings of insecurity. Most anorexia nervosa sufferers are female (only around one in ten are male) and they are often high-achieving, conscientious or perfectionist people who find it difficult to cope when they are not in control or who have difficulty in dealing with issues without family support.

Anorexia usually starts in adolescence or early adulthood, often at the time of leaving home, when the transition from a protective childhood to being an adult is most keenly felt.

How does anorexia nervosa develop?

There are usually three factors involved in developing an eating disorder:

- Firstly there will be *predisposing* factors in the person's personality, such as a natural inclination to apply self-control (for example, youngsters who are used to working hard and driving themselves), or a tendency to put others before themselves, or a sensitive, insecure or shy personality.
- Second, there is usually a *trigger* that sets off the desire to lose weight. This may

be an offhand remark about being chubby, sight of an unflattering photograph, or sometimes an emotional problem that causes an initial loss of appetite (a common effect of many stressful situations), but the person then realises that stopping eating actually makes them feel a bit better – it gives them a sense of release from the emotional problem. For some people the trigger is due to a difficult home life – perhaps parents who have gone through a turbulent divorce, or a parent with a mental illness, or perhaps the person has been subjected to emotional neglect or abuse. Triggers may be almost insignificant to an outsider or may be starkly obvious.

- Third, there will usually be circumstances that cause the eating pattern to become *a vicious circle*, so that there is a downward spiral of trying to feel better by not eating. This causes further problems – hunger, for a start, which produces guilt on eating, but also concern/interference from family, shortage of energy and other physical symptoms, plus an overwhelming anxiety and preoccupation with weight and food. But controlling appetite and weight seems the easiest way to blot out all problems and so the vicious cycle continues.

What feelings might a person with anorexia nervosa experience?

Whilst every person is different and the stresses that lead to an eating disorder vary enormously, there are certain things that most sufferers will experience:

- feeling hideously fat, regardless of what the scales may say
- a sense of pride or achievement from the initial weight loss
- feeling compelled to eat as little as possible and to exercise regularly in order to lose more weight
- inducing vomiting, taking laxatives or exercising even harder if the daily calorie 'allowance' is exceeded
- being deceitful about eating habits, hiding food, skipping meals and making excuses
- developing rituals to help control food intake, such as eating at the same time, and panicking if the ritual is disturbed
- finding ways to avoid social gatherings that involve food, and becoming withdrawn, isolated and irritable
- frequent weighing, with panic or depression produced by the slightest weight gain
- worsening concentration – apart from an obsessive focus on food, weight and calories
- a fascination with recipes, supermarket shelves and preparing food for others, but dogged refusal to join in the pleasure of a nice meal.

Some people with anorexia feel scared about the future, sometimes because the adults around them have difficulties of their own, so that adulthood appears even more frightening than adolescence. Humans have a tendency to protect things that are small and anorexia is a way of keeping small, both physically and developmentally. Many girls find that if their weight drops below a threshold, then periods stop or may simply not start at all. This is usually reversible, so that if weight is regained periods will begin again.

Which approaches might families try in order to help an anorexia sufferer?

Useful approaches to anorexia can be divided into three main areas:

1 seeking advice and understanding the condition
2 discovering alternative coping strategies for stress and building self-esteem
3 knowing how to deal with eating and food issues.

Seeking advice and understanding the condition

One of the most useful things for families is to be well informed. It will take time to build up an understanding of something as complex as an eating disorder, and reading leaflets, books and information on the internet will help. Ask other people such as friends and relatives, the family doctor and, if able, a therapist or counsellor if they have experience of eating disorders or depression, because sharing experiences is a very valuable way of gaining ideas and support.

It may not be obvious as to what approaches will help and it may take gritted teeth to stop nagging a person to eat when worried sick about how thin they are. In addition, the sufferer may hotly deny anorexia and hence refuse to go along to appointments or to open up when help is arranged. The more families understand about the condition, the easier it will feel to try new approaches, and it may be possible to do valuable groundwork that will help the sufferer to accept the diagnosis.

There are many organisations and websites directed at anorexia and bulimia sufferers and there are many local support groups in different areas. A family doctor may help in finding suitable support, or find information from a local Citizens' Advice Bureau, library or the *Yellow Pages* under 'counselling and advice' or 'charitable and voluntary organisations'. Many areas also have dedicated youth helplines that will also offer suggestions on local services.

Once families have begun to find some information this can be shared with the sufferer, making it clear that the family want to help, not add to the sufferer's problems. A good starting point is to ask to share worries, rather than try to change things, and to try and see how things look from the sufferer's viewpoint. Anorexia makes a person think in a sometimes bizarre and illogical way because it is an illness, not a whim. It can be frustrating to explain logical and sensible ideas and then find it makes no difference; acceptance and recovery can take a long time.

Guidelines for families

• Be clear as to your boundaries – your job as parent or family member is not to do the healing, but to show love and respect for the sufferer. It is not your job to make them eat. Instead, see your role as helping to improve understanding of what the problems really are. The sufferer fears food and weight gain, but you can help to show that this fear is part of a vicious circle – one that can be broken when they are ready.

• Involve professional help at the earliest opportunity, starting with your family doctor if you are uncertain whom else to try. Some sufferers have a sense of 'needing permission' to get better, which may need to come from a therapist of some sort, someone who can take over the responsibility for their feelings.

- See the future in at least two stages: the first is acceptance of the problem without trying to change the eating problem (but see caution below). Only when there is some acceptance will it be possible to move on to the second stage, which is to encourage weight gain.
- Show the sufferer that you are not expecting them to start eating, but you would like to help explore the reasons behind their unhappiness.
- Build trust – explain that you are concerned because you love and value your family, not because you feel let down in some way or because they are not doing what you want. Recovery will require the sufferer to build trust in themselves as well as others.
- Understand that someone with anorexia fears losing control over food, eating and their lives, and that most of all they fear recovery. To the sufferer, recovery means losing control. You can help change to a different interpretation of recovery – one that means no longer being obsessed with food and when eating no longer means suffering guilt.
- If the sufferer is adamant that they do not have an eating problem, change tack and explore the idea of improving low self-confidence or perhaps seeing their sadness as a form of depression, which may be easier to accept. Focusing on improving low moods, confidence and self-esteem without reference to weight may ultimately make it easier to accept that there is an eating disorder too.

Caution: anorexia is a chronic condition, which means it builds up gradually over a long period. However, some people can mask how much weight they have lost by wearing layers of baggy clothes and by withdrawing from friends and family. If a family suddenly becomes aware of dramatic weight loss, or if the person has become ill due to weight loss, with exhaustion, dehydration, breathlessness or fainting, or if they are so low that they have talked about or tried to self-harm, then urgent assessment should be sought, even if this is against the person's will.

Alternative coping strategies and building self-esteem

The huge internal pressure to control eating is a form of stress release for sufferers, although it creates more stress as a result. By developing alternative and healthier coping strategies for dealing with stressful emotions, a sufferer will have a better chance of breaking the vicious circle. Rebuilding self-esteem and developing better coping strategies can take time and will often need support from a trained counsellor, because it can be tough to change the way a person's mind works. Listed below are the areas that a counsellor may explore, reassuring a sufferer who may otherwise fear that counselling is simply a way of forcing them to agree to eat.

- *Self-value*. The way we see ourselves is crucial to the way we care for ourselves. Nobody looks after rubbish, so if people think of themselves as rubbish or unworthy then it will lead to self-neglect and even self-harm. They will also assume that other people think they are worthless, making them timid and withdrawn, which can lead to being ignored or bullied because of a lack of self-confidence. It is essential for a person with anorexia to find a sense of self-value once again. Some people achieve this by understanding themselves better through counselling, some put their faith in God, which gives them the reassurance that He values them, and others find that friends and family are able to give enough support to help them overcome their loss of faith in themselves. Many people find a combination is the most successful.

- *Acceptance.* It is easier to value ourselves if we are able to accept our flaws as well as our strengths. Acceptance means having realistic expectations of ourselves, our appearance and our abilities. It means that we can go along with the ups and downs of life, instead of cracking under the strain of trying to reach an ideal. Accepting our defects does not mean that we cannot try to improve them, it just means that we weigh them up alongside our strengths and that they are an acceptable part of us – not great, not terrible, just ordinary human weaknesses the same as everyone else has. Positive thinking – the glass if half full rather than half empty – is something that can be learned, and negative thinking is something that can be left behind.
- *Trust.* Trust is something that comes along with self-esteem. If we value ourselves then we learn to trust ourselves too, by having confidence in the thoughts we have, the opinions we reach and the decisions we make. Trust in ourselves means that we can rely on our own opinions, believe in facts we have learned (such as that the world is round, even though it looks flat) and can trust our sensations – for example, if something feels hot then it is hot and if the body is saying that it is hungry then it is reasonable to eat. Trust in others will often follow from regaining trust in oneself, so that a person becomes able to accept praise and appreciation and to believe others when they pay compliments or offer support – support that may have been rejected during times of feeling worthless.
- *Responsibility.* Taking responsibility for our thoughts and actions can be a way of both accepting our problems and beginning to recover. Children, by and large, are not fully responsible for what they do because they are not old enough to understand the consequences of many actions. But adolescence is a time when young people start to face the repercussions of what they do. Anorexia is a condition where the sufferer denies the consequences of not eating, shying away from the effects on physical health, family and on the whole of emotional life. Taking full responsibility can be a very daunting prospect, but it can be broken down into manageable chunks that can be built upon as recovery progresses.

How can someone with anorexia take responsibility for their actions?
This is easier than it sounds once it is clear what 'taking responsibility' actually means. It doesn't mean sorting out all the problems, pulling socks up or piling on more guilt!

In simple terms, it means registering in some way the consequences of an action. This may occur by talking more openly about things, by admitting things rather than covering them up or lying, or it may involve writing thoughts down and sharing them with a friend or counsellor (*see* Box 10.1), or sometimes saying sorry. Everyone should remember that, as part of a family, they are no more allowed to rant and rave than anyone else in the household. Upsetting behaviour means apologising.

Box 10.1 Keeping an eating–emotion diary

One established method that can help people with anorexia to reduce their fear and take some control over eating is to keep a diary.

Record what is eaten and, most importantly, the feelings and emotions before, during and after eating. This helps to clarify and predict the emotions that eating induces, in order to deal with those emotions rather than focus only on controlling the food. Instead of being overwhelmed by guilt and fear, the sufferer can tune in to how those feelings start, increase and fade, and then find alternative ways of modifying and dealing with them.

This can also help to reduce some of the rituals that develop around food, making meals less stressful even if food intake takes longer to change. Exploring some of the complicated thoughts that lead to elaborate mealtime rituals by writing them down can help to reduce the need for them to continue.

A very important aspect of being able to take responsibility for something is setting realistic expectations. It would be unfair to make someone responsible for circumstances way beyond their control. Helping a sufferer to set achievable targets is a valuable way of putting them in control, giving them reasons to feel proud and breaking up the long journey to recovery into small, manageable sections.

Positive and achievable targets might include the following:

- Start to attend family meals even if not actually eating with the family yet.
- Show someone what is eaten, with the understanding that they do not try to change things, rather than keeping food intake entirely secret.
- Take vitamin supplements, following discussion with a doctor, if it is agreed that current intake is too low.
- Aim to stabilise weight even if the thought of increasing weight is not yet an option.
- Agree to attend appointments with supportive health professionals even if participation in these is limited.
- Reduce the frequency of weighing. Perhaps try writing down weights and then looking at what was recorded, rather than checking again on the scales.
- Increase the variety of foods eaten even if the calories consumed are no greater.

From a parent's perspective, it will be hard for a young person to start taking responsibility if parents have been busy doing it on their behalf – blaming themselves, trying to change things, accepting blame from their child over things like food provision or for emotional problems within the household. But parents are not responsible for their child's illness and the process of gradually passing on this responsibility with guidance, love and support will help the sufferer come to terms with being in charge of their own life. This is an area where family therapy or support from other families through a local support group may help.

Knowing how to deal with eating and food issues

Surprisingly, anorexia is not really about food – not about flavours nor cooking techniques – so it is not a case of searching for food that might be tempting enough or nutritionally suitable to be eaten. In fact, the more tasty and appetising a food, the more likely the sufferer may feel guilt and anxiety about being tempted by it. The aim is to understand the emotions related to food, rather than to worry over the food itself.

Guidelines for families include the following:

- Because you are aiming to build trust between you and the sufferer, never be tempted to hide extra calories in the food you have prepared or to lie about the ingredients a meal contains. Most sufferers have an expert knowledge of the calorie content of foods, and are likely to stop eating anything you prepare if they feel you cannot be trusted.
- Do not feel pressured into changing your own eating habits just to pacify the sufferer. If you have always cooked certain meals in certain ways, continue to do so if you and the rest of the family wish.
- Recognise if you are being bullied by the sufferer, who may suggest that the reason for not eating is because you are a bad cook, or because food is off or made with fatty meat, etc. People with anorexia may resort to endless excuses to explain why they won't eat, whilst denying there is an eating problem. It is hard work to achieve this, and some mud slinging and creative lying are all part of the illness. It can be extremely hurtful to listen to the person you love deeply accusing you of being the cause of their eating problem. Talking to families of other sufferers may help you understand this.
- Avoid chivvying at mealtimes. If possible, establish before the meal begins what they are planning to eat and then keep quiet.
- Discuss eating a balanced diet even if portion sizes are far smaller than needed. Accepting varied foods will help in obtaining more of the basic essential nutrients and may also help to give a sense of value in eating.
- Never belittle any attempts by the sufferer to help themselves. Eating an extra segment of an orange might seem a pathetic drop in the ocean, but to someone with anorexia it may require avid determination.
- During recovery, do not swamp any early forays into eating with tempting treats and overenthusiastic portion sizes. Leave them in control of what they are doing – show faith so that they can continue to trust you.

Box 10.2 Lisa's experiences of anorexia nervosa

Triggers

Lisa had always seen herself as chubby, but whilst living at home she was cheerful, confident and highly successful, eventually gaining entrance to university to study law. A year before she went to university she began to have concerns about eating and firstly became vegetarian. She then went through a stressful period whilst sitting her A-level exams that took her appetite away, and she began to lose weight. Somehow, success in her exams, which she knew she wanted, would mean that she would have to leave home, which terrified her. The thought of failure, however, was equally unacceptable. She couldn't make sense of these two conflicting factors ahead of her.

At first Lisa liked the fact that she had lost weight. She felt good about her appearance, but still anxious about her exams. Her weight loss seemed to take away some of the stress of the exams and the looming prospect of leaving home.

The vicious cycle

Without realising, Lisa then found herself becoming concerned about maintaining her weight reduction, and that she could maintain it more easily if she exercised more. It was easy to do lots more exercise because everyone feels that exercise is a healthy thing and a good way to cope with exam stress, and so her change in activities was applauded.

Soon Lisa found that she would feel depressed if she had overeaten, but better if she then starved herself. However, as time went by, this depression began to occur if she ate anything at all, so that she became obsessed with the fear of overeating. The only way to cope with these feelings was to try to control her eating as much as possible. This meant avoiding eating with other people, who might notice her odd eating habits, and so she stopped socialising. This made her feel more isolated and added to her mounting feelings of depression. She set herself rituals about eating – ways to cope with the inevitable depression that eating brought. She ate only a very narrow range of foods, especially high-fibre foods that were largely fat-free. She had to eat at certain times, rather than because she was hungry. She became expert at lying about what and when she had eaten, and wore bulky clothes to hide her shape.

Lisa actually thought that her weight was about right for her – it was fear of weight gain that filled her with such dread, rather than a desire to be much thinner. She had now arrived at university where there were many more worries on her plate – financial pressures, the university workload, new friendships to make and no immediate family support. Initially she joined in sporting clubs, throwing herself into rowing and running as a way, on the surface, of joining in, but underneath, of keeping her weight firmly under control. Her mum was not around to share her worries or to cook her favourite foods and so starvation was even easier than when she was at home. And so her weight dropped more and more, until she became too exhausted to take part in sports any more. This added further to her depression as she now felt the only way to keep her weight controlled was by starving herself even more.

Acceptance

Lisa felt extremely unhappy and wished that she could stop focusing on food during every waking moment. She wanted something to change, but had no idea where to start or what to try. Her family noticed the changes in her weight, her depressed moods and her denial, but she insisted that there was nothing wrong and that her slight weight loss was related to the absence of home cooking.

She was aware of the risks of being underweight – her periods had stopped and she felt exhausted on the least exertion. However, she was able to push these concerns out of her mind, along with all the other worries, by focusing on controlling her food intake and weight instead. It was like a full-time job planning and coping with every mouthful.

When Lisa's father mentioned her weight she became very angry. She felt very threatened by his comments because she felt that if she agreed with him then she would have to do something about the problem, whereas if she carried on denying it then she could continue to cope with all her worries by focusing on avoiding weight gain. It was a real 'catch 22'.

Her family, worried to death by now, spoke to a variety of friends, relatives and professionals. Although, to start with, any discussion about Lisa's weight and eating would lead to arguments and tears, they began to help her to accept that losing weight had not made her happy. It was only when Lisa decided for herself that she was too thin that she was able to accept any help. Her family were very important in leading her to reach this conclusion though.

Acceptance that she was too thin came on gradually, over several months, and recovery from the illness took many months more – they were like two separate stages of recovery. It was easier to accept the problem when she was only required to do that – accept it for now but not to try to change it yet. She gradually realised that recovery could be a slow journey under her own control, rather than a hideous threat from other people.

Recovery

Lisa's family helped by focusing on her happiness rather than her weight, and by showing their love and support rather than suggesting criticism and trying to control things. They had to show respect and acceptance of Lisa's abnormal eating pattern, without trying to push her, in order for her to trust them, which meant the family arguments could then stop too. They invited her to join their meals, but without expecting her to eat anything, whilst she continued to eat alone. Once the pressure was reduced, she felt more able to eat with them again.

Lisa recognised, with the help of her doctor, that she had depressive symptoms and was prescribed antidepressants. It was easier to accept depression as a diagnosis than anorexia. The tablets took some of the pressure off. She still felt worried whenever she ate, but found she could cope with more varied foods and with eating slightly more. The anti-depressants also helped her to accept that she was too thin, so that she wanted to gain weight.

Talking to other people who had suffered with depression – not just anorexia – was helpful, as many feelings are common to both conditions. Lisa was referred for counselling sessions. These were supportive up to a point, but she found their main benefit was that of 'giving permission' to get better and learning different ways to help herself. However, it was several months before her first appointment, during which time she felt she wasn't supposed to help herself – there was no point in turning up to the appointment already cured – and so this in fact delayed her recovery at a time when she felt impatient to begin getting better.

Whilst many of Lisa's university friends had backed away as her illness worsened because they didn't know what to say, a few friends became staunch supporters – friends she hadn't really been close to until she became ill. Their support was great.

As she recovered, she very gradually built up how much she could eat. It took months. She found it hard to stop counting calories and objected to being chivvied over what she ate. But eating with other people rather than alone helped her to eat more. She found it a relief to eat more interesting foods – the guilt was the same as for bland foods, but at least there seemed more point in eating something tasty, and gradually it became easier as well as more enjoyable.

As Lisa's eating improved, so her confidence built up along with her strength. She realised that leaving home did not mean that her family were lost to her. Indeed, their support was stronger than ever, and eventually she reached a stage where the illness was behind her.

Lisa is no longer on antidepressants and feels far more confident about dealing with stress without resorting to controlling her eating. Although there have been ups and downs along the way, she has found that sharing worries early on is the best way to prevent niggling concerns from building up inside.

Bulimia and binge-eating disorder

The term 'bulimia nervosa' means 'nervous insatiable appetite' and it may often follow on from anorexia. It is far commoner in women than men and it usually begins when a dieter discovers that they can keep their weight controlled by vomiting after meals or by taking large quantities of laxatives.

Following bingeing and purging, which induce dreadful feelings of guilt and self-loathing, a sufferer will then starve themselves until their will-power fails and they binge again. This leads to a cycle of regular bingeing and purging, guilt and erosion of self-esteem, so that they feel they have no control over the way they eat, merely a miserable rescue plan after eating.

Bulimia is easier to keep hidden from other people than anorexia because many bulimics are of normal weight or are overweight, and this has led to many sufferers remaining undiagnosed and their misery continuing for years.

Binge-eating disorder (also known as compulsive-eating disorder) overlaps with bulimia, although people prone to binge eating do not resort to extreme behaviours to prevent weight gain, such as self-induced vomiting, misuse of laxatives and diuretics, or episodes of fasting. If binge eating happens regularly then it can lead to severe obesity.

Bulimia and binge-eating disorder include the following traits:

- bingeing on huge amounts of high-carbohydrate foods, or in fact anything that is to hand, including uncooked ingredients or food taken from other people's cupboards when sharing accommodation

- depression is a common additional problem because life becomes dominated by food cravings, loss of control over eating, feelings of guilt and a sense of being trapped in a relentless vicious circle
- irritability and poor concentration, leading to isolation, plus financial problems due to lavish spending on binges.

Additionally, bulimia involves the following:

- Apparently 'normal eating' in front of other people – bingeing is a secretive affair. Many sufferers take pains to keep it hidden by presenting an image of confidence and success.
- Disappearing after meals in order to induce vomiting. The sufferer may then appear irritable or exhausted.
- In a person who was previously anorexic, the weight that is gained through binges causes terrible distress, especially if they feel they have simply lost the will-power to remain anorexic. Meanwhile, their family and friends are congratulating them on their apparent recovery, despite the fact that they feel worse than ever. Now, in order not to disappoint or be found out, the sufferer has to mask their misery even more than when anorexic, which adds to overall stress.
- As bulimia is a hidden condition associated with very low self-esteem, sufferers will sometimes take part in other risky behaviours to try and find temporary relief from their misery, such as drinking excessive alcohol, trying drugs, shoplifting (usually food) or becoming promiscuous.
- Physical problems that arise from bulimia include tooth decay, gum disease and throat infections, plus strain on the heart and kidneys from inducing vomiting. Excessive overeating can stretch the stomach lining and may lead to obesity, which increases the risk of diabetes and heart disease in later life.

Finding help for bulimia and binge-eating disorder

Many of the approaches that will help someone with bulimia or binge eating are similar to those for anorexia, because low self-esteem is a central theme. Seeking help is an important part of changing things. Most of the organisations that help people with anorexia offer support for bulimia and binge-eating disorder too, so try any of the organisations listed in Appendix 2 and be prepared to keep trying until you meet with other people to whom you can relate. Finding a good support group run by other sufferers and ex-sufferers is one of the most successful ways of breaking the bulimia cycle.

Another helpful approach to bulimia and to binge-eating disorder is to try a self-help programme that uses 'cognitive behaviour therapy' techniques. Studies have shown self-help programmes to be helpful in at least half of people who work through them, particularly if they have some additional support alongside. The following self-help books contain treatment programmes:

- Cooper PJ (1995) *Bulimia Nervosa and Binge Eating: a guide to recovery*. Robinson, London.
- Fairburn CG (1995) *Overcoming Binge Eating*. Guilford, New York.

Many sufferers have commented that their family doctor did not seem to take their illness seriously, a reflection of bulimia being less well recognised than anorexia and that a bulimia sufferer's weight is often in the normal or overweight range. In addition, a bulimic may have become successful at covering up their feelings and appear well organised and capable – which is why they are able to fit an eating disorder into an otherwise 'normal' life. This makes the sufferer appear not to be in need of help.

If you are a sufferer or are helping a sufferer to get help, bear these things in mind and be prepared to find out about local support groups and to push for specialist support if self-help approaches are not enough.

Summary points

- Eating disorders are usually the result of emotional upset, where the abnormal eating pattern is a symptom of the underlying psychological problem. Low self-esteem is universal in eating disorders.
- Dieting is common and does not indicate the onset of an eating disorder in most people. If there is a suspicion of anorexia nervosa then expert help is vital.
- Bulimia is often hidden as weight may be normal and binge eating is usually secretive.
- The trigger for anorexia nervosa may vary from a trivial remark to a major upset in someone who tends to apply self-control or who is particularly sensitive, leading to a vicious cycle of feeling slightly better by controlling eating.
- The feelings of guilt and loss of control on eating lead to the development of complex rituals, deceit about eating and excessive exercise or self-induced vomiting, but these strategies make the guilt and misery worse, not better.
- Recovery can be seen in two distinct phases – acceptance of the condition (when the eating pattern may not alter) and the phase of weight gain. Weight gain will only be successful when the sufferer learns to break the cycle of guilt from eating.
- Alternative coping strategies can be learned by focusing on self-value, setting realistic expectations, rebuilding trust in both self and then in others and by gradually taking responsibility. Good family support can make a huge difference.

Chapter 11

An A to Z of conditions that affect weight and eating in young people

Each condition is discussed, some briefly and some in more depth, with details of how and when to obtain further advice.

- Abdominal pain
  - Abdominal migraine
  - Colic
  - Urine infection
- Acne
- Allergies
  - Egg allergy
  - Peanut allergy
- Anorexia or loss of appetite
- Appendicitis
- Coeliac disease
- Constipation
- Contraception
- Depression
- Diabetes
- Diarrhoea and gastroenteritis
- Inflammatory conditions of the gut
- Irritable bowel syndrome
- Polycystic ovary syndrome
- Premenstrual syndrome
- Teenage pregnancy and nutrition
- Thyroid disorders
- Tooth decay

Abdominal pain

Abdominal pain is a common ailment in all age groups – along with coughs and colds it features daily in every doctor's surgery. It is not an illness in itself, but a symptom. Sometimes there is an obvious cause, such as constipation or appendicitis (*see* below), but at other times no cause can be found. The first question to ask is whether it is a new problem or if it has been grumbling on for some time.

If symptoms have come on rapidly, with vomiting and abdominal pains, especially if the pain is worse on moving, then further advice should be sought promptly from a doctor or health helpline (*see* Appendix 2), who will discuss the symptoms and advise on how quickly to seek further help.

For milder or intermittent symptoms it is reasonable to try simple measures first, keeping the option of seeing a doctor in case symptoms persist.

Abdominal migraine

This is a term sometimes used to describe intermittent tummy pains that leave the sufferer feeling under the weather for a few hours but then subside as oddly as they arrived. There is nothing to suggest spasm of the gut as a cause, as in colic, and no other signs to suggest a urine infection or appendicitis. The pain may be accompanied by a headache; indeed, as children go through adolescence into adulthood, many sufferers find the headaches become more troublesome with each bout but the tummy pain gets less, until as adults they simply suffer migraine headaches. A doctor will have some suggestions about how to treat this condition, and happily many people grow out of the phase.

Colic

The gut does not sense things in the same way as skin – guts are not sensitive to touch or to hot and cold, but they are very sensitive to being stretched or to griping, for example when they are stretched by trapped wind or a hard motion, or if they clamp down in spasm. This causes a pain called *colic,* which usually comes in nasty waves that build up gradually, become a tight griping pain and then slowly ease off again. A person with colic tends to writhe around, finding it difficult to get comfortable.

Colic can be caused by a variety of things; constipation is by far the commonest cause, but it will accompany diarrhoea and sickness bugs, and sometimes seems to happen for no apparent reason. See the sections below on constipation and irritable bowel syndrome for ideas on treating colic.

Urine infection

The typical symptoms of a urine infection are pain or discomfort whilst passing urine, called cystitis, plus a feeling of urgency and passing small amounts of urine very frequently. Some people only get discomfort as they finish passing urine. However, sometimes these symptoms are vague or even absent and a person simply becomes unwell with abdominal pains, vomiting, a high temperature or even rigors – when the body shakes uncontrollably then sweats profusely whilst body temperature rises and falls. It is always helpful to take a specimen of urine along when visiting the doctor if symptoms are vague, as this may provide the answer.

Urine infection is far commoner in females than males because of the different designs of the urinary system in men and women. If a male is ever found to have a urine infection then, in addition to prescribing antibiotics, a doctor will arrange further tests such as an ultrasound scan to look at the kidneys and bladder. If a female suffers from a urine infection then simple measures to increase fluid intake and to fully empty the bladder may help to reduce the problem. Recurrent infections would usually be investigated with an ultrasound scan, as for men.

Drinking cranberry juice has been shown to help prevent cystitis from developing and can help to treat an infection once already established.

Acne

Acne is a common problem affecting about 90% of young people at some stage. It often settles down during the twenties, although some adults find it remains a problem in later life too.

There are many myths surrounding acne, in particular dietary myths, which is why it is included here.

What is acne?

Acne is due to blockage of the tiny pores of the skin, leading to blackheads and spots. It appears, after puberty, in response to a hormone called testosterone. All men and women have this hormone and so anyone can get acne. Blackheads are due to partial blockage of the pores with thick oil, or sebum, where the black discolouration is pigment rather than dirt. If the pore becomes completely blocked then the oil within the pore becomes infected, leading to redness, swelling and pus formation – otherwise known as 'zits'. Acne can leave scarring but it is not contagious, so there is no need to worry about contact with someone who has acne.

Some things can make acne worse:

- Sweating, humid climates or working in a hot, humid place such as a kitchen or steam room can have an effect.
- Some drugs worsen acne, such as steroids and some hormone treatments.
- Cosmetics, hair oils and some suntan oils can worsen blackheads and acne, so try test doses first.
- Some women find that acne is worse in the time leading up to a period.
- Over-washing of the skin can dry it out and make it sore, leaving it more prone to acne. Washing once or twice a day should be fine.
- Squeezing spots: it is okay to gently squeeze spots where yellow pus is visible, but it is not advisable to squeeze red spots because this can force infection deeper into the skin and increase the chance of scarring. Blackheads can be gently expressed, but avoid squeezing as this can lead to them becoming infected.

Other things have no effect:

- The diet has not been shown to cause acne, so excess chocolate, too many chips and a supply of other junk foods are not to blame.
- Having dirty skin is not a cause.
- Even though acne has a hormonal cause, it is not linked to sex or masturbation, so lots, a little or none at all will have no effect.

The following factors can help acne:

- Sunshine – acne often improves in the summer but gets worse in winter. However, make sure the skin does not burn.
- Lotions and potions from the chemist. Lotions containing benzoyl peroxide are effective for mild acne, although they may dry out the skin. Use with a moisturiser too.
- Antibiotics – these require a prescription and may be used on the skin in a

lotion form or taken by mouth in tablet form. They need to be used long term for at least six months in order to keep acne under control.

- Topical vitamin A gels or creams – these can reduce acne, but may also dry out or irritate the skin and so should be used with a moisturiser.
- The combined contraceptive pill, especially a high-oestrogen pill, can be very effective in controlling acne in women, although it can cause side-effects. This is only available on prescription.
- Oral vitamin A tablets are available through specialist dermatology clinics only and are usually reserved for the most severe cases due to side-effects.

Allergies to food

Allergies have become a common problem and may arise at any time of life. If a food allergy is suspected, seek advice from a doctor or registered dietician so that the condition can be diagnosed correctly. This ensures that avoiding the problem food will not result in a dietary deficiency and provides the opportunity to learn what to do if there is accidental contact with the problem food in future.

Most people who are allergic will suffer mild irritating symptoms, but occasionally, in severe allergy, a person can suffer an acute and sometimes life-threatening reaction called *anaphylaxis*. This is an emergency situation where the body reacts rapidly, causing swelling of the mouth and throat, which results in breathing difficulties and can cause collapse. It requires immediate help and an ambulance should be summoned if suspected. If a person has suffered an anaphylactic reaction, it is wise to wear a Medic-Alert bracelet and to consider carrying an emergency supply of adrenaline that can be supplied by a family doctor.

Box 11.1 Common foods that can trigger allergic reactions

- Seafood, especially prawns and mussels
- Peanuts
- Eggs
- Milk
- Wheat
- Citrus fruits and strawberries
- Soya products
- Bananas
- Food additives
- Chocolate

Box 11.1 lists common foods that can trigger an allergic reaction. Certain foods, for example milk, wheat, eggs and nuts, cause more of a problem than others because they may be hidden in many basic foods, making them hard to avoid.

There is currently no cure for food allergies, which means the food must be avoided in order to avoid the symptoms it triggers. Mild reactions can be improved by the use of antihistamine tablets, but it is preferable to avoid the allergen because of the risk of a mild reaction becoming more severe on repeated exposure. Common symptoms from any food allergy are similar to those described for peanut or egg allergy below.

Egg allergy

Egg allergy is significant not only because egg is hidden in many foods, especially cakes, biscuits, pastries, some breads and many sauces, but it is also used in the manufacture of some vaccines. If allergic to egg, then inform a doctor or nurse about egg allergy before any vaccinations or injections. Check the ingredients list of foods carefully and look out for the various alternative names that egg may be listed as (*see* Box 11.2).

Box 11.2 Some alternative names for egg derivatives

- Albumin
- Egg protein, powder, white or yolk
- Dried, frozen or pasteurised egg
- Globulin
- Livetin
- Ovalbumin
- Ovaglobulin
- Ovomucin
- Ovovitellin or vitellin
- Lecithin (also known as E322) may be derived from eggs, although it is more often derived from soya. This is usually clarified on an ingredients list

---

Peanut allergy

Peanut allergy is unfortunately becoming more common, although it is not clear exactly why. Anyone can develop it, even in later life, but it is commoner in people who have atopic (meaning allergy-related) conditions such as asthma, eczema or hay fever. These sometimes run in families (atopic families) and can be inherited.

Because there is a chance that eating peanuts in pregnancy and during breastfeeding may increase the risk of a child developing peanut allergy, the Department of Health recommends that a mother from an atopic family should avoid peanuts during this time. Children from such families should avoid peanuts and peanut products until they are at least three years old.

If allergic to peanuts there is a high chance of being allergic to other nuts too, such as walnuts, cashews or brazil nuts, and sometimes to hazelnuts, pine nuts and pistachios, so these are best avoided too.

What happens if a sufferer comes into contact with peanuts?

There can be two main reactions: a mild reaction or severe anaphylactic reaction.

In mild peanut allergy, varying symptoms come on quickly, with perhaps an itchy rash, tingling of the mouth, diarrhoea or sickness. In severe cases, the person may have facial swelling, difficulty breathing and even collapse. Both mild and severe reactions can happen up to six hours after eating peanuts, and even if only tiny traces of peanut have been consumed.

Peanut allergy is now well recognised and food manufacturers have improved the labelling of many foods to inform if peanut traces are present. Look for 'not suitable for nut allergy sufferers' or 'may contain nuts' as a guide, although some manufacturers have taken this too far and are labelling all their products so as to avoid liability.

Because there is no cure to the underlying allergy, an affected person should avoid any contact with peanut products. In particular, check the ingredient list of:

- baked foods, such as cakes and biscuits
- cereals
- oriental dishes
- ice-creams
- health bars
- pastry
- savoury snacks.

Some restaurants are following suit with clear labelling on menus, but others are happy to advise on particular dishes if asked.

Box 11.3 describes what someone should do if they witness a person having an allergic reaction to nuts.

Box 11.3 What to do if a person is found having an allergic reaction to nuts

Prompt action is essential:

- Remove any nuts from the person immediately.
- Ask for immediate assistance. Call 999 for an ambulance if the reaction is rapid or severe, with collapse, facial swelling or difficulty breathing.
- Do your best to keep calm and to reassure the person that help is being arranged.
- For a mild reaction you might contact the person's general practitioner (GP), the casualty department, or use the National Health Service (NHS) advice line, NHS Direct, on 0845 4647 for further guidance on what to do.

With a degree of care and caution, a person with peanut allergy can live a perfectly normal life. About 25% of children affected will grow out of their allergy, and others will suffer milder reactions as they get older. Consider wearing a Medic-Alert bracelet or necklace and make sure that schools and clubs are informed about the condition. More information and advice on treatment are available from the Great Ormond Street Family Resource Centre: 020 7813 8558, or on various websites (*see* Appendix 2).

Anorexia or loss of appetite

Anorexia means loss of appetite and is distinct from the condition anorexia nervosa, which is covered separately in Chapter 10.

Many things will cause appetite to tail off, especially infections such as coughs and colds, urine infection or appendicitis.

- If a person has a cough, cold or sickness and diarrhoeal bug, then loss of appetite is expected to some extent. As long as enough fluids are taken (which is shown by passing urine several times a day), short-term loss of appetite is not a problem. Even skinny people can tolerate not eating for a few days without coming to any harm, as long as they keep drinking. If appetite fails to return after a few days, then consider seeking advice from a doctor.
- Another reason why appetite may disappear is worry and sadness. Many young people as well as adults lose their appetite in times of stress, so if there are no physical reasons why someone should be off their food, then emotional problems may be responsible. New situations such as a change in school, or emotional upheaval such as parental divorce, will frequently be accompanied by a change in appetite.
- Illicit drug use may take away appetite and will sometimes be associated with weight loss and changes in behaviour or personality.
- Following a growth spurt, someone with a usually good appetite may go through a phase of eating very little, simply because energy requirements have tailed off. This is normal and will regulate itself if the person is used to eating according to what natural appetite dictates. If more energy is needed then appetite will increase again. Forcing food when not hungry teaches people to overeat.
- Following a prolonged illness that has caused significant weight loss, appetite can be slow to recover, sometimes because the sight of food is a reminder of the illness itself, but also because people get used to eating less. In this situation, the balance of foods eaten is just as important as ever – a recuperating person will need plenty of vitamins, minerals, fibre and protein to enable healthy growth to pick up. Rather than piling large amounts of food on the plate, go for foods that are more energy-dense, such as full-fat dairy products, creamy sauces and fried rather than grilled meat or fish, to increase the amount of calories eaten without having to eat large quantities. Plain foods are more likely to be acceptable than heavily spiced or strongly flavoured foods. If nausea remains a problem, then bland foods that have little smell, such as tinned fruit, milk puddings and breakfast cereals, may be better tolerated. Once a person gets used to eating more varied foods again, appetite should improve.

Appendicitis

This is the commonest reason for emergency surgery in young people, but it can affect people of any age. It is sometimes easy to diagnose, but at other times can be a real puzzle when the usual symptoms are not obvious.

The appendix is a small, blind-ended tunnel near to where the small bowel joins onto the large bowel in the bottom right-hand corner of the tummy. If it gets blocked then infection can seep into the walls of the appendix, which can even burst. The resulting peritonitis – when the whole abdomen becomes inflamed – can make a person extremely ill, so any suspicion of appendicitis must be carefully assessed and the appendix may be removed even when it is healthy if abdominal pain is not settling.

Appendicitis usually starts with vague tummy pains and loss of appetite. The pain soon moves down into the bottom right corner and may be accompanied by a slight temperature, vomiting and reluctance to move because it worsens the pain. Tummy pain with loss of appetite should always be checked out, but if there is a hearty appetite it is less likely to be appendicitis.

Once the appendix becomes inflamed it does not usually settle on its own, it simply gets worse until it is surgically removed. If in doubt, always seek help from a family doctor or discuss symptoms first with a health helpline (*see* Appendix 2).

Coeliac disease or wheat sensitivity

In the past, coeliac disease was always thought to show itself in early childhood, but it is now recognised as a cause of symptoms in older children and sometimes adults.

Coeliac disease is a condition where a protein called gluten, which is found in wheat, barley, rye, and to a lesser extent oats, reacts with the lining of the small bowel. The body's immune system starts to think the small bowel lining is foreign and so attacks it, so that it struggles to absorb nutrients and vitamins. In particular, if left untreated, there is difficulty in absorbing iron and folic acid (resulting in anaemia), calcium (which can lead to weaker bones and ultimately osteoporosis) and calories in general, because the surface area of the gut is reduced, leading to weight loss or failure to thrive.

Diagnosing coeliac disease

The diagnosis of coeliac disease is usually made by a gastroenterology specialist or paediatrician and involves blood tests and a biopsy of the small bowel, done under mild sedation. A positive blood test for antibodies (called tissue transglutaminase or TTG) will usually indicate coeliac disease is present, but a negative test does not rule it out, so biopsy is usually necessary too. A gluten-free diet should not be started without medical advice, in particular if confirmatory tests are planned, or else the diagnostic signs may disappear before the condition has been confirmed.

It is important to confirm the diagnosis because leaving it untreated may lead to serious complications, including an increased risk of cancer. This risk reduces if the disease is kept at bay by sticking to a strict gluten-free diet.

In addition, because a gluten-free diet requires commitment and understanding, it is not a diet to be tried on the off chance.

The gluten-free diet

Many foods are naturally gluten-free, such as fruit and vegetables, fresh meat, fish, cheese, eggs and milk, because they do not contain any wheat, rye, barley or oats.

Foods that contain flour, such as bread, cakes, pastries, biscuits and puddings, should all be avoided, but there are many hidden sources of gluten to avoid too.

In processed foods, flour may be used for binding ingredients, in fillings or as a carrier for flavourings and will not always be listed on the ingredients panel if only a small amount is contained.

Oats, whilst being low in gluten, are not entirely gluten-free, especially if milled or processed alongside other grains. There is some evidence that mild coeliac sufferers can tolerate small amounts of oats (up to 50 grams per day), but someone with more troublesome symptoms should avoid oats in addition to other cereals. This is best discussed with a specialist.

In addition, wheat or wheat flour can contaminate other usually gluten-free products if they are processed or manufactured in the same place. The Coeliac Society, www.coeliac.co.uk, provides a full listing of all gluten-free products, which is regularly updated.

Constipation

It is not how often a motion is passed, rather that the process works easily and with no straining or discomfort. As a general rule, people who go regularly to the toilet are less prone to constipation than those who go infrequently. There is a huge variation in 'normal' – some people go at least once or twice a day, but for others it may be a weekly drama associated with cramps, nausea and even blood in the motion.

If a person is straining to pass a motion and goes less than three or four times a week, it is likely that they are short of fibre in the diet. If this pattern continues throughout adulthood there will be an increased risk of piles, diverticular disease and even bowel cancer, so it is worth sorting this out at the earliest opportunity and learning a healthy approach to fibre in the diet.

Colic is common if the diet is low in fibre, because the gut has to work hard in order for motions to pass along. Eating more fibre and fruit and vegetables helps to 'bulk up' the motion, so that it can travel more smoothly through the gut with less griping.

In addition, encouraging plenty of fluids and exercise will help the gut to work more smoothly.

Getting the right balance of fibre is important because too much fibre may cause diarrhoea and colicky tummy pains. Some foods can trigger loose motions, whereas other sources of fibre may suit well. Try a variety of things to see if there are certain basic foods, such as wholemeal bread, higher-fibre breakfast cereals and certain fruits and vegetables, that reliably keep the bowel working smoothly and so should feature as daily basic foods. There is no reason why a tablespoon of a reliable higher-fibre ingredient can't be mixed with a whole variety of other lower-fibre foods if it tastes better that way. See Chapter 5, 'Nutritional basics for young people', for more information on high-fibre foods.

Contraception

Some methods of contraception can have an effect on weight, but there are many myths too. At the end of the day, we are a reflection of what we eat and as contraceptive pills do not contain much in the way of calories, they are not an obvious cause of weight gain. However, one method, the injectable progestogen called Depo-Provera, does seem to influence metabolism and so is associated with slight weight gain.

The combined oral contraceptive pill

The reason for so many myths about the Pill and weight gain is because of the age at which it is usually commenced – during the mid to late teenage years. In reality, the Pill has very little effect on weight and women taking it long term are just as likely to lose weight as to gain it.

All teenagers have a tendency to gain weight as they head into their twenties, whether girls take the Pill or not, but Pill takers tend to attribute this natural weight gain to their new Pill. Teenage weight gain is a biological safety net to ensure that women have enough body reserves to cope with pregnancy and breastfeeding. Other biological factors play a part too, such as humans evolved to store food when it was available and so living in an environment where food is plentiful results in biological temptation to overeat and store fat in case of future need. Hence with each decade a human will tend to get a bit heavier. By the time we add in society factors, such as sedentary jobs and inactive forms of entertainment, there is a multitude of reasons why someone will put on weight as they leave school and head into adulthood.

However, we live in a society obsessed with 'pill scares' and which encourages people to blame the Pill for any symptom going. Therefore the Pill has shouldered much of the blame for natural weight gain that would have happened anyway.

The progesterone-only pill or mini-pill

The mini-pill contains progesterone only with no oestrogen. It has a more unpredictable effect on symptoms, particularly bleeding pattern, which may cause periods to be regular, irregular or even absent. It is a very safe hormone and is usually suitable even if there is a reason why the combined pill cannot be prescribed.

Most women tolerate it very well with no side-effects at all, but a small number seem quite sensitive to progestogen, becoming bloated and moody with worsening acne, breast tenderness and fluid retention. They may notice weight gain of a few pounds, which is usually related to fluid retention. These women may settle on a different brand of mini-pill or find that they are better off looking for an alternative method of contraception.

Injectable progestogens

The most widely used injectable progestogen is called Depo-Provera, or just 'depo'. It is an extremely effective contraceptive with a very low failure rate and has been very popular with younger users because it cannot be forgotten once on board. It is given every 12 weeks and with prolonged use results in much lighter bleeding, if any, compared to a normal cycle. However, it can take a few months to settle down and, to begin with, may cause irregular spotting or sometimes heavy bleeding.

This method has been linked to weight gain of around a stone with long-term use, although it is by no means universal. This may result from hormonal changes from its action on blocking ovulation, which may also be related to insulin resistance, as found in polycystic ovaries.

It has declined slightly in popularity due to a possible link with thinning of the bones, or osteoporosis, caused by suppression of the user's own oestrogen. It is now considered advisable to stop depo after four years of use, especially if the user has had no periods at all for several years, and it is discouraged in younger people whose bones have not yet finished growing.

Progestogen-releasing implant

There is one device currently available, called Implanon, which consists of a single flexible rod inserted under the skin of the upper arm. It is highly effective, lasting for up to three years, and is fully and quickly reversible following removal. It is similar in some ways to Depo-Provera, with an extremely low failure rate, but because the hormone dosage is effectively lower it is not particularly linked to either weight gain or thinning of the bones. However, its lower dosage gives a higher risk of irregular, nuisance bleeding, with less chance of periods stopping altogether.

Intrauterine contraceptive devices (IUD) or coils

Whilst coils are extremely effective, very safe and have no effect on weight, they are not usually a first-choice method for youngsters, because fitting can be uncomfortable and periods may be a little more troublesome with a coil. Fitting a coil is more straightforward if the user has already had a baby because the neck of the womb is not so tight. However, there is a 'frameless coil' that is suitable for women who have not had a baby. A family planning doctor will advise whether a coil is suitable and arrange the fitting after full counselling about the method.

Other contraceptive methods

These include condoms, caps and crossing fingers! Neither of the first two methods affect weight. Condoms and caps are both barrier methods which are simple to use and widely available. A cap will need to be fitted and prescribed through a doctor and must be used with a spermicidal gel. Condoms and caps have a higher failure rate than the other methods listed above, but are still much better than crossing fingers (i.e. no contraceptive use at all!). Condoms can help reduce the risk of catching a sexually transmitted infection and can be used with hormonal methods such as the Pill to reduce failure rates even further.

The crossing fingers method is definitely associated with weight gain – that of an unplanned pregnancy.

Contraceptive advice may be obtained through any doctor; it does not need to be one's own family doctor if there are concerns about confidentiality. It is also available through family planning clinics and some school nurses. Many youth organisations are able to give advice and help with worries related to sex, contraception, relationships, saying 'no' and unplanned pregnancy. See Appendix 2 or the *Yellow Pages* for details of youth organisations.

Depression

Although there is a tendency to think of depression as an adult condition, it can affect younger people too. One problem is that it is not easy to diagnose – many youngsters have fluctuating episodes of unhappiness, even well-adjusted, straightforward people. But at the other end of the spectrum, some have sad, challenging home circumstances that would produce low mood in anybody. The distinction between going through a sad phase and actually suffering depression is still up for debate, but it is clear that some young people could be helped by seeing their sadness and despair as an illness, rather than as a 'bad mood' that should have passed off with a quick hug or a walk in the park.

What does depression feel like, and what has it to do with weight and eating?

Unless you have had depression, it is hard to imagine why the sufferer can't just pull their socks up and put a brave face on things. But shaking off depression is not the same as trying to cheer up after losing a football match. It is an illness and a surprisingly physical one too (*see* Box 11.4).

Box 11.4 Physical symptoms of depression

- Headaches
- Backache
- Tiredness and physical exhaustion
- Nausea and loss of appetite, leading to weight loss, or
- Excessive hunger, leading to binge eating and weight gain
- Abdominal gripes and diarrhoea
- Anxiety symptoms such as breathlessness, pins and needles and panic attack
- Blurred vision
- Tremor
- Hot flushes and mood swings

In addition to feeling sad, tearful and as though there is no light at the end of the tunnel, many people with depression feel that there is something physically wrong with them. Sometimes fear of an illness can be a reason why depression develops in the first place, and then the physical symptoms that depression brings make the sufferer quite convinced that the illness must be a reality. This can make it hard to accept that the real underlying problem is depression, but talking about these symptoms with a doctor can help to put the jigsaw together.

It is not just because depression can cause weight and appetite to fluctuate that it is included in this book; it is also very significant with regards to eating disorders, which are covered in Chapter 10.

In younger people who are not used to expressing how they feel and may not recognise how unhappy they have become, depression can appear as behaviour problems such as temper outbursts, an inability to get started with a task, school refusal, withdrawn behaviour, or aggressive or destructive tendencies.

A central problem with depression is loss of self-esteem so that the sufferer feels worthless and like a failure. They no longer feel able to face problems, feel a burden to other people and lack confidence in their abilities, thoughts and in other people. Following on from loss of self-esteem is a sense of pointlessness – it no longer seems worth making an effort because goals seem so distant and unobtainable as to be completely out of reach. This can cause family, friends and teachers to lose patience due to not understanding the reasons behind the lack of effort, which further adds to the sufferer's sense of being a failure and a burden and of being misunderstood.

In addition, when a person stops valuing themselves because self-esteem has vanished, it becomes far simpler to make the *easiest* choice rather than the *best* choice, and so the sufferer can be swept along into situations that they wouldn't usually have chosen.

Depression may come as a reaction to being in a difficult situation, such as being bullied or following family disruption, or there may be no obvious reason for confidence to vanish and for it to occur – it just happens.

What factors distinguish depression from sadness?

The main factor that distinguishes depression from sadness is the time-scale. Depression is not an occasional bad mood; it persists for weeks or, more usually, months, and occasionally years. It can be seen as a spectrum of symptoms, ranging from low moods, tearfulness and loss of interest at the milder end to suicidal thoughts and attempts to self-harm at the other.

Children and adolescents do not usually show the classical symptoms of depression that are found in adults – those of weight loss, sleep disturbance and strong feelings of guilt. Instead, they are more likely to be irritable, complain of headaches, run away from home, play truant or show a decline in schoolwork. These symptoms may also make a parent question whether their child has begun to experiment with drugs, because drug use can result in similar changes in outlook and mood. The fact that drug use can bring about depression and vice versa makes it harder still to understand what problems a person may be facing. Drug use will usually give other clues that depression alone wouldn't produce, such as a change in friends or problems with stealing in order to pay for drugs.

If symptoms have become persistent then it is advisable to discuss this with a family doctor. It is not a parent's job to diagnose the condition, rather to assist with finding help for problems that won't go away.

How may a young person with depression be helped?

'A problem shared is a problem halved.'

Talking about problems is a very valuable way to help anyone with depression. From a young person's view, life feels very complicated when facing complex grown-up problems with limited experience of how to deal with them – for example, caring for a disabled parent or being targeted by someone who is pushing drugs. Family support is less available nowadays because in many households both parents work, or they may live separately, so that youngsters do not get as much opportunity to share their feelings and problems. They may be more likely to seek guidance from equally young and inexperienced friends, through websites or from television, or to follow the example of celebrity role models than to ask a family member.

Putting time aside to share simple things with a depressed person may be a good way to show that a parent wants to listen and to help, whereas announcing a five-minute slot within which all issues must be done and dusted is likely to confirm their view that they don't count. In families that are not used to sharing emotional worries, it can take a bit of practice to 'open up' and the youngster may need reassurance that the person listening to their worries won't think they are silly or being pathetic.

Young people are often surprised to hear that adults also worry about silly things or may struggle to deal with problems. Having an emotional reaction to a problem is normal. Getting upset after a disaster is understandable and is something that everyone needs to work through. Anger may be justifiable, but it is essential to learn positive ways to deal with that anger and to put things in perspective.

Young people can learn techniques to help them cope better by using simple measures:

- Sleep will be improved by exercise earlier in the day and by fewer drinks late at night.
- Stopping watching scary films or playing violent computer games may allow nightmares or oppressive thoughts to fade away. Go for sports-related action entertainment if a buzz is required.
- Hiding the alarm clock will stop the irritation of clock watching in the small hours.
- Organising tasks to fill empty hours may give the day more structure and make it feel more manageable.
- Setting simple tasks that are easily achievable, such as making the bed or taking a daily shower, will generate both a sense of achievement and the start of feeling in control of life.
- Aggression can be eased by a physical workout – hitting a punch bag or kicking a ball.
- Positive thoughts can be practised – 'Is your glass half empty or is it half full?'
- Big problems can usually be broken down into smaller ones that are easier to tackle bit by bit – 'One step at a time'.
- There is no point worrying too much about potential problems that have not yet arrived – 'Cross that bridge when you get to it'.

Counselling is an effective approach, although gaining access to counselling on the NHS can be a problem because of long waiting lists. There are many youth services in most areas that can provide informal support and advice. See Appendix 2 for further information.

Unlike in adulthood, where antidepressant medication has been tried and tested and found to be beneficial, antidepressant use in people under 18 is controversial. Many studies have found very little benefit in giving antidepressants to this age group and some studies have shown worsening symptoms such that some antidepressants are no longer recommended in people under 18. However, they may be used in severe depression, where the benefits are more likely to outweigh the risks.

What is the risk of suicide in a young person with depression?

Suicide is rare in children and it is not strongly linked to depression. Suicidal attempts are more often related to aggression and use of alcohol or drugs, which can make a person react unpredictably and out of character. Teenagers are also at more risk of a suicide attempt following an emotional crisis such as a relationship split, than from a grumbling depression.

Never brush off a young person's remarks if they include ideas of self-harm, regardless of whether their low mood is a new problem or something that has cropped up before; seek advice promptly from a doctor or casualty department, or try phoning a support service such as The Samaritans (08457 909090), or see their website www.samaritans.org.uk or email them at Jo@samaritans.org. Alternatively, look in the *Yellow Pages* for a local phone number as they have over 200 local support offices.

Happily, there has been a reduction in the rate of suicide since the change in law regarding the sale of paracetamol in the UK, so that only small quantities can be sold. Despite wide scepticism amongst the general public about this legislation, it has been shown to be helpful. Making large quantities of tablets less easy to obtain – which includes keeping only limited supplies in the home too – will reduce the chance of both accidental and planned self-poisoning.

Diabetes

Diabetes (or diabetes mellitus, as it is sometimes called) occurs when blood sugar (glucose) is higher than normal. There are two main types: type 1 diabetes and type 2 diabetes.

Type 1 diabetes usually develops in children or young adults and is also known as juvenile or insulin-dependent diabetes. It is not uncommon, occurring in around one in 250 people. The problem occurs when the body stops producing insulin – which is the hormone that regulates blood sugar – and so blood sugar levels creep up and up until the person becomes very unwell.

It comes on quickly over days or weeks and common symptoms include thirst, passing a lot of urine, tiredness, weight loss and feeling unwell. If it is left untreated, the person will become dehydrated and may lapse into a coma. The condition requires treatment for life with daily insulin injections to replace the insulin that the body no longer produces.

Type 2 diabetes is usually a condition of later life and it is strongly linked to obesity. Because obesity is now very common and is affecting more and more young people, this has led to cases of type 2 diabetes being found in childhood too. It is also called late-onset diabetes or non-insulin-dependent or diet-controlled diabetes. The problem is that even though the body continues to produce insulin, it does not produce enough and the cells of the body are unable to use what is there. This is called 'insulin resistance' and causes blood sugar to gradually creep up, but this usually comes on more slowly than in type 1 diabetes.

Symptoms include thirst, passing a lot of urine, tiredness, weight loss and feeling generally unwell, just as in type 1 diabetes, but many people actually have no symptoms and the condition may go unnoticed for some time.

Both types can be detected by a simple 'dipstick' test on a urine specimen, which is then confirmed by a blood sample.

What problems does diabetes cause?

If diabetes is untreated or poorly controlled it causes problems both in the short and in the long term.

Short-term problems

- When sugar levels rise, it causes the body to produce more urine, causing thirst, dehydration and the need to pass more urine, especially at night. This can lead to drowsiness and a serious illness called ketosis, but it is very treatable if prompt help is sought.
- Some people wrongly believe that being off their food due to flu or a stomach bug will mean less insulin is needed because they are not eating. In fact the opposite is usually true – the illness makes blood sugar rise and so insulin often needs to be increased. If a diabetic person feels unwell for any reason, it is important to check sugar levels more frequently and adjust insulin accordingly.
- Too much insulin can cause problems too: if sugar levels go too low (hypoglycaemia) a person will feel sweaty, confused, unwell and may lose consciousness. This can be treated by giving sugar in the form of sweets, a sugary drink or an injection of glucagon – a hormone that has the opposite effect to insulin. Some young children have been saviours to their diabetic parents by knowing that if their parent becomes drowsy they should pop a sweet in their mouth and call for help.

Long-term problems

It is very important for anyone with diabetes to keep their sugar levels as well controlled as possible because good control reduces the chance of long-term problems.

Too much sugar in the bloodstream is a bit like having 'dirty' blood rather than 'clean' blood circulating. Using a hosepipe analogy: if dirty water runs through the pipe, eventually some of the dirt sticks to the walls and clogs it up so that less water can pass through. It is exactly the same with diabetes: high sugar levels make blood vessel walls become clogged up with something called 'atheroma' and this causes hardening as well as narrowing of the arteries. This can mean that some organs in the body gradually become short of blood and oxygen, causing heart attacks, stroke and problems with circulation in the legs. It can also damage the kidneys and nerves and create problems with vision.

However, atheroma is not only caused by diabetes: other problems that clog up blood vessels include a high cholesterol level, high blood pressure, smoking and getting too little exercise. Aiming to keep fit and healthy, keep weight under control and not to smoke are all very important aspects for someone with diabetes, because all these measures will help to keep their blood a bit 'cleaner' and reduce the chance of diabetic-related conditions.

How is diabetes controlled?

There are three main aims for diabetic treatment:

1 The first is to control blood sugar as carefully as possible. Type 1 diabetes requires lifelong daily insulin, which is given by injection because it cannot be

absorbed through the gut. After diagnosis, a newly diabetic person will have tuition in how to measure their blood sugar and give themselves injections. This can be hard to accept for some people, but support is available for those who are having difficulties. Sometimes poor control can be a sign that the person has not come to terms with their illness, and addressing worries and feelings may be more useful than another lecture on insulin. Type 2 diabetes is treated at first by changes to the diet, as outlined below. If this does not give enough improvement then tablets may be added, and some people also go on to insulin injections if their sugar levels remain hard to control.

2 The second aim for all diabetic people is to encourage them to be as healthy as possible in other ways. This means getting weight under control (which on its own can give a huge improvement in blood sugar levels in type 2 diabetes), avoiding smoking, monitoring and treating blood pressure, checking and treating cholesterol, and encouraging general fitness. Getting regular exercise has all sorts of benefits, including:
    • regulating blood sugar levels
    • helping insulin to work more effectively
    • reducing weight
    • improving cholesterol and blood pressure
    • keeping the heart stronger and healthier
    • reducing stress and promoting good sleep.

3 The third aim is to keep diabetes under regular review to check that control is good and to look out for any early signs of complications. The earlier problems are picked up, the sooner they can be tackled, and so regular monitoring is a vital part of diabetic care.

What is a 'diabetic diet'?

In days gone by, people used to believe that diabetics needed to eat a special diet, but that is not true. We could all do with eating a 'diabetic diet' because it simply means a healthy diet. *The Balance of Good Health* – referred to throughout this book – contains the ideal diet for someone with diabetes because it focuses on getting the right balance of healthy foods without too many rich ingredients.

In particular, someone with diabetes should:

• eat at least three meals per day, each including starchy foods such as multigrain bread, potatoes, rice or pasta. These foods release glucose into the bloodstream more slowly than sugary foods, so that the person's insulin has a better chance of working effectively
• eat plenty of fruit, vegetables, wholegrain cereals and pulses
• go for sugar-free drinks
• limit sugary foods or foods with a high glycaemic index (*see* the section on glycaemic index in Chapter 9). The more sugar a person eats, the more insulin that will be needed to deal with it, and so a low-sugar diet can help diabetic control for both types of diabetes
• reduce the fat content of the diet
• watch out for added salt and reduce salt intake because too much salt causes blood pressure to rise
• aim to eat healthily most days of the week, even if it doesn't happen every day.

Foods labelled 'for diabetics' are unnecessary and often expensive. Instead, sort out the basics of a healthy diet using *The Balance of Good Health*, and seek advice from a registered dietician to boost knowledge and confidence at the beginning. Most people who are newly diagnosed will be referred for dietary advice through their family doctor as part of their initial care.

Diarrhoea and gastroenteritis

The cause of most bouts of diarrhoea is usually viral, producing a sudden illness that may include vomiting, loss of appetite, abdominal gripes and watery diarrhoea. As with other viral infections, the symptoms usually drag on for several days but can last up to a fortnight. If diarrhoea persists for more than a few days, and especially if there is any blood in the motion, it is wise to get a medical check to ensure that there is no sign of dehydration and to clarify the cause of the symptoms.

There is no need to forbid solids, but be guided by appetite when deciding whether to eat. Encourage plenty of fluids, but avoid drinks that are very sugary as these can worsen symptoms. Very dilute squash is suitable for the first few days. If symptoms persist then oral rehydration sachets, which are available in pharmacies, will provide the correct balance of sugar and salt to replace what has been lost. Because viral infections cause flu-like symptoms, including aching and general malaise, paracetamol will help settle these and will not worsen the diarrhoea.

Most diarrhoeal viruses are infectious, so take care with hygiene and hand washing and avoid close contact. Avoid sharing towels and kitchen utensils with an affected person.

Inflammatory conditions of the gut

There are two diseases, *Crohn's disease* and *ulcerative colitis*, that cause ulceration of the small or large bowel, producing frequent bouts of diarrhoea, the passage of blood or mucus, weight loss and a general feeling of being unwell. There may also be anaemia, arthritis and some skin conditions. Neither condition is common but both may sometimes start in childhood. If a young person is unwell with persisting diarrhoea and weight loss, a family doctor will check whether these conditions could be present. If so, then specialist care will be arranged to plan treatment. This usually involves tablets but surgery is sometimes needed.

Irritable bowel syndrome

Irritable bowel syndrome, or IBS, is very common, affecting around one in five people at some point. Whilst it usually starts in early adult life, it can affect youngsters too. Symptoms include painful gut spasms, especially before passing a motion, bloating, and a change in motion with either diarrhoea or constipation, or sometimes an intermittent mixture of both. Some people find their motions become small and pellet-like, or may be mixed with mucus. Other people have urgency, meaning they suddenly have to dash to the toilet with little advance warning. Other symptoms include headache, passing excessive wind and feeling sick.

One symptom that is not part of IBS is the passing of blood from the back passage. If this occurs it should be discussed with a doctor.

Many sufferers find their symptoms come and go and are often worse during times of stress. It is not known what causes IBS, but overactivity of the nerves or muscles of the gut seems to play a large part. Occasionally, a person may discover that a food sensitivity triggered IBS, or it may have arisen after an infection of the gut that never seemed to fully settle.

What treatments are there?

- Reassurance from a doctor is often the only thing that many people require. Knowing that a more serious condition has been ruled out and then finding out some facts about IBS can help to put minds at rest, which can ease the severity of symptoms.
- Dietary fibre is a useful treatment that helps to bulk up the motion as it passes through the gut. This makes it easier for the gut to work without having to gripe and clamp down. There are two sorts of dietary fibre: soluble and insoluble fibre. Some sufferers find that insoluble fibre, such as that found in bran and wheat products, can make diarrhoea worse. It is worth seeing if soluble oat bran, such as in porridge, is more suitable. Some people find that eating varied wholegrain cereals or bread is the easiest way to incorporate fibre without worsening symptoms. Further information about fibre is given in Chapter 5 'Nutritional basics for young people'.
- Moving towards low-fat eating is often associated with an improvement in irritable bowel symptoms. It is not clear if this link is due to fat triggering symptoms or whether people who are focusing on low-fat eating tend to eat more wholegrain and high-fibre foods instead.
- Antispasmodic tablets are medicines that relax the muscles of the gut wall. There are several different types that work in different ways, so be prepared to try more than one if the first treatment seems ineffective. Some are available over the counter in pharmacies, but others need to be prescribed by a doctor.
- Relaxation techniques and counselling treatments can help some people to improve IBS, particularly those who find their symptoms are linked to worry and stress. Certain antidepressants have a calming effect on the gut in addition to their antidepressant action, and so may be prescribed if symptoms are persistent or severe.

Polycystic ovary syndrome

Polycystic ovaries are becoming more widely known about, partly because the condition is commoner in women who are overweight, which is on the increase, and partly because ultrasound scanning is performed more often, which is how the condition is picked up. An incidental finding of polycystic ovaries is nothing to worry about: approximately one in ten women will have them to some degree, and if there are no associated symptoms, weight is in the normal range and the menstrual cycle is regular, then nothing more need be said – they are a variation of normal.

Polycystic ovary syndrome (PCOS) is slightly different because it is linked with period problems, reduced fertility, hair growth and acne. It is also linked with being overweight, developing diabetes, high blood pressure and raised cholesterol because of its link with insulin control.

What is the cause of PCOS?

This is complex and is not yet fully understood, but there is a strong link with insulin – the hormone that controls blood sugar. In PCOS there is *insulin resistance*, which usually means there are higher levels of insulin circulating around the body. Not only does insulin act on fat and muscle cells to take in sugar and thereby keep the sugar level controlled, it also stimulates the ovaries to produce a male hormone, testosterone, which interferes with the normal hormone cycle. Higher insulin levels mean higher testosterone and this leads to some of the symptoms of PCOS – hair growth, acne and irregular periods.

Instead of releasing one egg each month, the ovaries become rather 'sleepy and indecisive', producing lots of small follicles or cysts (which can be seen on ultrasound scan), none of which become mature enough to release an egg. Therefore, women with PCOS may find that their periods are irregular, very infrequent or even absent, which may lead to difficulty getting pregnant.

What about treatment?

The best way to control PCOS is by weight loss, if overweight. This helps to reduce high insulin levels and hence testosterone too. This means that the normal hormonal cycle can settle back down again, so that periods are likely to return. Hair growth and acne are sensitive to testosterone and so these are likely to improve too.

Any weight-reducing eating plan can work, but for the best benefits weight loss should be maintained or the condition will return. Using *The Balance of Good Health* and the healthy eating tips listed in the diabetes section of this chapter will help insulin levels to improve and should boost long-term healthy lifestyle changes.

Happily, for those people concerned about their ability to get pregnant, PCOS is a treatable condition. The ovaries can be 'booted into action' using ovulation-inducing tablets if lifestyle changes alone do not regulate the cycle and stimulate ovulation. Also, there is increasing evidence that a treatment used for diabetes, called metformin, can improve insulin resistance and may boost fertility in PCOS.

For those women who do not wish to get pregnant, PCOS can be overridden by use of the combined oral contraceptive pill if lifestyle improvements have been difficult to maintain. A family planning clinic or GP will be able to recommend the most suitable pill, which will create a regular cycle and also keep the lining of the womb healthy. In a young woman, having no periods at all for a prolonged time, whilst sounding convenient, can lead to abnormal cells developing and this can, in rare circumstances, lead to cancer of the uterus (womb). Regular periods, whether from lifestyle improvements or from the Pill, will take away this increased risk.

It is important to use a method of contraception even if periods are very infrequent, because even sleepy, polycystic ovaries will sometimes release an egg, which could be fertilised if no contraception is being used.

Unwanted hair can be removed by shaving, waxing, using creams or by electrolysis or laser treatments. The combined oral contraceptive pill can also have a good effect on reducing hair growth as well as controlling acne, but may take months to build up improvement.

Further information is available through Verity, a UK self-help group that provides information about PCOS, at www.verity-pcos.org.uk.

Premenstrual syndrome

For the majority of women periods are a minor inconvenience, but for some the menstrual cycle is accompanied by a monthly pattern of weight gain, fluid retention, breast tenderness, bad moods and tiredness, otherwise known as premenstrual syndrome or PMS. Symptoms build up during the week leading up to a period and then resolve once bleeding begins. Some women find the symptoms are troublesome for a day or two only, but others find the symptoms seem to creep up from as early as mid-cycle and may hardly fade by the end of the period, so that they feel there is only one good week in every four.

These changes are linked to ovulation, and so using a contraceptive method that blocks ovulation, such as the combined pill, Depo-Provera or Implanon, should abolish premenstrual syndrome, as will pregnancy.

There can be a tendency to link too many symptoms under the same umbrella, such that each and every new symptom is somehow blamed on the main problem, even though they may be unrelated. For example, if someone is prone to painful periods and premenstrual syndrome, she may also think that her aching back or stress symptoms stem from it too, whereas they are more likely to be related to muscle strains or to the complexities of life. It is unhelpful to link too many symptoms to one problem because it makes that problem very hard to improve. Treating each symptom at face value and breaking problems down into small aspects are more likely to result in at least partial treatment success.

What treatments work for premenstrual syndrome?

As already mentioned, because premenstrual syndrome is caused by ovulation, blocking ovulation can be an effective treatment and many women find it is an unexpected benefit of the combined pill and Depo-Provera.

Although different varieties and strengths of cyclical progestogens (i.e. taken for part of the cycle but not every day) have been tried for many years, there is no convincing evidence of benefit in premenstrual syndrome. Progestogens given continuously for contraception may help if ovulation is blocked, resulting in periods stopping, although the mini-pill does not block ovulation in all women, hence the effect is not guaranteed. However, there are some dietary supplements that have shown some benefit. Vitamin B_6, or pyridoxine, in a dose of up to 100 mg a day, helps some women. This dose should not be exceeded because of the risk of toxic side-effects. Calcium, magnesium and vitamin E have all given some positive results in trials, as have St John's wort and homeopathic remedies.

Acupuncture has been of value for painful periods, but not other symptoms of premenstrual syndrome. The herbal remedy evening primrose oil has long been used for cyclical breast tenderness. Although the evidence behind this treatment is not concrete, some women may find it worth a try.

Teenage pregnancy and nutrition

Pregnancy during the teenage years puts a significant strain on a teenager's nourishment because she may still be growing herself and not yet have put down adequate fat, mineral or vitamin stores to support a pregnancy easily. This can mean that the teenage mother is competing with her growing baby for available nutrients. In particular, iron is in big demand, as are the B vitamins and folate, plus iodine and zinc. There is no need to 'eat for two' in pregnancy; rather, eating healthily for one is a good idea.

Dietary advice for pregnant teenagers

- Encourage a healthy, balanced diet and monitor this if necessary by adding up the daily intake of fruit and vegetables and looking at what protein-containing foods are eaten.
- Avoid restricting calorie intake. If a pregnant youngster has been concerned about being overweight before she became pregnant, encourage regular exercise to improve fitness and a balanced diet as above, but put any plans for weight reduction to one side until after the pregnancy.
- Monitor weight gain and seek advice from a doctor or midwife if it is poor in pregnancy, or if weight is low for height at the beginning of the pregnancy (i.e. BMI below 20).
- Advise folic acid supplements in the first 12 weeks of a pregnancy, but preferably start before the fetus is conceived. Folic acid is needed for healthy development of the baby's spine and so extra folic acid in early pregnancy reduces the risk of spina bifida and neural tube defects. 400 micrograms (mcg) is the recommended daily supplement, in addition to a folate-rich diet. Folic acid tablets are readily available in pharmacies or through a family doctor. It is found in leafy green vegetables, pulses, beans, nuts and citrus fruit, and also in yeast extract and spreads such as Marmite, as well as being added to many breakfast cereals.
- Encourage an iron-rich diet, which is discussed in Chapter 5 'Nutritional basics for young people'.
- Encourage plenty of low-fat dairy products to ensure a good source of both calcium and protein. If the pregnant person is underweight then choose full-fat dairy products.
- A multivitamin and mineral supplement designed for pregnancy may be advisable. Stick to well-known brands and discuss with a pharmacist if not sure which to try. Do not overdo vitamins as this can cause problems.
- A young mother will benefit from eating healthily after her baby is born, which will help breastfeeding and also set a good example for her own child to copy as he or she grows.
- Breastfeeding is the best start for any baby, so find out more from the breastfeeding organisations listed in Appendix 2. The companion book, *Weight Matters for Children*, also contains plenty of tips to help get breastfeeding established.

Thyroid disorders

The thyroid gland is a small gland at the base of the neck, which produces a hormone called thyroxine. Thyroxine controls many things, including our rate of metabolism, body temperature, growth and development. The thyroid gland can be both underactive, which is a fairly common condition, and overactive, which is less frequent.

If the gland is underactive this causes *hypothyroidism*, where metabolism and growth slow down. This causes tiredness, especially after exercise, weight gain, constipation, clumsiness, and poor concentration and attention. A goitre may develop, which is a soft swelling at the base of the neck due to bulging of the thyroid gland.

If the gland is overactive this is called *hyperthyroidism*, where the metabolic rate is too fast. This can make a person feel very unwell, with weight loss, tremor, difficulty with concentration, and agitation that may lead to disruptive behaviour and poor school or work performance.

Both conditions may run in families and are usually an *autoimmune* condition, where the body's own immune system has started to think that the thyroid gland doesn't belong. The body's defences attack the gland and either stop it from working (hypothyroidism) or actually make it go into overdrive (hyperthyroidism).

If there is any suspicion of a thyroid problem, the diagnosis is easy to confirm with a blood test and treatment can then be arranged. If a person has a tendency to be overweight and is then found to have an underactive thyroid, do not expect thyroxine replacement to solve the weight problem on its own. Weight always needs a concerted effort for it to change, although health drives may become easier once the thyroid is better controlled.

Tooth decay

Although teeth seem incredibly hard, they are susceptible to attack in the form of both tooth decay and gum disease. This creates problems in four areas:

- the cosmetic appearance of teeth
- their ability to do their job, i.e. to chew food
- pain and discomfort from infections of the teeth and gums
- loss of teeth altogether from decay, dental abscess or gum disease.

When affected by tooth decay (also known as dental caries), brown patches develop on the tooth's surface, which leads to collapse of the underlying part of the tooth, forming a cavity. Cavities can be treated by a dentist, using fillings of either silver-coloured amalgam or a whitish material that matches the rest of the tooth. However, if left untreated, infection can travel down the tooth and into the jaw where it can form an abscess. Once an abscess forms, the tooth usually has to be pulled out altogether unless root canal treatment is possible. Either way, the condition is painful and unpleasant, but happily is very much avoidable.

What causes tooth decay?

Tooth decay is caused by a combination of bacteria in the mouth plus sugar. Mouth bacteria produce plaque acids which dissolve minerals in the tooth's hard surface, leading to the brown patches referred to above. However, bacteria alone do not do much damage. It is only when there is a steady supply of sugar in the mouth that tooth decay really becomes a problem, as bacteria use sugar to produce the plaque acid that does the damage. The acid attack that bacteria plus sugar produce takes about 20 minutes to fade away, and each time more sugar arrives in the mouth, bacteria wake up and do more damage. It is best to eat food, sweets, treats and sugary drinks only at mealtimes so that the mouth can remain empty in between meals in order to reduce the amount of tooth decay.

Eating acidic foods causes further damage in a slightly different way, by causing dental erosion. This is where the hard enamel surface of the teeth is thinned or worn away, leaving teeth that feel sensitive to hot and cold and are at greater risk of tooth decay.

What causes gum disease?

Gum disease is caused by plaque, which is the slimy film of bacteria that builds up on teeth. When this forms next to the gum it can cause infection and damage, making the gums sore, sensitive and likely to bleed easily. If gum disease persists, it can lead to teeth becoming loose and thus at increased risk of infection.

It is best to use a toothbrush with a small head and soft bristles, in order not to damage the gums when brushing teeth.

How can tooth decay and dental erosion be avoided?

There are three different approaches that, in combination, will greatly reduce the chance of tooth decay and dental erosion:

1   *Tooth brushing.* Teeth should be brushed twice a day using fluoride toothpaste, ensuring that impacted food is completely removed from the surface of the back teeth in particular. Fluoride toothpaste will help to refresh the mouth in addition to strengthening teeth against decay because fluoride is an essential part of tooth enamel.
2   *Eating and drinking.* Sugar between meals causes tooth decay and so cutting this out is a great way to protect teeth. The longer the mouth is empty between meals, the better it is for teeth. Sugary foods can be eaten at mealtimes without worry, but if snacks are wanted in between meals then they should be low or preferably absent in sugar. See the section on safe snacks in Chapter 7, 'The Food Frequency Framework', for further ideas. Candy, sweets, chocolate and sweetened drinks should all be reserved for mealtimes in order to have least effect on teeth. If they are eaten between meals, they should be consumed as quickly as possible instead of sucked or eaten slowly, in order to cause least damage. Fizzy drinks, even low-sugar varieties, as well as fruit juice, have a bad effect on teeth because they are acidic, which can lead to dental erosion in addition to tooth decay, and so they are best kept to a minimum and consumed at mealtimes rather than in between meals.
3   *Visiting the dentist.* Regular dental check-ups are important for everyone, even if teeth appear to be in good shape. The dentist will look for any early signs of tooth decay and will give help and advice on good tooth brushing and general mouth hygiene. The dentist may recommend 'disclosing tablets' to teach people to clean teeth well and find out if there are areas that their toothbrush tends to miss.

▶▶The Top Teen Health Plan◀◀

The Top Teen Health Plan shows you how to work out your health strengths and weaknesses and then explores different ways to look at problems before going on to find practical and workable solutions.

Introduction

Are you worried about your weight? Have you been teased because of your appearance? Do your parents nag about the way you eat? Have you already tried dieting?

If the answer to any of these questions is 'Yes' then you are not alone.

Up to a third of young people are teased or bullied because of their appearance and at least a third of girls in the early teenage years are trying to diet, with many more young people having tried dieting at some time or other.

But think of the extreme of anorexia nervosa. Dieting isn't the key to happiness; it isn't the answer to feeling good about yourself or feeling in control. It's just a good way to pile on more pressure.

The Top Teen Health Plan looks at healthy ways to make a difference to how you feel; it looks at understanding how to make good choices – sometimes surprisingly easy choices in fact. Living healthily isn't a mystery and doesn't require regular doses of raw cabbage, spray-on Lycra or colonic irrigation. Read on to find out easy routes to feeling happy inside as well as looking great on the outside.

Start with finding out facts about yourself before looking for solutions

The first step is to sort out your baseline – what are you like right now? Once you know where you stand then you can plan some changes. The Top Teen Health Plan will guide you through the following five questions, suggesting solutions and improvements along the way – but before you read on, why not answer them very briefly now? You can then look back at your answers when you've finished reading the whole Plan to see if you still think the same way.

Your baseline questions

What is your current eating pattern like?	Great	So so	Dire!
Is your weight okay for your height and age? Do you think you are:	Overweight	About right	Underweight
What is important to you about your health?	Looking good	Feeling good	It isn't important
What aspects would you *really* like to change?	Your weight	Your fitness	Nothing much
Whose opinions count most?	Your own	Your friends' opinions	Your parents' opinions

Fill in your food diary score sheet

Find out if you are a nutritional angel or a junk-food demon with this easy food diary. If possible, fill out the diary each day for a week, then add up each row's score and tot up the running total. Your score will give you a good idea of where you are starting from – but bear in mind the comments in the scoring guide. The food diary gives plenty of points for regular exercise, which could cover up a diet of junk food.

You could cheat and get a rough idea by estimating your usual diet and filling in the diary at one sitting, although this may give you false reassurance about your lifestyle if you're not honest with yourself.

As you will find, you can score easy points by simply drinking water or eating breakfast – but points are equally easy to lose if that breakfast consists of a hash brown and breakfast burger from a fast food outlet!

Note: some foods will not fit obviously into the food diary so use your common sense about what type of food it is – perhaps think what might replace it as an alternative to see where it should fit on the chart.

It doesn't matter that all foods are not classified because the purpose of the food diary is to give an idea of how healthy your basic diet is, rather than a detailed nutritional analysis of it.

Some foods will score a positive and a negative point at the same time. For example, eating a burger in a fast-food restaurant would score a point each for the bread roll and the burger (but to call half a lettuce leaf or a pickled gherkin a portion of salad would be stretching things!). However, you would lose points if the burger was accompanied by chips and a shake or fizzy drink, plus lose another point for visiting a fast-food outlet. Overall, such a visit would score either no points or negative points because fast food does not contribute much to a healthy balanced diet.

The colour version of the food diary score sheet is available for printing/downloading at www.radcliffe-oxford.com/youngpeople

Food diary score sheet

Item	Points available per portion	Monday	Tuesday	Wednesday	Thursday	Friday	Saturday	Sunday	Points scored	Running total
Nutritional basics										
Portions of fruit and vegetables	1 each portion									
Slices of bread, rolls, naan, pitta, plain crackers	White = 1 Wholegrain = 2									
Potatoes (not chips), rice, pasta, noodles, couscous	1 each portion or 2 if unpeeled potato or wholegrain									
Breakfast of any description (not mid-morning snack)	1 point									
Dairy products Milk – each 200 ml or ⅓ pint Yoghurt – 150g pot or milk dessert Cheese portion	1 each portion Size of a small matchbox/25 g of hard cheese									
Meat, fish and other protein sources Processed, e.g. burgers, fishcakes Unprocessed, e.g. steak Quorn	1 2 1									
Pulses, lentils, kidney beans, nuts, seeds	1 each portion									
Eggs	1 per egg									
Water, tap or bottled	1 per glass									*

Total of nutrition points = 'yellow' nutritional basics score =

Food diary score sheet (*cont.*)

Item	Points available per portion	Monday	Tuesday	Wednesday	Thursday	Friday	Saturday	Sunday	Points scored	Running total
Lifestyle points										
Exercise (that makes the heart beat faster, rather than a stroll)	1 point for each 5 minute bout									
Smoking										**
Long-term non smoker (for at least three months)	5 points daily									
Ex-smoker or currently trying to stop and not smoked in last week	1 point									
Occasional smoker, smoking most weeks	Minus 2 points									
Current smoker, most days or every day, regardless of amount	Minus 5 points daily									

Total of lifestyle points = 'green' lifestyle-uplift score =

Junk foods – take points away!										
Crisps or savoury snacks – 30g packet	Minus 1 per packet									
Chips	Minus 1 per portion									
Sweet snack items such as chocolate bars or doughnuts. NB up to 1 slice of cake or three biscuits score zero, but larger daily amounts score 1 for each extra portion	Minus 1 point									
Can or bottle of fizzy drink (not diet) or highly sweetened or alcoholic drinks	Minus 1 per portion									
Chewy sweets or other confectionery	Minus 1 per packet									
Any visit to fast-food outlet	Minus 1 per visit									***

Total of junk foods points = 'red' reduction score =

Scoring

Add the 'yellow' nutritional basics and 'green' lifestyle-uplift scores then take away the 'red' reduction in order to calculate your overall food diary score. But it is not just your final score that tells you about your current lifestyle: look at the nutritional basics score in the 'yellow' box (*), the lifestyle-uplift score in the 'green' box (**), and the red reduction in the 'red' box (***) when working out what your score means.

	Perfect lifestyle	Passable lifestyle	Poor lifestyle
'Yellow' nutritional basics score*	Eating recommended amounts of the basics would score around 145 points.	Scores over 70 will contain a reasonable amount of good nutrition.	Scores under 70 are likely to be short on essentials.
'Green' lifestyle-uplift score**	The recommended hour of activity every day would score 84 points, with 35 bonus points for not smoking.	Scores above 42 will indicate a rough average of half an hour of exercise most days. Active attempts to stop smoking will add another 7.	Scores below 42 are well short of healthy activity levels and regular smoking may push this into negative figures. Occasional smoking scores badly because nicotine is so addictive that most occasional smokers will eventually smoke regularly.
'Red' reduction score***	The healthiest diets will contain only one or two rich treat items daily, giving a score of less than 14.	Keeping the 'red' reduction below 21 will prevent junk food from ruining the overall balance of the diet.	'Red' reductions over 21 indicate that junk food is replacing healthier basics.
Total score	An ideal well-balanced diet and lifestyle would give a score of around 250 – a nutritional angel!	Scores over 100 show that at least the minimum is there, but there is plenty of room for improvement.	Scores below 100 need looking at because the basics are missing! See below.

Score between 50 and 100

Low 'yellow', high 'green' and moderate 'red' reduction: 'running on empty'! This is the 'lifestyle-uplift' score. Any good nutrition shown by your 'yellow' score is cancelled out by your 'red' reduction, leaving you with a score that reflects your active lifestyle. Although you might get away with this lifestyle as an active youngster, your diet will let you down in the long run if your exercise levels reduce or if you start smoking. If you are keen on sports then your performance could improve if you boost the nutritional side of things. Are you getting enough dairy products, fruit and vegetables, and protein to match your activity levels? Currently you are 'running on empty'!

Moderate 'yellow', moderate 'green' and big 'red' reduction: 'running on rubbish'!

This score suggests you are not that bothered about your lifestyle. You eat as you want without paying much attention to details. This means you are eating more junk than is healthy and as you get older (when exercise levels may reduce) your lifestyle could start letting you down. Smoking may be cancelling out the benefits of any exercise you get. Junk food is making up a significant part of your diet – are you happy to run the risk of becoming overweight? Right now you are 'running on rubbish'!

Score below 50

Low 'yellow', low 'green' and big 'red' reduction: 'standing still and gasping'!

Oh dear! If you haven't seized up already then it won't be long. How can you expect to get through life with no petrol in the tank? It's all very well oiling the engine parts (with all that junk), but you have to run the engine (get some exercise) and put some decent fuel in the tank (nutrition) in order to keep your body machinery going. If smoking is piled on top of a poor lifestyle then you are begging for trouble. Your body has to last your whole lifetime – you can't just trade it in for a new model.

There are all sorts of avenues for improvement, whether it is adding in some of the nutritious things, reducing some of the junk or simply putting activity higher up your priority list. You may already be carrying too much weight for your height and age (see following section), but don't panic because it is never too late for young people to change. Read on for lots of ideas on what you can do.

Action points

Aim to increase your food diary score by pushing up the 'yellow' and 'green' scores and making sure you don't lose too many 'red' points. Getting the balance of your diet right is a crucial part of eating healthily – a bit of junk food is not a problem if there are plenty of the good things there too.

For further information, read about *The Balance of Good Health* in Chapter 1. There is also plenty more nutritional information in Chapter 5, 'Nutritional basics for young people', and information to help people stop smoking in Appendix 2.

Is your weight ok for your height and age?

The best way to monitor growth is with growth charts

The best way to check out your growth is by plotting height and weight measurements on a growth chart that covers your age group (*see* Appendix 1). Once you reach the age of 18 you can use adult guidelines, as described below.

When looking at a growth chart, whether for weight or for height, there will be a series of centile lines ranging from the 0.4th centile right up to the 99.6th centile. The 50th centile line represents the national average (as things stood in 1990) for white British children. Unfortunately, as so many children and young people are developing weight problems today, we now find that far more than half the population fall above the 50th centile line.

There are slightly different trends for children of other races, with Asians tending to be lighter and shorter and African-Caribbean people tending to be heavier and taller on average.

If a person is within a healthy range then their height and weight will fall on roughly the same centile lines. So if weight is on the 95th centile, it is not a problem if height is also on the 95th centile. In the same way, a person whose height and weight both fall on the 3rd centile may be petite but perfectly healthy, rather than underweight.

If height and weight fall on different centile lines then you will need to calculate your body mass index in order to see if you still fall within a healthy range.

What is body mass index?

The body mass index, or BMI, gives a good (but not perfect) idea of how much body fat you are carrying in relation to your height.

$$\text{BMI} = \frac{\text{weight (in kilograms)}}{\text{height squared (in metres)}}$$

For adults over 18 years, BMI provides a simple guide to whether weight matches height appropriately, as outlined in the table.

Adult body mass index guide (this does not apply under age 18)

BMI under 18.5	BMI between 18.5 and 24.9	BMI between 25 and 29.9	BMI between 30 and 39.9	BMI over 40
Underweight	Normal weight	Overweight	Obese	Morbidly obese*

* Morbid obesity means that there is a very high chance of developing weight-related illnesses, especially diabetes.

For younger people, the BMI is more complex because it varies from birth to adulthood and is different between boys and girls. But it is still useful when plotted on a chart for comparison against the appropriate expected range. BMI charts for boys and girls up to 20 years of age are given in Appendix 1. An online calculator for working out and interpreting a young person's BMI is also available at www.healthforallchildren.co.uk on the parent's page.

Get a rough idea if measurements are not available

If there are no weight or height measurements available, you can still gain a rough idea about your shape from the following aspects:

• Clothes size. Whilst there is enormous variation in both people and clothing manufacturers' sizing of clothes, they can still give an idea about whether you are near the average or way off. Once you stop growing in height your weight should start to plateau too. A sign that your height and weight do not match up is if waistbands are always too tight when leg length seems to fit. For girls, if your clothing size is keeping pace with your age then you are probably developing a weight problem. Check things out with proper measurements to be sure.

- Compare with friends of the same age. Once again, with such huge variations in healthy growth patterns, it may not be helpful to compare one person next to another. However, if you physically stand out from all your mates of the same age, monitor height and weight more accurately to see whether it is you or the rest of them that are way off average.
- Teasing from others. Sadly, tact is not always a strong point of young people and anyone who stands out from the crowd is likely to know about it. Teasing about weight or height is very common and can lead to loss of confidence and unhappiness at school or college, with reluctance to take part in physical exercise or swimming. If you have started to feel self-conscious and worried about your appearance because of teasing, then there are plenty of ways to help yourself without needing to go on a diet. The Top Teen Health Plan looks at building self-esteem so that teasing and bullying will have less impact. By improving health, fitness and overall diet, you will become more confident in yourself even if your weight does not change significantly. Bullies do not tend to pick on confident people, however they look.
- Family trends. If family members tend to be on the large size then the same tendency may apply to you too. It is very common for children of overweight parents to become overweight themselves due to learning the same eating habits. In addition, the family genes may be partly, but not wholly, responsible.
- Worrying signs. No one needs to store rolls of fat even if they are in the middle of a growth spurt. It is far more efficient to store excess food in kitchen cupboards than lug it around all day on your person. Watch out for signs of a 'spare tyre' around your midriff or a tummy that hangs over your waistband. Your ribs should normally be visible as you raise and lower your arms.

What do your findings mean?

Now that you know whether or not your height and weight match up, what does it mean? Were you surprised to find that you are about right or concerned to find that you are overweight? What should you do if you are underweight for your height and age?

The section below gives you an idea of which direction to follow.

Overweight for your height and age

So you are overweight. Were you surprised? Are you bothered?

It would be good if you *were* surprised because that means you will begin to think about an aspect of you that you simply hadn't thought about before. The sooner you start to put in some good ground rules for yourself, the healthier and happier you will become. Change doesn't happen quickly, so prepare yourself for gradual improvements rather than a quick fix.

If you weren't surprised and find that you do not feel too bothered either, the best place to start is to work on your interest in taking good care of yourself. We tend to look after the things we really value, so boosting the way you feel about yourself may help you see that lifestyle changes are worth the effort – *you* are worth the effort. You might like to read the next section on where you would like to be and then come back to this section later.

Action points

Look at your food diary again. Was your final score on the low side? This means that the *balance* of your diet is letting you down.

One simple approach to improving things is to try to improve your average food diary score. You can choose how you get your score to increase, but it doesn't need to involve dieting – just adding more nutritious foods *into* the diet rather than worrying about cutting things *out* is a great first step.

Filling up on healthier ingredients first will reduce your desire for the less healthy ingredients. There is no need to ban anything – just improve the balance of foods you eat overall. Simply changing the order in which you eat a meal could make a difference – clear the vegetables off your plate before tucking into the pie or mash. Eat the apple before your sandwiches, crisps and bar of chocolate in your packed lunch. This way you are more likely to eat the nutritious items, rather than getting full up on stodge and leaving no room for the healthy things.

The second way to improve your score is to add in more exercise and activity. Regular short bursts are a better bet than a rare marathon.

But hang on! This is starting to sound like a diet! Be very clear that improving your food diary score is a way to get *healthier*, rather than a direct route to weight loss. The next section talks much more about where you want to be and how you might get there – improving your food diary score is plain good sense, not a miracle cure!

Talk about your findings and your plans with someone you trust. Lifestyle changes are most successful if they apply to the whole family, so wherever possible discuss things with your parents. If your parents are also overweight then family changes are even more likely to reap rewards and you will be able to share your feelings, your difficulties and your triumphs together.

About right for your height and age

Just because your height and weight match up does not mean you automatically feel happy with yourself. Almost half of girls who are about right feel unhappy about their shape and try dieting. And 10% of *under*weight girls feel like that too.

How did you feel when you worked out that your height and weight are about right? Were you relieved or did you put this knowledge to one side and continue worrying about your bits of flab and whether your bum looks big? There is something disturbing going on if even the people who are in good shape feel pressured to change. The next section looks at this in more detail.

If you are happy with your shape then good for you! Check up on whether your diet is working for you in other ways by double-checking your food diary score. A low score, even if you are about the right shape now, could put you at risk of health or weight problems as you get older. You are worth taking care of, so a bit of fine-tuning over how you eat and exercise will be a good investment for your future. Remember that the best way to improve your score is to add in more of the healthy things, rather than worry about cutting things out.

If you feel dissatisfied with your weight even though you shouldn't, then your next step is to find out where that dissatisfaction is coming from and whether changing your weight is the best way to improve things. The next section will help you do this, so read on.

Underweight for your height and age

You may be the envy of your friends, but are you happy? Were you aware that you are underweight? Have you always been on the skinny side or have you become underweight by controlling how you eat?

The most important question to ask yourself right now is: 'Could I go and talk to someone about being underweight?'

Yes? If the answer is 'yes' then it suggests that being underweight is more likely to be due to a physical or dietary reason, rather than an emotional problem. Do go and talk to someone you trust about your weight, perhaps a parent or other relative, or make an appointment with your family doctor. Between you, you can make sure you are not dangerously underweight and also check if there is a medical reason why your weight is low. You may also find it helpful for someone else to monitor your weight, to assess why your weight has been too low and to work out what a healthy target weight would be.

No? If the very thought of talking about your weight makes you feel anxious or upset, or if you feel that being underweight is an achievement rather than a problem, then you may have an emotional eating problem. Emotional eating problems get worse the longer you live with them, so you should really try as hard as you can to share your feelings. Remember that sharing your feelings doesn't mean that you will be forced to eat – no one will expect your feelings or worries to evaporate after a quick chat and a cuppa.

The whole of Chapter 10 looks into eating disorders, such as anorexia nervosa, and you might like to read this next if you feel reluctant to share your feelings straight away. Have you tried to talk to someone and had your worries brushed aside? It is usually a good idea to tell parents if you feel really low, but they may not always know what to say or how to help you. It may take a little while to find the right person to share things with.

Sometimes it helps to write down how you feel rather than say things out loud. Sometimes it is easier to talk to a stranger rather than someone you know, in which case you could start with The Samaritans. Try phoning 08457 909090. Alternatively, look in the *Yellow Pages* for a local phone number as they have over 200 local support offices. They also give email support on Jo@samaritans.org and have a helpful website at www.samaritans.org.uk. They could put you in touch with a local support group that helps people with eating problems.

Whatever it takes, being unhappily underweight is worth tackling and it is much easier to sort out if you have support. Talking about being underweight is the first step to finding the support you need.

What is important to you about your health – and why?

Most young people are far more concerned about their outward appearance than their inner health – and why not? Diseases of old age are a long way off. Blood pressure? Cholesterol? Boring. Whereas looking great is likely to make a difference to how you feel, your ability to fit in with the right crowd and your chances of impressing a potential boy- or girlfriend. So back we come to dieting again . . .? No, no, no!

'Health' is really a concoction of feeling good as a whole – there is no point living on lettuce and lentils, farting like a trooper, and feeling left out and lonely. The best way to look good is to be 'whole-time healthy' – meaning being healthy in mind, body and outlook. Most of us are a long way off perfect and however hard we diet, have cosmetic surgery, slap on foundation, have our eyebrows plucked or invest in a wig, we will still be faced with what we are – ordinary people trying to look our best despite wonky noses, big bums, knobbly knees, spotty shoulders, crooked teeth, sticking out ears and flabby bits that wobble.

It is quite possible to feel happy and healthy despite all these 'failings' and the SCOFF Check is the next step to finding out how.

The SCOFF Check

The SCOFF Check gives you a score out of 10 for how you feel about yourself. Try it now before working anything out – how do you rate yourself today, right now? Give yourself a score out of 10 for how you feel in general.

Score group	What this means
Scores between 7 and 10	You are pretty happy with yourself, feeling content and life is okay. Life could be better, but it is no big deal if things stay much the same.
Scores between 4 and 6	You are not feeling great, but not terrible either. There may be one or two things on your mind or problems that you would like to sort out.
Scores between 1 and 3	You are feeling pretty low and things are getting you down. You can't seem to find solutions to the problems on your plate. If you have been feeling like this for a while, talk to somebody about how you feel because this can help.
Scores of zero or below	Oh dear, you are feeling terrible – as if there is no light at the end of the tunnel. You must tell someone how you feel because things could get better if you do. Sharing problems is the best way to finding solutions.

Now you have a basic idea, we are going to break up the score to see where your sense of how you feel comes from.

For each individual component you score 0, 1 or 2, where 0 means rubbish, 1 means okay and 2 means fine. Put a circle round your score for each.

The SCOFF Check

Shape	0	1	2
Confidence	0	1	2
Outward appearance	0	1	2
Fitness	0	1	2
Feelings	0	1	2

Now add up each component and see if it matches your first score. It might not be exactly the same, but should be roughly in the same score group.

Note that body shape is quite a different thing from outward appearance. Just because you do not like your thighs or tummy doesn't mean you can't dress for impact or make a statement with your hair. In the same way, confidence is separate from feelings. Just because you are shy or loath adventures doesn't mean you are doomed to misery.

Shape

Shape is only a small part of how we feel about ourselves, yet some people feel it is the answer to everything. The most important thing about the SCOFF score is that it shows that you can feel happy and healthy without being a perfect shape. You could give yourself 0 for your shape, but still feel good about other areas of life such that your total score is high. What is more, changing your shape, for example by going on a diet, may only make a small difference to your overall score if the other factors do not change.

If you focus too much on your shape, you are at risk of forgetting other good aspects about yourself, such as your sense of humour or your successes in other areas.

Going on a diet (where you eat in a restrained way in the hope of losing weight) might seem like a good way to boost self-confidence, outward appearance and therefore your feelings, but it often doesn't work like that. Dieting requires effort and determination, and weight loss is often much slower than hoped, leading to frustration and a sense of failure, which worsens self-confidence and creates unhappiness.

Even when people are successful at dieting, they are often disappointed that life is not much different after all. Boyfriends are no different, money worries are the same and, after the initial congratulations, people quickly get used to the new you, so the increased attention does not last long. What is more, many restrictive diets are complicated or dull, leading to a sense of missing out on the good things. This means the motivation to keep going with restrictive diets gets less, until you give up and the weight piles back on . . .

The solution is to develop a taste for and enjoyment of healthy things for their own sake, rather than to help with weight loss. If you enjoy a healthier and better balanced diet there will never be any reason to stop eating that way. A bonus is that your shape may gradually improve too.

Confidence

Confidence is the aspect that is most likely to come from either your own personality or from other people – approval from friends, being relied upon and taken seriously, doing well in exams or in performance, being rewarded for the amount of effort you put into something. Feeling confident about things you have already done sets you up for trying other things. Reminding yourself of achievements in your past is a perfectly reasonable way of giving yourself a bit more confidence for the future.

Outward appearance

Outward appearance is the factor that you have most control over. Looking good on the outside can help with feeling better inside. Think of packaging in a shop: whatever the goods are like inside, your first knowledge will be the condition of the outer package itself. People are more drawn to items that look good on the outside, presuming the contents inside will match up. Grotty packaging might mean grotty contents too. But not always.

You can often tell when people are fed up or bogged down because they take less trouble over their dress and grooming and are more likely to slouch along with their heads bowed low. People who are full of beans, however, are more likely to make the effort to look good both physically and in their body language. It is worth remembering that if you feel down you can give yourself an easy lift by pampering yourself to boost your appearance. Then lift your head up high and put your best foot forward.

Fitness

Fitness is one of the most productive ways to boost health. By increasing exercise and stamina there is a good chance that all the other scores will improve too: people who get regular exercise are most likely to value themselves, which means they are likely to take pride in their appearance and be in better physical shape, resulting in better self-confidence and general happiness with themselves. There are degrees of fitness though. Do not feel put off by those scrawny long-distance runners – a bit of cycling or a regular swim alongside your usual walking will make a huge difference to general fitness.

Feelings

Feelings are the most variable of all the factors. The teenage years are a time when emotions surge from one extreme to the other. Normal feelings range from absurd excitement and enthusiasm to grumpy frustration, disinterest, cynical contempt and plain anger. However, there are some good ways to get feelings under control and increase the chance of feeling happy on occasion.

First you need a few friends who like you for who you are, warts and all – perhaps friends who have known you for a very long time or who have shared a difficult time with you.

Secondly, you need to listen to them on their bad days, i.e. you need to be a good friend in return.

Thirdly, you need an outlet for when anger, frustration or moodiness builds up. Shouting and being unreasonable is *not* an outlet – it is a sign that you *need* an outlet! Outlets are often physical things like dancing, kicking a football or hitting a tennis or golf ball, but also include things like a punch bag, a dartboard with your least favourite person's face on it, a stress ball or a phone. Phone your mates and have a moan. Get it out of your system.

What aspects would you *really* like to change?

Now you know how you really feel about yourself, what would you like to do to improve things? Or were you surprised to find that you are not so bad after all? Do you still feel your shape is worth working at? Are you carrying more weight than you should for your height and age? Did your food diary highlight a disaster zone that needs attention? Should fitness be pushed up your priority list?

Just because this book discourages 'dieting' does not mean you should not try to improve your eating habits and your body image. In fact there are loads of healthy things to try that can make you feel more positive and in control.

There are two types of action points:

- changes to how you think about things
- practical changes to what you actually do.

Change how you think about things

Putting your thoughts straight will help you feel clear about what you are aiming for and where the drive to succeed is coming from. These steps will increase the chance of any practical changes actually working.

1 Discover pride in yourself. Who bothers to look after rubbish? Unless you really care about yourself then you won't feel that you are worth looking after. If you have a low opinion of yourself, improving this is your first and most important target. Once you find some pride in yourself then keeping healthy will start to feel a lot more worthwhile. Try the 'Dare or Care?' quiz in the next section to see how you score on valuing yourself. Chapter 2, 'Testing times', gives lots of ideas on boosting self-esteem, dealing with bullying and coping with emotional turmoil.

2 Only ever set yourself targets that you know you *can* achieve. There is nothing like an early failure to set you back. Starting with achievable targets is a great way to boost confidence and get you feeling motivated. Instead of starting with plans to lose a stone, aim to eat more healthily whilst wearing clothes that help you look trim.

3 Only ever set yourself targets that you *want* to achieve. Why bother trying to do things that are pointless for you? Be careful about setting your *own* targets, rather than aiming for other people's ideals. Just because the world is full of skinny role models doesn't mean that being skinny is the ultimate aim. Think of Dawn French – success and happiness are not the sole domains of the underfed.

4 Take the pressure off by rating yourself less by how you look and more by the person you are underneath. Remember that your really good friends won't care whether you are drop dead gorgeous or wear a bag over your head – but they will care if you are moody, selfish, spiteful or unkind.

5 Watch out in case other people are busy giving you *their* problems. Bullying is the commonest example of this: bullies feel very insecure so they act tough to cover up their insecurities. This is why they try and score points off other people who seem weaker, because it makes them feel better. But all they are doing is handing out their problems to their victims – the victim is not the one with the problem but is just suffering from the bully's problem. Another example is being burdened by a friend's difficulties when you are not in a position to help, despite wanting to. There's a difference between being a supportive friend and being responsible like a parent.

6 Work out what your comforts are when life is tough. If comfort eating is your most reliable consolation then you are heading for trouble. Put some other reassuring methods of support in place so that tucking into comfort foods does not get out of hand. Options include writing worries down in a personal diary, reading a favourite book again, playing favourite tracks far too loudly, or asking your mates to come round for a sleep-over so you can put the world to rights in the small hours.

7 Don't be taken for a ride. Learn to take a sceptical view of miracle cures,

fantastic offers, 'unbeatable' value items and new essential trends. Young people are now a highly prized target audience for heavily marketed rubbishy goods or bizarre concepts. Think twice before lining the pockets of some rich executive with your hard-earned money. Being cynical about food is a good thing – the foods that are most heavily advertised are the ones containing most fat, salt and sugar. Have you ever seen an ad for a plain old carrot?

Practical action points to change what you actually do

1 Start with easy things that you can stick to. Simply drinking more water is helpful – especially if this makes you less thirsty for fizzy sugary drinks. These are a big source of useless calories – 'flab-fillers' that do not banish hunger but do fill teeth with cavities . . . Get ideas from your food diary for some easy points, such as adding in breakfast or changing to wholemeal bread.
2 Put in some structure to how you eat. Hunger varies according to what you are expecting as well as to when you last ate. If you were expecting a feast and were served a slice of toast you would feel disappointed. But if you were expecting a piece of toast it would seem just right. The more each meal follows a predictable pattern, the less hungry you will feel. So if lunch is always a sandwich, piece of fruit and a biscuit then that will begin to seem just right once you are used to it. However, if lunch varies from a lettuce leaf one day to a vast fry-up the next then hunger will feel worse due to not knowing what to expect.
3 Avoid snacking for the nation. Chips and burgers are main-meal items, rather than appropriate snacks for in between meals. Check out your regular snack foods to see if they would be better forming part of a proper meal, whilst choosing more nutritious foods for in between meals, as outlined in Chapter 7 'The Food Frequency Framework'.
4 Never skip meals. Studies show that people who skip meals overeat at the next meal. By allowing yourself to get over-hungry you lose self-control when you do allow yourself to eat, leading to more snacking as well as eating extra at the next proper meal. People who skip breakfast have poorer concentration than those who start the day with something to eat.
5 Make your food work for you. This means eating food that has some value apart from its taste. There are lots of examples, such as eating high-fibre foods to avoid tummy ache by keeping motions regular. Check out the 'glycaemic index' (*see* Chapter 9, p. 130) to stave off hunger for longer – a low GI food, such as baked beans, takes longer to be absorbed by the gut than a high GI food such as a Mars bar. Drinking orange juice (which contains vitamin C) alongside a main meal can help you absorb more iron and other nutrients from your food.
6 Think about the 'energy density' of what you eat. Fat has twice the calories per mouthful than carbohydrate or protein. Pad fatty foods with healthy low-calorie ingredients, so that after eating the same number of mouthfuls you will have taken in fewer calories but feel just as full. Examples are putting some salad into sandwiches, adding a can of sweetcorn, some frozen vegetables or a tin of kidney beans to a stew or curry, and using skimmed or semi-skimmed rather than full-fat milk on cereals.

7 Don't con yourself when you've done some exercise. Five minutes' footie will not justify a shed load of chocolate. Look at the calorie table for the bad news! Instead, think along the lines of : 'healthy exercise – healthy snack'. The best way to achieve this is to take a healthy item with you when you play sports. This means that even if you buy something from the fleece-the-teens-snack-machine, you will have had something nutritious alongside – that is, if you eat it.

Calorie table

Activity (minutes)	Calories used up	Snack (grams)	Calories contained
Moderate cycling (30)	100	Mars bar (62.5g)	281
Moderate running (20)	148	Kit Kat chunky (55g)	290
Swimming (30)	130	Snickers (64.5g)	323
Table tennis (30)	160	Packet of crisps (34.5g)	181
Golf (60)	160	Lucozade energy original drink (380 ml)	277

Whose opinions count most?

Are you driven by anxiety about what everyone else thinks? Are you curious about the world – and to hell with the risks? Or do you have a strong sense of what is right for you? Try the 'Dare or Care?' quiz to see if your self-esteem is zero, under attack or a safety net keeping you out of harm's way.

The 'Dare or Care?' quiz

1 You are at a party and someone you are vaguely interested in makes a move on you but starts getting physical without bothering with introductions. Do you:
   a. Feel flattered until half your clothes are missing, then back off in a panic?
   b. Grab the chance to get some action?
   c. Realise your early interest was misguided if that is all the person is after?
2 Your mates are all smoking and offer you a cigarette even though they know you don't smoke. Do you:
   a. Say no but wish you had said yes, feeling that your mates will think you are feeble?
   b. Take one – it looks cool and the risks are bound to be overstated. Anyway, one couldn't hurt, could it?
   c. Tell them you don't want a mouth like an ashtray, thanks?
3 Without asking, your mum buys you some new spot cream and leaves it in your room. Do you:
   a. Feel upset that this must mean your skin is terrible, but don't have the nerve to talk to her about it?
   b. Feel flattered that she bought you something personal at last?

c. Feel confused because teen spots are normal and you didn't think your skin was that bad, so go and ask her what she thinks?
4   You had a 'close moment' with your new partner, although didn't have full sex. Now you have itching and a rash down below. Do you:
a. Panic about what you could have caught, but feel just as anxious about sorting it out?
b. Not worry – it's bound to go away if you leave it long enough?
c. Ask your mum/school nurse/older sister/best friend's mum/do an internet search as to whether you need a check-up with the doctor or cream from the chemist?
5   Your parents feel strongly about which course you should do next, but you disagree and keep arguing about it. Do you:
a. Back down and go along with their views, feeling belittled and resentful?
b. Use it as an excuse to give up education altogether and look for a job instead?
c. Get hold of leaflets and information about the course you want to do and where it might lead, to convince your parents that you are making a serious choice?

Your replies

Mainly a's

It's not your self-esteem that is letting you down, but your self-confidence. You know what you want for yourself, but sometimes you are not confident about sticking up for those views. Be true to yourself always – you are only answerable to yourself at the end of the day. Remind yourself regularly how much you value and care for yourself because this will boost your confidence when other people are trying to sway you. You would like to be on the right track, so don't let others push you off it.

Mainly b's

Your self-esteem is at an all-time low, which is shown by your lack of self-respect. You may have found some confidence to get on with life in one way – but at what cost? Why are you putting your values to one side just to appear cool, tough and popular? Be cautious about letting curiosity about the world lead you into danger. Pace yourself and think things through before acting on impulse or going for a quick buzz. If you don't show respect for yourself then don't expect other people to respect you either. Ask yourself whether your actions will make you feel proud before deciding how to act.

Mainly c's

Your self-esteem is one of your strengths because you think about what is best for you when making decisions. Even when those close to you want to influence your views, you are clear about your ultimate goal – to treat yourself with respect and make sure other people do the same. You will do well in life because your sense of value will guide you well and other people will recognise that you are not to be mistreated.

Conclusions

Now you have read through the Top Teen Health Plan, why not go back to the baseline questions at the beginning to see if you feel the same way?

Set yourself some goals – both short term and long term – and see if your family or your pals would like to join you in putting health on the priority list. A team approach is the best way to have fun as well as boost motivation to keep up with good routines and leave unhealthy habits behind.

Weight Matters for Young People contains many more ideas about enjoying a healthy lifestyle and putting good habits into practice. It also advises you on what to do when things are going wrong or if illness strikes. If you are keen to put the Top Teen Health Plan into action then dip into the rest of the book for extra tips and guidance.

Be happily healthy and be yourself!

Height and weight charts showing normal growth

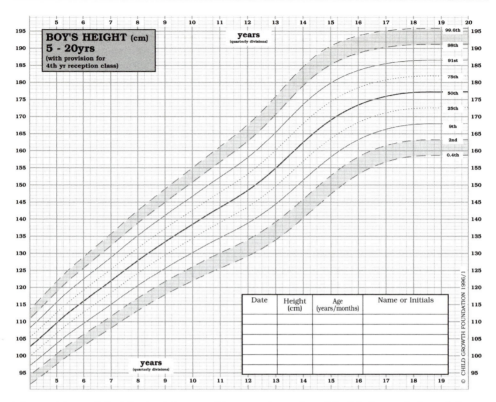

Figure A1 Boy's height (cm) from 5–20 years. Reproduced by kind permission of the Child Growth Foundation.

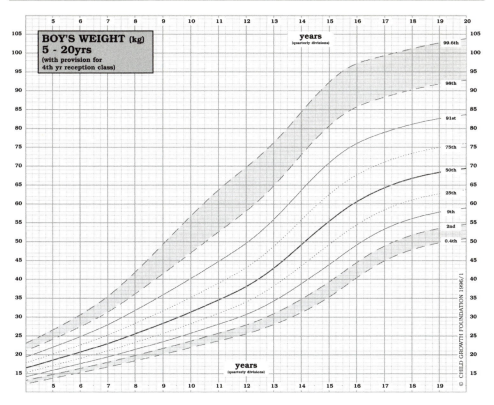

Figure A2 Boy's weight (kg) from 5–20 years. Reproduced by kind permission of the Child Growth Foundation.

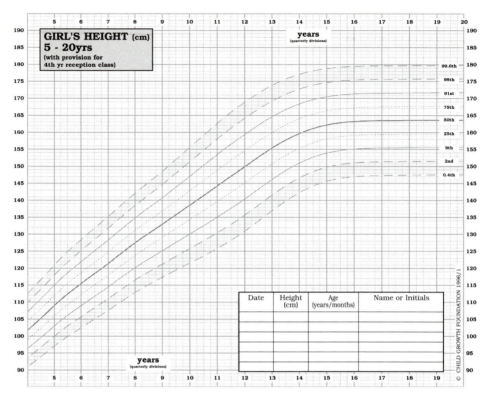

Figure A3 Girl's height (cm) from 5–20 years. Reproduced by kind permission of the Child Growth Foundation.

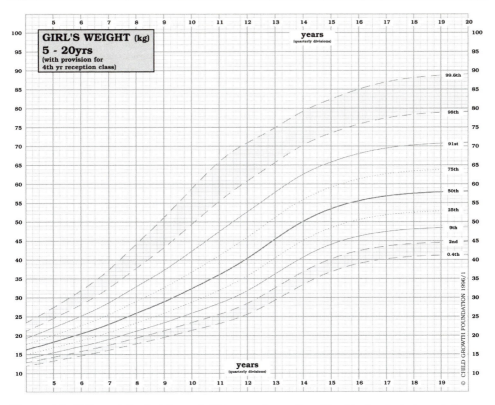

Figure A4 Girl's weight (kg) from 5–20 years. Reproduced by kind permission of the Child Growth Foundation.

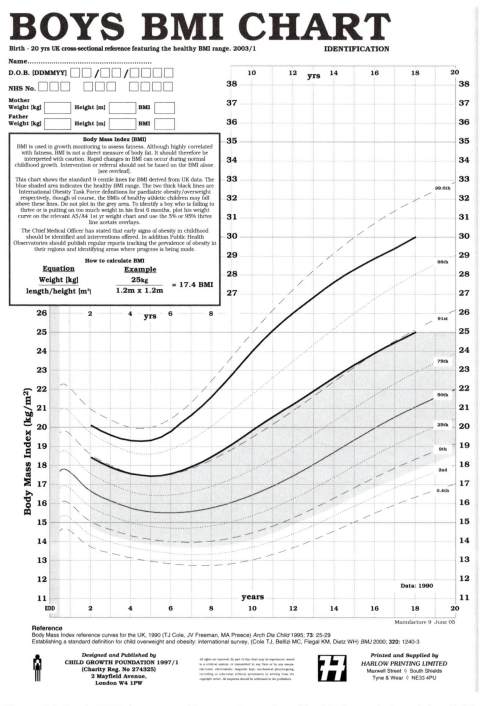

BOYS BMI CHART

Birth - 20 yrs UK cross-sectional reference featuring the healthy BMI range. 2003/1

IDENTIFICATION

Name...

D.O.B. [DDMMYY] □□ / □□ / □□□□

NHS No. □□□   □□□   □□□□

Mother Weight [kg] □   Height [m] □   BMI □
Father Weight [kg] □   Height [m] □   BMI □

Body Mass Index (BMI)

BMI is used in growth monitoring to assess fatness. Although highly correlated with fatness, BMI is not a direct measure of body fat. It should therefore be interpreted with caution. Rapid changes in BMI can occur during normal childhood growth. Intervention or referral should not be based on the BMI alone. [see overleaf].

This chart shows the standard 9 centile lines for BMI derived from UK data. The blue shaded area indicates the healthy BMI range. The two thick black lines are International Obesity Task Force definitions for paediatric obesity/overweight respectively, though of course, the BMIs of healthy athletic children may fall above these lines. Do not plot in the grey area. To identify a boy who is failing to thrive or is putting on too much weight in his first 6 months, plot his weight curve on the relevant A5/A4 1st yr weight chart and use the 5% or 95% thrive line acetate overlays.

The Chief Medical Officer has stated that early signs of obesity in childhood should be identified and interventions offered. In addition Public Health Observatories should publish regular reports tracking the prevalence of obesity in their regions and identifying areas where progress is being made.

How to calculate BMI

Equation	Example	
Weight [kg]	25kg	= 17.4 BMI
length/height [m²]	1.2m x 1.2m	

Data: 1990

Manufacture 9 June 05

Reference
Body Mass Index reference curves for the UK, 1990 (TJ Cole, JV Freeman, MA Preece) *Arch Dis Child* 1995; **73**: 25-29
Establishing a standard definition for child overweight and obesity: international survey, (Cole TJ, Bellizi MC, Flegal KM, Dietz WH) *BMJ* 2000; **320**: 1240-3

Designed and Published by
CHILD GROWTH FOUNDATION 1997/1
(Charity Reg. No 274325)
2 Mayfield Avenue,
London W4 1PW

Printed and Supplied by
HARLOW PRINTING LIMITED
Maxwell Street ◊ South Shields
Tyne & Wear ◊ NE33 4PU

Figure A5 Boy's BMI chart up to 20 years. Reproduced by kind permission of the Child Growth Foundation.

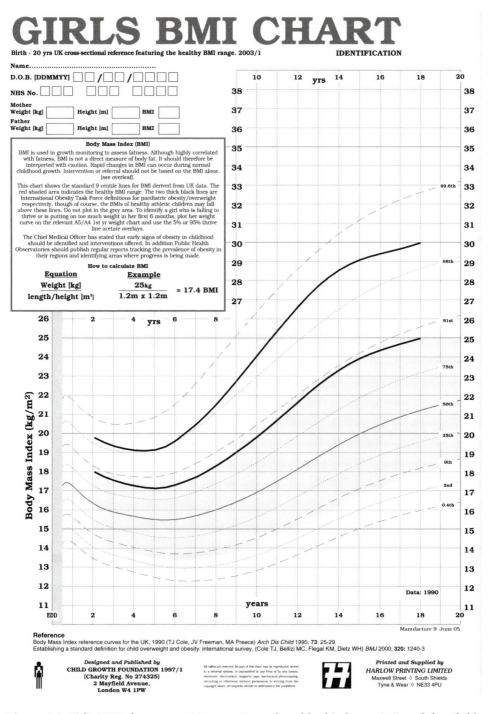

Figure A6 Girl's BMI chart up to 20 years. Reproduced by kind permission of the Child Growth Foundation.

Useful resources

Nutrition

The Dairy Council
Gives information about dairy products, including providing healthy vending in schools.
www.milk.co.uk

The Food Commission
94 White Lion Street, London N1 9PF
Tel: 020 7837 2250
A national non-profit organisation that campaigns for the right to safe, whole-some food. The Food Commission publishes *Food Magazine*, which is the UK's leading independent food magazine covering product investigations, the latest news on diet and health, and ideas on how people can help campaign for safer, healthier food for themselves and their family.
www.foodcomm.org.uk

Food Standards Agency
Tel: 020 7276 8000
This is an independent food safety watchdog set up by an Act of Parliament in 2000 to protect the public's health and consumer interests in relation to food. Their main website is www.food.gov.uk. They also have a great site for families and young people, giving a wide range of nutritional information plus the chance to post your own email questions, at www.eatwell.gov.uk.

Health Education Trust
Tel: 01789 773915
A UK registered charity formed to boost the development of health education for young people. It campaigns on topics such as improvements in school meals and action on healthier school food and drink vending.
www.healthedtrust.com

La Leche League
For breastfeeding information and support.
Helpline: 0845 120 2918
www.laleche.org.uk

National Childbirth Trust (NCT)
Enquiry line: 0870 444 8707 (8:30 am to 5 pm, Monday to Thursday; 8:30 am to 4 pm, Fridays)
Breastfeeding line: 0870 444 8708 (8 am to 10 pm, seven days a week)
Membership hotline: 0870 990 8040 to join the NCT using a credit or debit card
www.nctpregnancyandbabycare.com/nct-online

Organic food and farming

Information about organic food and farming is available through the following:

Fish stocks and safe fishing practices
Further information about sustainable fishing and how consumers can help can be found at www.fishonline.org.

Henry Doubleday Foundation
www.hdra.org.uk

The Soil Association
www.soilassociation.org

The Vegan Society
Donald Watson House, 7 Battle Road, St Leonards-on-Sea, East Sussex TN37 7AA
Tel: 01424 427393
www.vegansociety.com

The Vegetarian Society
Parkdale, Dunham Road, Altrincham, Cheshire WA14 4QG
Tel: 0161 925 2000; Fax: 0161 926 9182
www.vegsoc.org

Recommended cookbooks

- *Annabel Karmel's Favourite Family Recipes*. Ebury Press. An ideal guide to easy family meals.

- *Ainsley Harriott's All New Meals in Minutes*. Dorling Kindersley. Quick meals that will go down well with all the family.

- *Sophie Grigson's Country Kitchen*. Headline. Fabulous ideas for incorporating fruit and vegetables into meals throughout the year.

- Nigel Slater. *Real Fast Food*. Penguin. A timeless guide to fast easy nutrition for busy families.

- *Delia Smith's Complete Cookery Course*. BBC Books. The ultimate reference book for anyone wanting to cook fail-safe traditional meals that the whole family will appreciate.

Health

Asthma UK
Advice line: 0845 701 0203 (9 am to 5 pm, Monday to Friday)
In addition to their telephone advice line, they have an email information service through the website, plus useful information for young people.
www.asthma.org.uk

The British Heart Foundation
Tel: 0870 600 6566
This charity has many initiatives to boost health for adults and children, including funding research and promoting education. For further information about all the BHF materials, see www.bhf.org.uk/youngpeople. The website has lots of activity and nutritional information too.

Coeliac UK
PO Box 220, High Wycombe, Bucks HP11 2HY
Helpline: 0870 444 8804
Gives comprehensive information on the diagnosis of coeliac disease and ways to manage a gluten-free diet.
www.coeliac.co.uk

Diabetes UK
Macleod House, 10 Parkway, London NW1 7AA
Tel: 020 7424 1000; Email: info@diabetes.org.uk
Supports people with diabetes, funds research and campaigns to improve the lives of people with the condition.
www.diabetes.org.uk

Health Education Authority – Wired for Health
This is a series of websites run on behalf of the Department of Health and the Department for Education and Skills. There are four sites for young people, covering a range of health topics for different age groups ranging from 5 to 16.
www.wiredforhealth.gov.uk

Health for All Children – online growth charts
This is an ideal site for plotting height and weight and calculating body mass index (BMI) in people under the age of 18. Go to www.healthforallchildren.co.uk and choose the parents' page.

Hyperactive Children's Support Group
71 Whyke Lane, Chichester, West Sussex PO19 7PD
Tel: 01243 551313; Email: hyperactive@hacsg.org.uk
This charity organisation provides support for ADHD/hyperactive children and their families, encouraging a dietary approach to the problem of hyperactivity.
www.hacsg.org.uk

Institute of Child Health and Great Ormond Street Family Resource Centre
Institute of Child Health, 30 Guildford Street, London WC1N 1EH
Tel: 020 7242 9789
Great Ormond Street Family Resource Centre, Great Ormond Street, London WC1N 3JH
Tel: 020 7405 9200
The combined website of these two organisations gives comprehensive information on a huge range of illnesses in its Health A to Z, plus many other issues such as what to expect if a trip to hospital is needed.
www.childrenfirst.nhs.uk or www.ich.ucl.ac.uk

NHS Direct
Tel: 0845 4647
This freephone service is staffed by nurses to give immediate information and guidelines on health and illness. There is also a comprehensive website giving health and illness advice at www.nhsdirect.nhs.uk.

Teenage Health Freak
This website talks about general teenage health worries and has an email service where health concerns are answered by an online doctor.
www.teenagehealthfreak.org

Contraception, sexual health and relationships

Brook Advisory Centre
Tel: 0800 018 5023
Provides free, confidential support on all sexual health matters for the under-25s. The website gives details of local branches.
www.brook.org.uk

Caledonia Youth
Scottish service that provides information and support on any aspect of contraception and relationships, and gives details of clinics in Scotland.
www.caledoniayouth.org

Drug problems

D-2K
Tel: 0800 776600
Run by Health Promotion England, it gives information on drugs for 14–16 year-olds. It links to **Frank**, which is a drug information telephone and email support line for young people and parents.
www.d-2k.co.uk or www.talktofrank.com

Release
Tel: 0845 450 0215
Provides information for drug users, their families and friends, as well as information about drugs and the law. It has a free and confidential heroin helpline in addition to other forms of support.
www.release.org.uk

Smoking cessation advice services

ASH – Action on Smoking and Health UK
In addition to English-speaking services there are a number of support lines in foreign languages. Details are on the website.
www.ash.org.uk

NHS Pregnancy Smoking Helpline
Tel: 0800 169 9169 (12 noon to 9 pm, seven days a week. Answerphone out of hours)

NHS Smoking Helpline
Tel: 0800 169 0169 (7 am to 11 pm, seven days a week)

Quitline
Tel: 0800 002200
www.quit.org.uk

Activity and exercise

Disability Sport England
This organisation gives information on getting involved in sports for disabled people, charity information and details on sponsorship. It also lists a calendar of Disability Sport England events.
www.disabilitysport.org.uk/

Sport England
This organisation takes the strategic lead for sport in England, creating opportunities for people to start, stay and succeed in sport. Its website gives details of clubs and facilities in local areas.
www.sportengland.org

Sport Scotland
This national organisation has responsibility to develop sport and physical recreation in Scotland.
www.sportscotland.org.uk

Sports Coach UK
For information on coaching at every level in the UK.
www.sportscoachuk.org

Sports Council for Wales
This organisation is responsible for developing and promoting sport and recreation in Wales.
www.sports-council-wales.co.uk

Sustrans – cycle routes
Information service: 0845 113 0065; Email: info@sustrans.org.uk for details
This charity works on practical projects to encourage people to walk, cycle and use public transport, and gives ideas on cycle routes in local areas.
www.sustrans.org.uk

Emotional health

Alateen
Tel: 020 7403 0888
Advice and support for young people affected by someone else's alcohol problem. Alateen and Al-Anon are branches of Alcoholics Anonymous that support the families of alcoholics.
www.al-anon.alateen.org

ChildLine
Helpline: 0800 1111
ChildLine is the UK's free, 24-hour helpline for young people in distress or danger. Trained volunteer counsellors comfort, advise and protect children and young people who may feel they have nowhere else to turn.
www.childline.org.uk

Cruse Bereavement Care Youth Line
Helpline: 0808 808 1677 (9:30 am to 5 pm, weekdays)
A confidential support service that helps young people find their own road to dealing with the loss of someone close. They have a free helpline or will reply to emails through their website.
www.rd4u.org.uk

Eating disorders

Anorexia and Bulimia Care
This organisation provides information, support and a befriending service for sufferers and their families from a Christian perspective.
www.anorexiabulimiacare.co.uk

Eating Disorders Association
Youth line: 0845 634 7650
Text messaging service: 07977 493345
This national charity provides full information and advice on seeking help for eating disorders, which includes finding a local self-help group and sharing concerns on their message board.
www.edauk.com

National Society for the Prevention of Cruelty to Children (NSPCC)
Helpline: 0808 800 5000 (with support also available in Welsh, Bengali, Gujurati, Hindi, Punjabi and Urdu)
The NSPCC has a great website that gives advice on dealing with bullying and on safe web surfing, plus a helpline that can support victims of both physical and sexual abuse or advise people who are worried that a friend may be in danger.
www.nspcc.org.uk

Parentline Plus
Freephone helpline: 0808 800 2222 (available 24 hours a day)
This national charity works for and with parents to give guidance on a wealth of topics from bullying, divorce and discipline through to drugs and talking about relationships. An email reply service is available through the website.
www.parentlineplus.org.uk

Samaritans
Tel: 0845 790 9090; Email: Jo@samaritans.org
Confidential emotional support is available 24 hours a day by telephone, letter, email and minicom, if people are experiencing feelings of distress or despair, including those which may lead to suicide. Some local offices also provide face-to-face contact.

Look in the *Yellow Pages* for a local phone number as they have over 200 support offices.

www.samaritans.org.uk

Young Minds

Tel: 0800 018 2138

This national charity is committed to improving the emotional health of all children and young people. They provide leaflets and booklets plus a parents' information service. The website has pages for young people and for parents, as well as information for professionals involved in helping young people.

www.youngminds.org.uk

Index

Page numbers in *italic* refer to tables or figures.